# The Great Within

# THE
# GREAT WITHIN

by

## MAURICE COLLIS

## FABER AND FABER LIMITED
24 Russell Square
London

First published in mcmxli
by Faber and Faber Limited
24 Russell Square London W.C.1
Second impression mcmxlii
Third impression mcmxlvi
Fourth impression mcmli
Fifth impression mcmlvi
Printed in Great Britain by
Bradford and Dickens London W.C.1.

To
His Excellency

DR. QUO TAI-CHI

Formerly Chinese Ambassador
at the Court of St. James
now Minister of Foreign Affairs
The National Government of China
with grateful thanks
for his hospitality and kindness

# Prefatory Note

This essay on the interactions of China and Europe from the seventeenth century till the present day is founded upon the authorities quoted on page 343. These will tell the sinologue at a glance the book's limits. It is not, as he will perceive, addressed to him, for it contains no facts with which he is unfamiliar. If he is not amused to read it for its presentation and its argument, let him leave it with indulgence to that large and intelligent public whose reading takes it occasionally upon a tour of China. That such people should find it clear, and sound within the limits above stated, is the whole extent of the author's ambition.

Much use has been made in the first eighty pages of that brilliant and absorbing book, *Annals and Memoirs of the Court of Peking* by E. Backhouse and J. O. P. Bland, which was published twenty-seven years ago. No-one attempting a sketch of the Ming's fall can do otherwise than treat it as an original authority, unless he is able to procure and read the Chinese sources upon which it rests or produce others which override them. There is no European writer who has done either of these things and it is extremely unlikely that we shall see one in our time. The present writer has, therefore, quoted from the documents translated by Messrs. Backhouse and Bland, where he is treating of the Ming, as freely as he has done from the authorities for other chapters.

This first part does not deal with the interaction above mentioned, but has been inserted because it seemed that unless the reader were first taken inside China he would be unable to observe in their proper perspective the visitors from the outside who came to make demands on or lay their views before the Son of Heaven.

Moreover, the fall of the Ming is the first act in a great historical drama, the elements of which are inherent in the present narrative.

# Contents

9

# Contents

# Illustrations

# Illustrations

# Maps

PART ONE

## *The Ruin of the Great Ming*

# The Porcelain Box

In the year 1928 I was appointed Deputy Commissioner of Sagaing by the Burma Government. Sagaing is a small country town on the west bank of the Irrawaddy, a few miles south of Mandalay. The great river, though four hundred miles from its mouth, is there a full mile across. On the opposite shore is Ava, the shell of a once capital city, the site now occupied by rice fields and small villages.

From my house on the Sagaing bank I could see Ava over the water, its wall split by banyan roots, its western gate a ruin. In my study I had a circular box of Chinese porcelain, decorated in enamels with red dragons among green scrolls. On the vase was inscribed in blue idiographs the imperial mark—Ta Ming Ch'ung Chên Nein Chih, made in the Ch'ung Chên reign of the Ta Ming or Great Bright Dynasty—a rare mark among Ming porcelains.

The Emperor Ch'ung Chên was the last ruling sovereign of the Ming. He committed suicide under the most tragic circumstances in 1644. So low had the Mings sunk that they were overthrown by a bandit, who in turn was displaced by an invasion of the Manchus. For the first nineteen years of their dynasty, called the Ch'ing or Pure, cousins of Ch'ung Chên struggled to re-establish their House. The last of them was Prince Kuei, who assumed the reign title of Yung Li. Losing his last battle he fled in 1659 to Burma. Its capital was then Ava and its king Pindalé. Yung Li placed himself under the protection of Pindalé, who sent him to live across the river at Sagaing.

It was, therefore, with very particular interest that I used to handle the porcelain box on which was inscribed his cousin's name. That it should find its way to Sagaing was strange, but stranger was the long story of how Yung Li himself happened to come there. The principal characters of that story are boldly cut; its details are a lexicon of human conduct; the whole reveals a world in miniature. Ch'ung Chên the Emperor, and Wei the Chief Eunuch, with Li the bandit, and Wu the General, Jui the Regent, Shih the Grand Secretary—these with Yung Li are the high personages who occupy the stage; their voices still reach us clearly across the centuries.

# The Eunuchs

The first scene is in Peking, some years before the fatal year of 1644. The Ming had been reigning for two centuries and a half. Their empire was the largest and richest in the world. In no other realm was there such a huge population, so many great cities, such a high standard of living. Everything that men could desire was supplied in superfluity by the most talented artisans. Right across the north the Great Wall, strongly manned, protected them against the raiding nomadic tribes of the Steppe, which in the past had so often burst in with terrible results. The west and south-west were flanked by endless chains of mountains, nor was there any threat from the far kingdoms in that quarter after the death of Tamerlane in 1404. The ocean guarded them on the east and south-east. Though adventurers from Portugal had arrived to trade, these 'Red Barbarians' caused no real anxiety. There was little apparent reason why the Ming should not rule for ever. Their civilization was still superior to any other, though Europe was beginning to catch them up. It is customary to say that the great creative age of China was under the T'ang, a thousand years earlier, that during the flowering of the Sung in the twelfth century everything conceivable had been said and done. That may be true, but the Ming had, as it were, gathered up and preserved what was most significant and beautiful in their past, the capital becoming a vast museum of the arts, ceremonies, rituals and manners which had been evolved during two thousand years, and which now, backed by that long usage and precedent, seemed unalterably fixed and powerful.

But in spite of their intense sophistication, their passion for the amenities and decorations of life, the Ming had begun more and more by the seventeenth century to neglect one thing of first importance, the efficiency of the administration. Under their system, derived from the T'ang model in the seventh century, which in turn had grown out of the Han model of the first, the provinces were governed by a hierarchy of officials selected by open public examination. At the capital were six Boards or Ministries, the heads of which, supplemented by certain noble-men, formed the Imperial Council. The system resembled our own Government of India before the introduction of Diarchy in 1921. It generally worked well enough, but there were occasions when a rival authority, situated under the shadow of the throne, but which had no legal place in the admini-strative machinery, was able to interfere for its own corrupt pur-poses.

The corps of eunuchs, who were meant to be no more than Court attendants, was that rival authority. The Presidents of the Boards were supposed to have the Imperial ear. But living as the etiquette of ages demanded, a cloistered being in a Forbidden City, the Emperor, surrounded by his Concubinate and its eunuch servants, was liable if he were credulous or weak to listen more readily to them than to those in charge of the depart-ments of state. When that happened—and it happened several times in the long course of Chinese history—the eunuchs were able to obtain official appointments and so to influence policy, meddle with the civil service, tamper with the army and distri-bute state patronage

The late Ming period was such a time of eunuch dominance. Honours, titles and rewards fell to those who bought their good-will, while imprisonment and torture awaited the Minister or official who attempted to balk them or enlighten the Emperor. Provincial officials, forced to purchase their appointments and to continue making costly presents in order to keep them, re-couped themselves by misappropriating the revenue, selling justice and oppressing the people. Hence, the best class of officials were driven out of the service, while commanding the armies were placemen instead of soldiers.

The extent to which orderly administration was disrupted at this time may be illustrated by citing the case of Wei Chung-hsien, who was Chief Eunuch in 1624 and against whom one of the Censors sent in a memorial to T'ien Ch'i, the youthful Emperor who was then on the throne.

The Censorate was a department of the Government, and it was the duty of the Censors to memorialize the Emperor on any topic which was agitating the country or about which he was held to lack information or require guidance. No matter how disagreeable might be their advice or remonstrance, he was obliged to consider it without prejudice. As there was no as-sembly representative of public opinion, these Censors held a position of great importance, and took their duties with every seriousness. There were occasions, however, when it needed more than ordinary devotion to duty, when, indeed, it required great courage, to draw the Emperor's attention to some abuse. Such an occasion had arisen when the Censor, Yang, memo-rialized against the Chief Eunuch, Wei.

'The founder of our Dynasty', he begins, 'desired that eu-nuchs should not interfere in affairs of government. But the eunuch, Wei, behaves with arrogance and treats such dynastic ordinances with contempt.'

He then proceeds to particularize under sixteen heads the eunuch's main crimes. The first head contains the pith of the indictment.

'Wei is a very common fellow who, after being emasculated in middle life, won a position in the Palace by blatant intrigue. He wheedled his way into Imperial favour by displaying zeal in trivial matters, thereafter becoming a traitorous villain, until now he is practically dictator, even issuing his own decrees, whereby the Government has been thrown utterly into con-fusion.'

Such decrees, it is alleged, Wei issued either by word of mouth or, if they were drawn up on paper, by endorsing them with the Vermilion Pencil, the sign-manual of the Emperor himself.

The enumeration of Wei's misdeeds which follows makes formidable reading.

'He has removed all honest officials from your Court, until not a soul is left who dares warn Your Majesty. At a word from him you dismiss everyone who incurs his displeasure. He fills official posts with youths still smelling of their mother's milk or with illiterate members of his own family.'

Then comes a list of his murders, illegal beheadings, forced suicides, smotherings of infants, even an allegation that he poisoned the previous Emperor Wan Li by pretending to cure his sickness with red pills.

Not only had Wei become enormously rich, the indictment continues, but 'at his native place he has erected triumphal arches in his own honour, on which are carved Imperial Dragons and Soaring Phœnixes. His sepulchre on the Western Hills, roofed with yellow tiles, is like an Imperial Mausoleum.' Further, he had recruited a secret police of his own, a pack of bravoes who beat and assassinated at his pleasure.

In his sepulchre and his arches he had aped His Majesty, and when he 'was sent to perform sacrifice at Cho-chin, the road was cleared for him, as for an Imperial progress. Heralds announced his advance and yellow earth was spread upon the highway, so that the people believed that he was the Emperor himself. What manner of man does this Wei fancy himself to be?'

'Why should you nourish a tiger to work his evil will at your very elbows?' exclaims the Censor in conclusion. 'Humbly I implore your Majesty to show your displeasure and appoint an official Commission under the chairmanship of some nobleman with power to subject Wei to the closest examination.'

But Wei was too strong. Backed by a concubine who bore the title of 'Lady of Divine Worship', he persuaded T'ien Ch'i to believe that the memorial was a gross calumny lacking any foundation in fact. Soon afterwards his secret police seized the

Censor and flung him into the palace prison. Two other prominent persons were seized along with him. One of them, his colleague in the Censorate, had submitted a supplementary memorial containing the sentence: 'Can your Majesty employ as your right-hand man a creature whose flesh the whole Empire desires to eat?' The other, a distinguished scholar of the day, had written: 'It comes to this, that you, the Son of Heaven, have surrendered yourself and your consorts to the keeping of Wei. The peril of our State makes my blood run cold. You are become like an orphan in a friendless world.'

These three leading personalities of the official and scholar class were tortured every fifth day to make them confess to having taken bribes, so that they could be formally charged before the Board of Punishments. They refused in spite of horrible sufferings to accuse themselves falsely, until one of them, Yang's fellow Censor, unable to endure his torments any longer urged that it would be better to confess, because they could then hope for a regular trial, at which, perchance, the truth would come out. The others agreed and they all made false confessions. But their compliance did them no good. Wei ordered the torture to continue. Yang was eventually killed by the piling of great sacks of earth upon his stomach and the driving of nails into his ears.

This incident shows how far T'ien Ch'i had fallen under criminal influence. Wei was entirely irresponsible. He did not care what happened to the State. Men of his type, indeed, experience a deep pleasure in destruction. They create about them the atmosphere of the orgy. Gold, blood, wine, lust, torture—these equally intoxicate them: their manner of life is a sort of frenzy. In China they represent the opposite pole to the Confucian ideal, which is compounded of sanity, moderation, fairness and duty. T'ien Ch'i, at the time of Wei's indictment only nineteen, was undersized and of poor constitution. Surrounded by flatterers, by intrigue and lies, what chance had he, the wretched youth? His hobby was carpentry, and while he was planing and joining, a harmless occupation which Wei encouraged, the eunuch worked in collaboration with the Lady K'o, already referred to as the 'Lady of Divine Worship', who was the Emperor's foster-mother, a concubine of his father's. This adventuress was one of that line of formidable women which ended with the Dowager Empress Tzu Hsi. She used to supply T'ien Ch'i with aphrodisiacs and laugh heartily when his sweetheart, a concubine called 'Precious Pearl', a mild good little thing, would urge him to make friends with scholars and take lectures in the classics.

As the Censors' memorials show, all that was best in public opinion was profoundly shocked by this state of affairs. The resulting disaffection towards the throne, along with the decline in the efficiency of the administration, prepared the way for the rebellion which was to destroy the Dynasty.

# III

# *The Bandit Li*

Tien Ch'i, after a reign of seven years, died in 1628 aged
twenty-three, being succeeded by Ch'ung Chên, fated, as we
have read, to be the last ruling Ming Emperor.

He began well by taking steps against Wei's supporters
which so terrified that evil bully that he fled the Court and
committed suicide. But he did not make a clean sweep of the
eunuchs; nor was he able to repair the damage done to the administration. Public opinion was not reassured. The stage was
ready for the appearance of some such figure as Li, the bandit.

Li's banditry was of a particular kind. One meets it often in
Chinese history. It occurs, too, in the history of Burma. During
my residence in that country, I had experience of two such
bandits, Bandaka in Sagaing and Saya San in Tharrawaddy,
and have given some description of them in another place. Such
people are not just highway robbers. They regard themselves as
having a mission. They appear when a political change is imminent and believe they are fated to effect that change. This
belief they derive from astrology. Great changes in eastern States
are always foreshadowed by astrologers. In Europe we do not
pay attention to prophecies; in Asia they arouse the closest
interest. Individuals, also, all have their horoscopes. If a man, at
a time when a general prophecy declares the fall of a state, finds
it written in his chart that he will rise to great eminence, he may
believe that he is the coming ruler, who is destined to bring in
the new order. This encourages him to turn bandit, for in that
way he secures followers. If he is a successful bandit, his followers increase. One day he finds himself at the head of an

army. At this stage he declares his political mission and becomes the leader of a rebellion, taking in advance the title of king. That is as far as most of such bandits get. Li was one of the few whose success continues.

We may be certain that from the accession of Ch'ung Chên or earlier, many astrologers had begun to predict the fall of the Ming. Such prophecies must have been common knowledge throughout all the vast provinces of China. In 1628, the date of the accession, Li was a man of twenty-two, an obscure peasant of the Province of Shensi. But his horoscope was highly remarkable. There could be no doubt, he was told; with such signs he would rise to the top, a throne was surely waiting for him. So potent were his astrological measurements, they whispered, that he must become—yes, the Son of Heaven!

When a youth grows up believing that he is fated to become Emperor of China, brooding over that tremendous destiny and watching for portents to fortify his belief, he lives a strange inner life apart from his fellows. To a chosen few he confides the startling secret. These also believe and swear to follow him.

Li took the first step towards his goal by becoming a bandit in his own Province of Shensi, which is remote from Peking, on the north-west by the Great Wall. The local officers, corrupt and unpopular for the reasons already given, were too inefficient to hunt him down and he was allowed to lay the foundations of his future power. No report was made of his depredations to the Central Government, or when report was made, no sufficient action was taken.

It was in these early days that an event occurred which strengthened his certainty that fame awaited him. In an engagement with Government troops, his left eye was pierced by an arrow. An old prophecy was current that the Empire would be conquered by a one-eyed man. The auspicious wound, therefore, profoundly impressed his followers. It was like a finger pointing to him: the empty socket marked him as a man of destiny. Slowly the future began to take shape. But it took time to disclose itself. For ten years Li was no more than a bandit.

By 1641 he commanded a large army. Every year more men had joined him, men whom maladministration had turned into enemies of the régime. That year he marched out of his province and began to attack important cities on the road to the capital. He had now become clearly the leader of a rebellion, and he assumed the title of 'By Heaven's Grace, Grand Captain of Righteousness'.

It would be a mistake, however, to imagine him as better than a ferocious and uneducated ruffian; nor could he have made headway if the generals of the Imperial troops sent to oppose him had been other than dishonest or incompetent amateurs. He advanced towards the metropolitan province of Chihli. During his progress he took the capitals of Honan and Hupei, the Governors of which were relatives of the Emperor. In the former it was Prince Fu, Prince Good Luck, and this unlucky gentleman was captured as he tried to desert his troops. While he was being conducted to Li's presence, he passed the Commander of the city garrison, who had remained at his post and now waited his fate in chains with the courage which marked some of the Ming officers, venial and inefficient though most of them were.

'Prince,' said this man as Fu went by, 'a person in your exalted station has a duty to the state to fulfil: he must never submit, he must die bravely.'

This admonition, which was strictly in accordance with Confucian ethics, the gentleman's code of China, steadied Fu, and when Li asked for his submission he refused to answer. Whereupon the bandit dispatched him, and that night, flavouring his soup with a cupful of his blood, playfully named it 'Good Luck Red Soup', as we might say, 'Potage rouge à la Bonne Chance'.

At the capital of Hupei it was Prince Hsiang who was Governor. When he was brought before Li or, rather, Li's lieutenant, Chang, for the rebel army operated in two divisions, the latter, offering wine, addressed him in this way:

'I have no grudge against your Highness, and you are a

harmless person enough, but I have a fierce longing to see the head of your general, Yang, separated from his body. But, alas, Yang is not available at this moment, so I propose to substitute your Highness's head. For if I now remove it, the Emperor, enraged at the killing of one of his kinsmen, may see fit to order the death of Yang, who should have been able to prevent this abomination. Will your Highness kindly drink as much wine as you can carry?'

When Prince Hsiang was intoxicated, his head was taken.

From Honan and Hupei, Li advanced closer. Having spilt the blood royal twice and sacked such notable cities, he was preceded by panic: the Court for the first time began to tremble. He knew that he was about to engage in the decisive battle of his career. What he had done so far was to overcome provincial garrisons and defeat those Imperial troops which had been sent against him. Now he had to engage the Ming on their home ground. He was nearing his final objective, the Forbidden City.

Before making that last fling for glory, he paid a visit to his native village in Shensi. There his ancestors had been buried and he now sacrificed at their tombs, informing their spirits in accordance with Confucian custom that he was about to strike for the honour of the family and that if he won the Dragon Throne he would confer upon them, to seven generations, grand posthumous imperial titles. Thereafter, calmed and assured that they would lend him all their countenance, he set out again and, on the first day of the year 1644, dressed in Imperial Dragon robes, assumed a dynastic style, calling himself Yung Ch'ang of the Ta Shun or the Great Obedient Dynasty. At the same time, in earnest of his promise to raise seven generations of his ancestors to the purple, he raised four generations. They had been farmers in a small way.

There was a one further measure for him to take, a measure which in my experience all such mystical bandits as Li always take before their main battle. He appointed his Empress, his ministers and a court nobility. Then at the head of several hundred thousand men, he marched on Peking, distributing as he went a leaflet containing these words: 'His Majesty, the present Emperor, cannot be called an utter fool. He stands alone, but the exactions of his officials are like the heat of a furnace. His Ministers do not care that the prisons are full of the innocent. The people are so oppressed that they flee their homes miserably.'

Meanwhile in Peking there was growing dismay. It was the richest city on earth, the most sophisticated, the most beautiful. As its scholars and artists, its merchants and its bankers, sat in their courtyards surrounded by their families or looked at their porcelains, their jades and their books, they could not believe that within a few days' march was a man who sought to take all these from them, that they were on the edge of ruin, degradation and death. Such things could not happen in their time. The Ming had been reigning nearly three hundred years. There had been peace and plenty, long days without fear. How could it be that all was tumbling down? Could nothing be done? It was too incredible. Their Emperor, Ch'ung Chên, surely he would save them? He must—they were not yet lost—the walls were well defended—the main army was in being; they were still undefeated.

Then the news reached them that Li had actually proclaimed himself Emperor, and on the same day worse was reported—an earthquake had occurred at the birthplace of the founder of the Dynasty.

On paper, however, the situation was far from desperate. The Ming disposed of enormous forces. For some time the taxes had been very heavy, and it was understood that the army was at full strength and well equipped. The public did not know that, in fact, all the garrisons between them and Li were disgracefully depleted because the taxes had been either wasted or misappropriated.

Ch'ung Chên began to lose his nerve. On the day when it was reported that Li had set up a new dynasty, he sent for a Grand Secretary and almost in a state of collapse exclaimed:

'My conscience is clear. I have not deserved to forfeit the Man⁄date of Heaven. Yet ruin confronts me, the Empire is slipping from me. The inheritance which my ancestors won, after being "combed by the wind and bathed by the rain", is rapidly dis⁄solving. How can I dare to face them in the next world?' And he burst into tears.

The Grand Secretary, who was a very rich banker, tried to comfort him.

'I myself will march on the rebels,' said he, 'and you can debit the expenses to my account.'

This reassured the Emperor for the moment.

'I will see you off,' he said, almost gaily. 'There are pre⁄cedents, I will see you off.'

As soon as all was ready, the departing troops were reviewed outside the south entrance to the palace⁄city. The Court was in attendance, bands were playing. Ch'ung Chên stationed him⁄self on the tower of the Ch'ien Gate, which commanded a pros⁄pect of the whole parade. Later in the day he presided at a ban⁄quet and after passing the wine seven times, thrice pledged the Grand Secretary's health and handed him a patent inscribed with the words: 'Acting as Grand Marshall on our Imperial behalf.'

The troops then marched away past the Temple of Heaven. But it was no good omen that the pole of the Grand Secre⁄tary's sedan⁄chair should break when he was hardly clear of the outer city.

In spite of this effort, the news continued to be bad. During the next few days T'ai Yuan⁄fu, one of the bastions of the metropolitan province, fell to the rebels. When the Emperor was informed, he is reported to have said: 'In the watches of the night I mourn over these things and my self⁄abasement knows no limit. From this day forth I am resolved to reform myself and to avert the consequences of my errors. I mean to strengthen our resources by employing able men in office and by adherence to honoured precedent to avoid evil.' He went on to command that those who had been unjustly dismissed should be re-instated and offered a marquisate to anyone who should capture Li.

Worse news, however, began to come in, desperate news— Ming Wu-fu was fallen, another bastion of the capital. The Grand Secretary had totally failed, which was not surprising as he knew nothing of soldiering. In his distress the Emperor lost all sense. He placed an eunuch at the head of a fresh army, a creature called Tu Hsün, a coward and a traitor, who was totally ignorant of military affairs and had already advised his master to surrender.

'You had better abdicate,' the fellow had said. 'You and I, we have plenty to live on in retirement.'

Tu Hsün was ordered to go to Hsuan-hua, the last fortress between Li and the capital, and hold it at all costs. When he got there, however, he ordered the Governor to open the gates and himself in court robes went out ten miles to meet the rebel army. Li entered the city unopposed and in such an excellent temper that he did not allow a massacre. The inhabitants in their joy burnt incense in welcome, but the Governor, who was an old Ming die-hard and had refused to have anything to do with the surrender, though he could not prevent it, now wrote a valedictory memorial in which he implored the Emperor to call upon his subjects for a supreme effort, and then hanged himself from a beam.

Li now debouched into the plain of Peking, which stretches for thirty miles north of the city. Halting at the Ming tombs, he plundered them, a desecration calculated to strike at the Emperor's morale, for his ancestors would be highly incensed by the affront. While he halted, confidential agents were working for him in the capital. There was treachery everywhere. The Board of War could not issue a confidential order, but its terms were communicated to him at once.

The Grand Secretary, who was back again at Pekin, strongly advised the Emperor to leave. Let the Court move to Nanking out of harm's way. Their immense resources could be rallied there. Li would collapse in time. He was only a marauder.

When he had got his plunder he would take himself off. Better to lose property than your life.

But inept though the Emperor was, he possessed a reserve of dignity. To these too politic suggestions he replied with the lofty formula: 'The Sovereign must die for the Altars of the Tutelary Deities.' And pressed to send, at least, his children to safety, he said firmly: 'It is the duty of the Emperor and his family to die for the state. I order the Princes to remain in Peking.'

But the situation was not yet wholly desperate. The Ming possessed another army, an excellent army of 200,000 men, and under, so it happened, a most capable general. This was the force commanded by General Wu San-kuei, which was stationed on the eastern frontier of the metropolitan province, where that marched with Manchuria. It was there for a very good reason. We have had our eyes fixed on Li advancing from the west, but actually a great, though less instant, danger existed in the east. That was the direction in which the Ming had long been looking, and the danger there explains in part why the arrangements to stop Li were so entirely inadequate. The fact was that Manchuria had for years been a source of anxiety. When T'ien Ch'i was on the throne, that country, which was the home of several Mongolian clans, had been unified by a great man, Nurhachi. Aware that the Ming administration was breaking down, he saw a chance of making himself Emperor of China. During the years which followed he extended his dominion, improved his army and got ready for the great day. He died in 1626, two years before Ch'ung Chên became Emperor. His successor, T'ai Tsung, carried on his policy with vigour, and there were preliminary battles in which the Ming got the worst of it. By 1644 T'ai Tsung was dead, and a Regent had been appointed, as the heir was a child. This Regent was Prince Jui, a man of great ability. When he saw the strait to which the Ming were brought by the rebellion of Li, he knew the time was come and massed his troops for an invasion.

That was the very good reason why General Wu with the

best Imperial army was watching Manchuria. However, as Jui on the frontier was not so immediately alarming as Li at the gates, Ch'ung Chên sent an urgent message to Wu, bidding him hasten to his assistance. In the same letter he created him an earl. Wu was distant hardly more than two hundred miles. But he did not come. Why he did not, we shall see later, for General Wu is one of the principal characters in this story. We must return now to the Forbidden City to witness the last act of the drama there.

## IV

# *Suicide*

The capital was strongly fortified and there was no reason, if it were stoutly defended, why it should not hold out till Wu arrived. But Ch'ung Chên, in spite of his ardent desire to act rightly, could not act with common sense, and appointed another eunuch to the command of the garrison. The whole corps of eunuchs was in communication with Li. They hoped to save themselves and their money by a private arrangement. But Ch'ung Chên still believed in their devotion.

When Li was satisfied that his agents had done their work and that there would be little resistance, he covered the few miles which separated him from Peking. Having dispersed three regiments which were outside the walls and intimidated by his artillery fire those manning the top of it, he raised his scaling ladders near the south gate of the outer city and established himself easily inside that part of the capital. North of him was the Imperial City, the core of which was the Great Within, as the Forbidden City or Palace was called. The key to both was the Ch'ien Gate, from the tower of which Ch'ung Chên had watched his troops parade. Li had no difficulty in seizing this gate. The fall of the inner cities was now certain.

A fortnight previously the Court of Astronomers had submitted to the Emperor a memorial indicating his astrological position. This was as serious as well could be imagined. He was atrociously aspected. In reply he had issued a feeble rescript calling on his officials to repent. What he should have done was to dismiss them and put loyal men in their places, a course which he had promised to take and which was quite feasible, for he had devoted supporters, as will appear.

With the fall of the Ch'ien men the Emperor realized that the end had come. There was no word from Wu. The garrison troops began deserting. He now changed his mind about his children and sent for the Heir Apparent and his younger brother. They arrived in Court robes, when he ordered an eunuch to dress them in rough clothes. They must escape from the city.

'To-morrow you will be one of the people,' he told them, 'homeless wanderers. Do not reveal your names, pretend as best you can; say "sir" when spoken to. You must try and live so as to right my wrongs.'

He was very distressed after this parting and called for wine. Night had fallen. All round the doomed city were the watch fires of the rebels. How his children were to escape he did not know. He himself did not intend to try. He meant what he had said about his Tutelary Altars.

The wine was brought; he drank several cups. His thoughts went to his imperial ancestors. They had never forgotten their dignity. When the hour struck, they knew how to die, turning a final verse, quoting a classic phrase. There was no lack of precedents to guide him.

He called for more wine and more again. Now, instead of mellowing, it seemed to be maddening him. That coarse ruffian out there, Li—what was it he now called himself?—Yung Ch'ang of the Ta Shun!—that rebel, that murderer—how many of the Royal House had he not already massacred? All whom he had laid hands on in the towns he had looted. And now he was about to loot the Palace, the Purple and Forbidden City, its stacked riches, gold, jewels, choice jades—why, there were rooms of lacquered boxes, which had never been unpacked, never been opened, tribute presents from the Outer Barbarians, treasures not yet even catalogued, dating back to the beginning of the Dynasty, such a superfluity had there always been of jade gongs, antique porcelains, pearl necklaces, bowls of lapis-lazuli. Well, Li would have his pick of them now. But there were certain treasures which the fellow should not have, and as he thought of them, he caught up a sword.

'Send for the Empress Consort and my Ladies,' he commanded.

While they were coming he drained a last beaker, and when they had entered and knelt, they saw him standing with a drawn sword, on his pale face the madness of desperation.

'All is over,' he cried. 'It is time for you to die.'

The Lady Yuan, who was in the first rank of the Concubinate and the first in that rank, screamed at these frantic words, and began to run back, but he pursued her, whirling his sword, and shouting—'You must die!'—struck her a blow across the shoulders. She continued to run till he caught her again and this time thrust her through and through. His intention was then to kill the others, but they were already in flight across the courtyard. The Empress Consort reached her own apartments and in the Pavilion of Feminine Tranquillity hanged herself.

But his frenzy was not yet sated. He told them to fetch the Princess Imperial. When the girl came—she was only fifteen—he was glaring, his embroidered boots soaked with blood, his sword stained dark.

'Ah!' he sighed, standing over her, 'you were unlucky, unlucky to be born a Ming. Had your father been a cultivator or a camel-driver, this storm would have passed high over your head. But now . . . !' and suddenly he cut off her arm.

Then he went raging through the courtyards to the Pavilion of Charity Made Manifest, where he killed his second daughter, the Princess of Feminine Propriety. Thence, sending ahead a eunuch to salute her, he turned towards the Empress's Pavilion. When he saw her body hanging dead from the rafters, he stopped and said softly, 'Death is best. She did well. She has pointed the way for Us.'

The day was nearly breaking when he returned to his apartments.

'Take off my dragon robe,' he said, and when they had done so, he chose a short tunic, a cap and a plain purple and yellow robe. The bell sounded for the dawn-audience. He took his seat, but no one came. It may have been that following the events of the night, it had seemed incredible that he should hold an audience, or the courtiers were too terrified, or they had abandoned him.

He became very sorrowful. After his debauch of wine and blood, he was very tired, very low. It was the muddy bottom of the ebb. And at any moment the rebels might burst in. But Li would never take him alive. His mind was made up on what he must do.

When a king comes to his end, it often happens that death is made less bitter for him by the presence of some faithful servant. Ch'ung Chên was now supported in his agony by a eunuch called Wang Ch'eng⁄en, for it happens, too, that worthies are found among the most unworthy. Together they left the Great Within by its northern exit, known as the Gate of Divine Military Prowess. That part of the Imperial City into which they entered was not yet occupied by the rebel troops, who were congregated to the south. Close by stands the Coal Hill, an artificial mound which had been constructed at that par⁄ticular spot for reasons of geomancy to shield the throne from the dangerous influences, which come from the north. At the base of it was the Imperial Hat and Girdle Department. They went into this pavilion and closed the door.

Before an Emperor of China died it was customary for him to write a valedictory decree. Ch'ung Chên now told Wang to give him writing materials. There should have been plenty in the Hat and Girdle Department, but the eunuch could only find a brush and some ink. As there was no paper, the Em⁄peror wrote the valedictory decree on the yellow lapel of his robe. These were the words he used in his farewell:

'I, feeble and of small virtue, have offended against Heaven. The rebels have seized my capital because my Ministers have deceived me. Ashamed to face my Ancestors, I die. Removing my Imperial cap and with my hair dishevelled about my face, I leave to the rebels the dismemberment of my body. Let them not harm my people.'

He then strangled himself with his girdle and Wang did the same.

The student of human nature will compare this scene with that which was enacted five years later in London. Charles I of England, having been condemned by those who had risen in rebellion against him as a 'tyrant, traitor, murderer and enemy of his country', was sentenced to be decapitated. 'The dignity which he had failed to preserve in his long jangling with Brad-shaw and the judges returned at the call of death,' writes Green. 'Whatever had been the faults and follies of his life, 'he nothing common did nor mean, upon that memorable scene'.'

Though the Emperor died out of sight of the Court, the news became known immediately, and distraught, as he had been at the prospect of Li's imminent arrival, many hastened to make an end of themselves. The Lady Wei, a member of the Con-cubinate, rushed out of her apartments to the Imperial Canal, and crying, 'All who are not cowards will follow my example,' threw herself in. Two hundred other ladies did the same. The minister, Yi Yuan-lu, hurried to the Palace and writing on a desk, 'My duty is to die. Do not wrap me in grave clothes, let my corpse be exposed,' sat down with his face to the south, the quarter of happy augury, and strangled himself. The President of the Censorate did likewise at the shrine of the Patriots of the Dynasty, where he wrote: 'In the hour of my country's disaster, I here commit suicide, asking permission to wait on you, worthy gentlemen, at the Nine Springs.'

The President of the Court of Revision went to his library and taking down his favourite books, burnt them so that they should not be defiled. Then, dressed in his Court robes and with his badge of office, he wrote to his father and put an end to his life.

Such desperate courses, which these latter days of Europe have made less unfamiliar to us, were in conformity with the canons of Confucian conduct. Many more took them than those already mentioned, such as the Director of Sacrificial Worship, the Censor, Ch'en Liang-mi, and the Marquis Liu, who, returning home that morning and finding that his mother, wife and sisters had hanged themselves after setting fire to the house, threw himself down a well in company with his uncle, a grandee of the Palace, when he had changed from military into court dress out of respect for the Emperor's spirit whom he was about to join.

# V

## *Li enters The Great Within*

At rĺoon that same day, mounted on a piebald horse and attended by his staff, the rebel Li entered the Imperial City by the Gate of Heavenly Peace, which had been opened to him by the eunuchs. His appearance was that of a ruffian of melodrama. Over the empty socket of his lost eye he wore a black patch. His other eye was large and phosphorescent, so that he was often called 'Owl-eyed'. He had a beak of a nose, ferociously aqui- line, a high forehead and a sunken jaw. The eunuchs escorted him with abject alacrity to the throne-hall of Imperial Supre- macy, and invited him to take the Dragon Seat. Striking an attitude, he bade them search for their Majesties, for he had not yet heard that they were dead. When he was informed of this, he ordered the bodies to be brought for his inspection. Con- trary to what the Emperor had feared, he did not decree dis- memberment and allowed a funeral, though he refused to sanction a Treasury grant for the expenses.

Two days later at dawn, taking the Dragon Seat in the throne-hall of Heavenly Purity, the centre of the Great Within, he summoned the Court to audience. It was only a minority which had committed suicide. The bulk of the officials were ready to submit and hoped to serve the new sovereign in their present appointments. All trooped in, depressed and servile, to the open space in front of the hall and went down on their knees and elbows to perform the kotow. Li, in his triumph, decided to snub them and let them grovel there, nor condes- cended even to reply to their congratulations. As he continued to slight them, not deigning so much as to look in their direction, his soldiery strode in among the crouching figures, kicked them on the neck and pulled off their hats. Among those kotowing were an Imperial Duke and two Grand Secretaries, who were prodded with swords, and kicked with the rest. It was the most humiliating spectacle which had ever been seen at the Court of China.

Shortly afterwards Li delivered the whole city to massacre and rape. While his soldiers were so engaged, he proceeded methodically to despoil those citizens who had money. The wretched officials who had hoped to save themselves by im/ mediate submission were seized in batches. Eight hundred of them were drafted into a camp presided over by one of his com/ manders and tortured until they disclosed their hidden wealth. An Academician was beaten to death because he was too slow in answering questions. Members of the Imperial Family, after they had delivered up all they had, were put to various kinds of death.

At the end of a week of horror, notice was issued by the President of the Board of Rites, calling upon all officials and notabilities to submit a memorial praying Li formally to ascend the throne. With this order they hurriedly complied, and he was graciously pleased to appoint a day, astrologically the best in the immediate future.

In spite of his glittering success in seizing the most ancient throne in the world, Li was not altogether easy. When long ago an astrologer had whispered that he would become Son of Heaven, he had been warned at the same time that his reign would be brief. The possible fragility of his triumph had been in his mind the day he rode on his piebald horse through the Gate of Heavenly Peace, for as he approached it and saw above him on the lintel the great ideograph signifying 'heaven', he be/ thought him of the early title he had taken—by Heaven's Grace Grand Captain of Righteousness—and suddenly anxious for a sign that heaven was yet favourable, bent his bow, declaring that if his arrow should hit the ideograph it would be proof that grace was still to be extended to him. Since the character was, as I say, large, and he was close and a good shot, there was small risk of his arrow missing, and when he did miss, striking just below it, he was appalled, as, indeed, was his staff, and could not suppress a foreboding that, in accordance with prophecy, his triumph would be short. However, what can mortal do but work out his destiny? He must continue on the assumption that all would be well. So had he arranged to be enthroned. True, there was a possible alternative which he might have taken, one which other kings of the East had been known to adopt. He might have postponed his installation and so, though he should be ruling *de facto*, his reign would not have started *de jure* and therefore the prophecy of its brevity would not have begun to run. But he dismissed this expedient or else it did not occur to him, and fixed a day in the circumstances stated.

# VI

# *General Wu and the Round-faced Beauty*

The scene now changes to the Sino-Manchurian frontier and the principal characters are General Wu and the Regent, Jui.

It will be recalled that during the last fatal days before the capture of Peking Ch'ung Chên had sent urgently to Wu bidding him leave the frontier and hasten to his assistance. Why had Wu not come? Had he turned traitor? The answer to these questions is full of human interest.

Wu was in command of 200,000 seasoned troops. His army, based on the frontier town of Shan Hai-kuan, lay halfway between the Chinese and the Manchurian capitals, being some 180 miles from Peking and 220 from Mukden. When Li came battering in, Wu, who was a man of great personal ambition, found himself suddenly the deciding factor in a game where the prize was the Chinese Empire. There were three alternatives before him. He might hasten to his Emperor's assistance, defeat Li and then return to the frontier in time to prevent a Manchu invasion. Or he might join Li on terms, the two together holding off the Manchus. Or he might join the Manchus on terms and so make them masters of the situation. Which course he took, and why he took it, the following citations will make quite clear.

It seems that he received the Imperial summons only a few days before Li's appearance outside the capital. He did not obey it, but remained where he was, biding his time and waiting on events. Four days after the fall of Peking, he wrote to his father, who held an important military appointment at Court.

'It is rumoured here that Peking is fallen, but of this we have no definite news. No doubt the city is being besieged. If you can manage to escape, do not bring much money with you, but bury your treasure as best you can. Please tell the Lady Ch'en that I am in good health and bid her keep up her courage.'

Lady Ch'en was his concubine and he was deeply in love with her. She was sometimes known as the 'Round-faced Beauty', and had been a professional singer.

Next day Wu heard definitely that Li had entered the city and that the Emperor was dead. He sent a messenger galloping to his father with a note advising him to submit to Li, should the women of the family be in danger. 'I am most anxious about the Lady Ch'en,' he adds.

His father had written him a letter two days after the entry of Li, and this now arrived. Wu replied immediately:

'I have received your letter of the 20th and note that you have surrendered to the new Emperor. Under the circumstances, it was the only thing to do, so as to save our womenfolk. . . . But your letter goes on to say that the Lady Ch'en has left Peking on horseback on her way to my camp. I have seen and heard nothing of her. Oh father! how could you be so reckless as to allow a delicate girl of her age to start on such a dangerous journey?' He then states the proposition that the truly great man will always frame his actions with regard to the exigencies of the moment, adding: 'I have been seriously thinking myself of submitting to Li, but your news about the Lady Ch'en has greatly upset me.'

Two days later he wrote again, saying he had heard that a rebel general had captured Lady Ch'en on the road. 'It is a frightful thing. I shall never see her again in this life. I could never have believed that you, father, would have been guilty of such folly as to let her go.' He then explains that on the previous day he fought an engagement with a detachment of rebel troops in the vicinity, worsted them and had planned to march on Peking in alliance with the Manchus. 'But I have hesitated to do so because of the possible consequences to the Lady

Ch'en.' If her captor had taken her back to Peking, Li would probably treat her well, when he learnt who she was, so as to induce him to surrender. 'But if I once move my troops, he will certainly kill her.'

On receiving his father's answer he wrote: 'I have your letter, in which you tell me that the Lady Ch'en has been appointed a concubine in the Palace and am glad to hear that she is being kindly treated. . . . You also say that the Ming Heir Apparent is in the Palace; have you seen him or not? Now that you have submitted to the Shun Dynasty, you should memorialize the new Emperor in audience and tell him what I wrote about coming over to his side. All I ask is that he hand over to me the Heir Apparent and the Lady Ch'en. Let him do this and I will loyally submit to his dynasty at once.'

These extracts make clear what was passing in Wu's mind. Deeply agitated about his sweetheart, his first impulse on hearing that she was in rebel hands was to join the Manchus and march against Li. Reflection showed the danger to Lady Ch'en of this course and he asks his father to negotiate terms with Li, these to include the surrender of Lady Ch'en and the Ming Heir. The latter, having been captured when the city fell, had failed to escape as his father had planned. Wu's desire to control his person should be explained as a plan to restore the Ming Dynasty in a modified form, by placing the youth on the throne. Li would be allowed to have, say, half the empire. By that arrangement he, Wu, would become Regent of the Ming half, for the Heir Apparent was not more than sixteen.

Shortly after sending this letter and before his father could have approached Li, Wu received a despatch from the new Emperor, dated eleven days after the fall of Peking. It was sarcastic in tone, full of bluff and threats, though accompanied by a present of 40,000 taels, a sum of about £15,000.

'You have indeed been favoured by fortune', it begins, 'in rising to so high a position, since you have never rendered any pre-eminent service to your Sovereign. But as you happen to be in a position to call in the Manchus, you are worth bribing, a course for which there exist classical precedents, since earlier rulers have been obliged to reward subjects of doubtful loyalty.'

After this offensive opening Li changes to menace.

'At present you have a large army under you, but it has only a spectacular value. If my troops march on you, they will be victorious. Here, therefore, is my offer and it is my last—surrender to me and you will be rewarded as I promise; should you fail to do so, I will defeat you one morning and in the same afternoon decapitate your father. A pressing message.'

To this letter Wu did not reply, waiting until his father should have seen Li and communicated his terms. This must have been done, for seven days later Li, who by then had been master of the capital for eighteen days, and was already using the imperial title, wrote to Wu:

'The Ming Heir is safely esconced in the Palace, so you may abandon all hope of using him for the furtherance of your schemes. We have given him a princedom, and we have made over to him your wife and women for him to dally with as he pleases.'

Li perceived very well why Wu wanted the Ming Heir, but he had no intention of dividing the empire or, if he should think it politic to use the young prince in some capacity, it would be for him, not for Wu, to judge what that should be. By giving the youth Lady Ch'en he made it clear that between him and Wu there was an issue which only the sword could decide. In fact, three days later he marched against him with 100,000 men.

When Wu saw that he could not come to terms with Li, he was obliged to turn to the third course which was open. Accordingly he wrote to Prince Jui, the Regent of Manchuria. The letter, which was in the classical style, for Wu had some pretensions to scholarship, began by a reference to the capture of Peking by 'pilfering dogs', and continued in these terms:

'The accumulated virtues of our dynastic line have inspired feelings of loyalty and devotion in our people; volunteers are flocking to my standard against the foul invaders and I, who

A CHINESE BEAUTY
*From a painting in the Musée Guimet*

have received such favours from the Throne, have endeavoured to raise an avenging host which shall attain the decisive victory that all men desire. But I regret to say that my forces are insufficient and therefore, weeping tears of blood, I implore your assistance.'

'Weeping tears of blood!'—but this is the grand manner and, as we shall see, the Regent knew the value of it. The letter swept on: 'For two centuries our States have been allies.' (In fact for sixty years they had been on the worst of terms.) 'Surely you will never suffer bandit traitors to work their evil will. Your duty to Heaven requires you to exterminate these wrong-doers. Generosity and justice urge you to rescue the people from this scourge of fire and blood. To restore a foreign State and renew an extinct lineage, that is real glory, that is virtue.'

The final paragraph is more splendid still:

'Your Highness is endowed with heroic qualities. I beseech you to pay heed to this loyal entreaty of the orphaned servant of a ruined dynasty.'

The Regent's reply, though also classical, contained certain hints of a realistic kind.

'The tidings of the capture of Peking and the lamentable death of the Ming Sovereign have caused my hair to stand on end with horror,' he wrote with exquisite politeness, but with an entire absence of truth; and then: 'Our present purpose is to establish the fortunes of your state and to take your people under our protection.' This sentence was an urbane way of stating that he proposed, not to restore the fallen state of the Mings, but to establish in China his own dynasty. As an inducement to Wu to second this intention, he offered him a feudal Princedom.

In his reply Wu pretended that he understood the Regent to be actuated by the loftiest of motives. 'Your righteous action will bring you eternal fame,' he exclaims, and declares that, of course, he will second him in every way, not because he has any desire to become a feudal prince, but solely on account of his loyalty to the Ming.

Six days later Li came up, his army having been considerably reinforced. By that time certain Manchu brigades had
joined Wu, and in an engagement which was fought near Shan
Hai-kuan Li was worsted. Realizing immediately that Wu
backed by the Manchus was too strong, he sought to detach
him by sending to his camp, as he had been asked to do a
month earlier, the Ming Heir and the Lady Ch'en.

Wu immediately reverted to his former plan. He arranged
for the Heir to take the reign title of Yi-Hsing and to appoint him Regent. Acting as such he entered there and then
into a secret alliance with Li, it being agreed that Li should
evacuate Peking (though he could take his loot), and withdraw to the provinces to the westward. If the Manchus attacked
they should join forces against them. By this arrangement China
was divided between the two of them, a vastly better proposition, as far as Wu was concerned, than a feudal Princedom.
Moreover, he had got his sweetheart back.

The alliance being signed, Li returned at once to Peking.
Wu publicly represented this as the result of his defeat, and for
the moment the Regent suspected nothing and went on with
his preparations for a major invasion. He did not even ask why
Wu had not pursued Li, or if he did was satisfied with whatever excuse was given him.

Back in the capital Li began to wonder whether his alliance
with Wu was as sound as it looked on paper. His agents
brought in copies of two proclamations signed by the General
on the same day, in one of which he styled himself Ming
Regent, and in the other a Manchu Prince. This looked queer,
so queer that Li began to suspect treachery. If Wu, in spite of
his promises, were to join forces with the Manchu main army,
he might attack him in overwhelming strength. It had been a
mistake to give up Lady Ch'en. Then he remembered that he
had another lever, old Wu. He seems to have sent a message to
say that unless Wu complied with certain demands, he would
kill his father.

This part of the story has never wholly been cleared up.

Suffice it to say that when Wu learnt that his father's life was in danger, he refused to take the steps, whatever they were, which Li required. It is possible that one of them was the temporary surrender of Lady Ch'en as earnest of his good faith. Colour is lent to this by the fact that Chinese historians, writing from the Confucian standpoint, have accused Wu of putting her before his father. But if we do not possess the precise sequence of events, Wu's last letter to his father is extant. It seems to have been in reply to one sent by the old gentleman, wherein he reminded his son of the duties of filial piety. In the context of that day, when a son's duty to his parents took first place, Wu's letter was shocking, and even to-day, when the passion of romantic love is put forward as an excuse for any aberration, it is unlikely to recommend the General for our admiration.

Let the reader judge: 'Father dear, your unfilial son weeps tears of blood' (this was evidently one of Wu's stock classical tags) 'and offers his duty at your knee. Since childhood I have benefited by your teaching, and striven night and day to do my duty in the field, in the hope of repaying something of my Emperor's favours.' As at the moment he was in alliance either with the bandit who had seized or the foreign enemy who hoped to seize China, these are mere phrases. He then proceeds to contrast his father's behaviour with his own, or rather with what he pretends is his. 'You, dear father, were one of the military commanders and had a large force at your disposal. How comes it that you surrendered so quickly? A mighty city like Peking should not have fallen after a single day's siege. I have learned with shame of His Majesty's death and of the massacre of his subjects. You, father mine, have enjoyed a reputation for loyalty; if you could not have repelled the invader, surely you should have cut your throat at the Gate? Then I should have hastened in deep mourning to avenge your fate or perish in the attempt.'

When we remember that Wu had already commended his father for his good sense in submitting quickly, the hollowness of his present indignation is only too evident.

The letter now becomes harsh and disgraceful.

'You have failed to act as a loyal Minister; why should I be a filial son? Henceforward I disown you. Even though the rebels place you on the sacrificial altar, so as to make me submit, I shall ignore your fate. Respectful greetings from your son.'

In fact, old Wu was executed. As soon as Li found that Wu refused to pledge Lady Ch'en or do whatever it was that was required of him to prove his loyalty, he ordered the decapitation of his father and all the women of the family.

# VII

# *Li discards the Dragon Robe for another*

This act of revenge shows that Li was now convinced there was nothing more to be gained from Wu, and as he could not maintain himself at Peking against his army combined with the Regent's, he decided to decamp at once. Orders were given to pack the loot. But he was not going without being enthroned. His reign, indeed, would be very brief, for he would have to leave the morning after. Yet he would have been *de jure* Emperor of China at least for a day. Nothing thereafter could expunge his name from the ancient roll of the Sons of Heaven.

As he was in a great hurry, he could not wait for the date already selected. The ceremony would have to take place at once. The arrangements in consequence were somewhat perfunctory. The gold coinage bearing his reign title was not ready in time. That part of the ritual, where utensils manufactured specially for the occasion were necessary, had to be omitted. It was the shabbiest enthronement in Chinese history. However, he had his hour of triumph. He sat on the Dragon Seat dressed in the Dragon Robe; the whole court kotowed; and in the Temple of Heaven he announced his accession to the supernal powers. Nor did he forget his promise to raise seven generations of his ancestors to imperial rank.

Packing meanwhile had been in vigorous progress. He could not remove everything of value. He had to select, take what would travel well, as the soldiers of the European allies found when in 1900 they sacked Peking. Porcelains, pictures, bronzes

—such works of art were hardly to his purpose, and he melted down all the gold vessels in the Palace. As bullion they went easily into his saddle-bags. It is said that he loaded altogether ten million ounces on to his mules. But that was not by any means the total of his loot. Camels, ponies, bullocks, carts, sedans, wheelbarrows—it was a multitudinous caravan that set out westwards. His last act was to set fire to the main halls of the Palace.

When Wu heard that the horrid gang was clear of the city, he moved down from the frontier ahead of the Prince Regent, revolving an extension of his previous plans. If he could put the Ming Heir on the throne quick enough, he might be able to present the Manchus with a *fait accompli*. But it was a forlorn hope. Prince Jui was much too clever a man. When he received information that Wu had arranged for the Heir to enter Peking in the Imperial Sedan and be conducted to the Palace, he issued orders that no such state entry was to be permitted, and himself hastened to Wu's camp outside the city. Next morning, when the notabilities collected at the Front Gate to receive the Heir, whom they had been told to expect that day, they saw a palanquin arrive. In it were the Regent and General Wu. There was dead silence, when the former ordered them to conduct him into the Palace. Obliged to comply, they formed a procession and at the Meridian Gate the residue of the eunuchs—for Li after robbing had killed most of their order—came forward in their abject way with the Imperial Sedan, in which Prince Jui was carried to one of the throne-halls. Since his army was known to be approaching, certain officials thought it prudent to offer him the throne there and then, which he accepted on behalf of his ward, Shun Chih. From that June day of 1644 until 1912 the Ch'ing Dynasty ruled in China.

The Regent's first act was to confer upon Wu the promised Princedom, which was handsome enough of him considering the General's tricky vacillations. His second act was to send him after Li, to rob that robber, get back the loot. This task

Wu eventually accomplished. Li, defeated in a series of actions, lost everything and, a beggared fugitive, fled back into the wilds of Shensi, from which he originally had come. Two years later, still pursued, he went south to Hunan with thirty followers and sighting one day a lonely monastery on Mount Chia in the An-fu district, bade his retinue farewell and took the yellow robe, as many another Eastern bandit has done. He did not tell the Abbot who he was, that he was Yung Ch'ang of the Ta Shun, but settled down quietly to his new life. For twenty-eight years, till his death in 1674, he remained in the monastery. What a host of memories must have lain in wait to distract his mind from the Buddhist way! As he sat in his room conning the Scriptures—it is said that the canonical books dealing with ecclesiastical discipline interested him the most—or droning the Sutras or in meditation, his thoughts must often have wandered to his astounding horoscope, to the day he became a rebel and began his march on the capital. What pictures must have risen up of triumph and disaster!—the first breaking in, his bowshot at the gate, the eunuchs, the Concubinate, the Court, the Dragon Throne, his defeat at the frontier, his flight with the gold. Well, he had been the greatest, the most glorious bandit ever heard of in China's story, which meant the premier bandit in the world! The Great Within, what a thing to have sat there! To have been the Dragon, if only for a day! Hard to believe, when one was dressed in saffron in the bare room of a hill monastery, surrounded by a sheepish crowd of monks, and having to obey a rustic Abbot. What would they say, how would they look, if he revealed his strange identity? Well, he'd never tell them, not a word. The secret would go with him down to the grave.

It is recorded that after he had been at Mount Chia for some years, one who was once his follower in the wild romping days —his name was Yeh Fu—took the robe also and became his servant. Now he had somebody to talk to, a man of his own kind, a fellow who knew his wonderful story. And they must have gone over every detail of it. What was Li's big mistake?

How often they must have debated that. When Peking was his, where had he gone wrong? One can see them arguing, Li on his mat, his single eye still bright, his nose more hooked than ever; at a respectful distance Yeh Fu cross-legged, his glance deferential, though they were now cronies. What was the mistake? Li had been so careful. He knew that the moment was astrologically dangerous, and had tried his utmost to circumvent his stars. Yet after his reverse on the frontier, a defeat by no means, a mischance he could have righted, what did he do but send Wu back his girl! That was the very root of all his ruin. At the time he had thought it a brilliant notion. Wu would be so pleased. He doted on the lady, the Round-faced Beauty, and she was a beauty. Li had been so sure it would bring him round; they would be close friends and divide the Empire. If he had kept the girl, promising to give her up only when Wu had openly joined him, Wu would have stayed, must have stayed his ally, and together they were fully a match for the Regent. So a pretty girl had been his ruin, as of so many men before him; not because *he* loved her; no, but because the one man in China who was a danger to him loved her to distraction, for her sake would have come to heel, and though he held that trump card, he had thrown it away, played it too soon and lost the game.

On the day before his death—he had reached his seventieth year—he addressed to Yeh Fu a valedictory decree, using the style of a Son of Heaven. In this document he declared that following the example of the Blessed One, who as Prince had renounced his kingdom to seek the Truth, so he after becoming Emperor of China had deliberately and for the same reason abandoned all. The Buddha's kingdom had been small and unimportant, his the most gorgeous heritage in the world. His renunciation, therefore, had been very great, greater—let it be said reverently—than the dear Lord's. And because it was clearly greater, and because for twenty-eight years, a monk of the Order, he had sought the Truth, night and day meditating on ultimate things, until now he had pierced the last illusions and knew his life to have been a true pilgrimage away from the errors which entrap the self, condemning it to endless empty births, might he not therefore hope to enter forthwith the blessed state of a Boddhisattva, so to dedicate himself for ever to the deliverance of mankind?

Thus died the old ruffian in the odour of sanctity and was buried in the temple precinct. Though he had enjoyed the consideration of the monks—for his portrait had been hung in the library—he had never revealed his secret and now on the dagoba which they erected over his grave, Yeh Fu cut the style he had assumed on taking the robe, Jewel of Heaven's Grace, an adaptation of and, perhaps, an allusion to his first style, By Heaven's Grace Grand Captain of Righteousness. In front of the tomb a tablet was erected, on which was written: 'None can tell the family name or origin of the priest who lies buried here,' proof that even after his death Yeh Fu was not tempted to tell the story. But the secret came out twenty-one years later when the portrait was seen by an official who had known him.

It is interesting to note that the dagoba and the two inscriptions remain to this day.[1]

[1] It is possible that this story of his later years may be apocryphal, because officially he was stated to have been killed in battle.

# VIII

# *The Death of a Confucian*

To return now to the year 1644. The Manchus had entered Peking without drawing a bow. The Regent, however, realized well enough that to take the capital was not to possess China. The provinces were full of Ming partisans. There was also another army stationed at Nanking on the Yang-tse, six hundred miles to the south, which had been too far away to affect the issue. To conquer what were vast territories, if these should refuse to recognize the new régime, would mean, he knew, a long war. But they might be persuaded to recognize it by a show of moderation and a parade of reason. Accordingly, he gave orders that the late Emperor and Empress should be canonized, and gave them a state funeral in accordance with the full rites. His troops were strictly forbidden to loot, the markets were kept open and the peasantry encouraged to continue their work. Grandees and high officials were confirmed in their old appointments. There was no proscription and no seizure of women. Everything was done to underline the difference between Manchu and rebel behaviour, the Manchus being held up, moreover, as the saviours of China.

But in spite of this conciliatory programme, he was unsuccessful in winning over certain of the provincial officials, men who were inspired by Confucian ideals of loyalty to their dynasty, and who in any case objected to foreign rule. In their eyes the Manchus were mere barbarians from beyond the Great Wall: any culture they possessed had been copied from China. The Heir Apparent having escaped from Wu's custody and his whereabouts being unknown, some of these men selected a cousin of their late sovereign, and enthroned him at Nanking as the rightful Emperor, under the reign title of Hung Kuang. The southern army, commanded by a resolute general called Shih K'o-fa, rallied to them and they prepared to resist any further advance of the Manchus. When the Regent learnt of this he decided to get into direct touch with their general. If he had been successful with General Wu, why should he not have the same success with General Shih? Could he but induce him to come over, the whole south would submit as the north had done without the necessity of drawing a bow. There-fore, in October 1664, he addressed to Shih a letter, taking the greatest care with his style, for reasons which will become apparent.

'Long ago at Mukden,' he opens, 'I heard of your high reputation in Peking as a scholar and since our victories over the rebels I have taken occasion to find out all about you in the literary circles of the metropolis. Last week I sent you a letter of condolence over the late sad events and His Majesty's death, but now I hear with surprise that the Ming dynasty has re-established itself at Nanking and that a new Emperor has been chosen.'

At this point the writer introduces a classical quotation, a passage from one of the Confucian Books, which is meant by analogy to cast doubt on the propriety of Hung Kuang's acces-sion while Li was still at large, for the letter was written before Wu had defeated him. That an *obiter dictum* of the Master with regard to a particular situation in the fifth century B.C. should be thought to govern absolutely a situation in the seventeenth century A.D. may appear to us odd. But it was less odd to the correspondents, both of whom had received a classical educa-tion still narrower than that dispensed, say fifty years ago, by an Oxford Tutor in *literae humaniores*. The Regent's object, how-ever, in introducing the quotation was less to convince Shih of its continuing validity than to create an agreeable atmosphere of learning before coming to the pith of what he had to say.

Having displayed his erudition in this way, and, he hoped, made the right impression, he comes to the point:

'Who could have dreamed that you, a scholar and a gentle/man, should be so short/sighted as to seek the temporary con/tinuance of your dynasty at Nanking. I greatly deplore that you should be thus blind to visible dangers, and permit yourself to cherish vain and deceptive illusions.'

He begs him to consider the facts: 'It hardly needs an astro/loger to foretell that the destruction of the Ming's poor rem/nant by our victorious armies is inevitable, since, while still masters of China, they were obliged to capitulate to Li and his rabble. They should face the situation and gracefully yield to the fortune of war.'

Cannot Shih advise them to do this, he suggests. If the Ming Prince who has taken an Imperial title will renounce it, 'our dynasty proposes to assign to him suitable revenues and a resid/ence, and will treat him as an honoured descendant of the dis/possessed dynasty. I undertake that the highest honours shall be lavished upon him by our Imperial bounty and that precedence shall be accorded to him over all Princes at our Court.'

There follows a direct inducement to Shih himself:

'As for you and other distinguished gentlemen of the south, if you will repair to our Court and swear allegiance to the Ch'ing Throne, you will be rewarded with the highest rank and hereditary fiefs. Is not our treatment of General Wu an earnest of our good intentions towards you?'

The Regent had appealed to Shih's good sense and to his self/interest: he now appeals to his humanity. 'Nowadays, many scholars and statesmen are apt to forget their duty to the people in their desire to win for themselves fame as men of un/wavering principles,' he says. The misery into which China would be plunged by a struggle between the Ch'ing and the Ming can be avoided provided that Shih will refuse to be mis/led by high/flown conceptions of honour and will contemplate realities. 'Our troops are ready to march against you if needs must be; everything now depends on your decision.' Again he quotes the classics: ' "Only the superior man can fully appre/ciate good advice." ' And ends: 'Therefore I lay bare my inmost heart and respectfully await your decision. Across the Yang-tse's flood I turn in spirit to your Excellency and entreat your early reply. There is still much that remains unsaid.'

Yet it is doubtful whether by adding more he could have heightened the effect. Every argument which might persuade a general to turn traitor had been masterfully adduced.

If the Regent's letter is remarkable, General Shih's reply is no less so. Indeed, the two letters are to this day held up as a model of how such a correspondence should be conducted, having regard to the best Confucian standards.

The exordium of Shih's reply may be quoted verbatim, for it suggests the weight of the curious occasion. 'Shih K'o-fa, Commander-in-Chief of the Great Ming Dynasty, President of the Board of War and Grand Secretary of the Eastern Throne Hall, prostrating himself respectfully before your Highness, the Regent of the Great Ch'ing Dynasty, has the honour to reply as follows: On receipt of your valued letter I sent it at once to General Wu in order that I might take his opinion.' (This suggests that the truth about Wu was not yet known.) 'I hesitated to indite an immediate reply, not because I failed to appreciate your kindness in writing to me, but out of regard for the principle enunciated in the *Spring and Autumn* classic, that a Minister of one state ought not to carry on a secret correspondence with the representative of another.'

The *Spring and Autumn* classic is, of course, one of the Confucian Books, and was precisely the work which the Regent had quoted when he sought to prove from authority that Hung Kuang should not have been enthroned. It was therefore a neat riposte for Shih to select from the same volume a demonstration of the Regent's solecism in having initiated such a correspondence at all.

After administering this preliminary snub, all the more crushing for being presented in the form of a literary allusion, he allows himself to compliment the Regent on his style. 'At a time of urgent military preparations like the present, your elegantly worded composition was a delightful distraction, and

I have perused it again and again, full of admiration for the sentiments it conveys.' Coming to a direct consideration of the passage quoted by the other against Hung Kuang's assumption of the Dragon Seat, he professes to 'admire the aptness of the allusion', but demonstrates that it is very far-fetched. 'The Sage never meant it to apply to a case in which the Sovereign Lord of the whole Empire had committed suicide in such circum-stances as the present. Slavish adherence to the letter of the prin-ciple in question is to be deprecated among men of affairs. Historical instances of the truth of this will readily occur to Your Highness.'

Assuming for a moment that the Regent's motive for enter-ing China had been only to help Wu against Li, whom he refers to by his nickname, the Prince Harrier, Shih next com-poses this well-turned sentence: 'If now, taking advantage of our misfortunes, you covet our territory and hope to benefit yourselves by annexing parts of our dominions, you will be open to the reproach that your good intentions were but tran-sient and that your actions which began in righteousness have ended in cupidity, which makes them indistinguishable from those of the rebels. I am reluctant to believe this of you Manchus.'

Finally he makes a concrete proposal. If the Manchus will agree to join forces with the Ming and destroy Li, then negotia-tions can be begun by the two Governments and a treaty be signed to the advantage of both. What concessions would be granted to the Manchus is not stated, but, says Shih, 'we shall do what in us lies to reward you'. Not until the postscript does he refer to the Regent's offers. 'I treat with the contempt of silence your ignoble endeavour to lure me with promises of rewards and dignities.'

It goes without saying that from first to last the Regent had always intended to take advantage of Li's rebellion in order to overthrow the Ming Dynasty and take possession of its Empire. The ease with which he had entered the capital had encouraged him to hope that the rest of the country would fall to him as

easily. But when he read Shih's letter, he saw that he would
have to fight for it. Li presented no difficulty; Wu was dealing
with him successfully. The struggle would be solely against the
Ming pretender, and the Regent began preparations for marching upon him the following spring.

General Shih, when aware of this, warned the Court of
Nanking of the approaching conflict, and urged that during
the winter an effort should be made to enlarge the army and
perfect its equipment. If this were done and he received the full
support of the Emperor, he felt sure that he could prevent the
Manchus from crossing the Yellow River or could defeat them
in the country between it and the Yang-tse. His army was
drawn up on the Huai, between the two great rivers and a
hundred miles north of Nanking. Yang-chao was in his rear; it
was the key of the capital.

One would have thought that in such circumstances the
Ming would have given their Commander-in-Chief every support. His army stood between them and final ruin. Well provided with men and materials, encouraged and well fed, it
might not only stem the tide, but serve as a rallying point for all
their adherents throughout China.

But the Ming had not changed: they had learnt nothing from
their disasters. Indeed, the Emperor seemed even less alive to
realities than had been Ch'ung Chên. He was an amateur of
the drama, and it is said that nothing could depress him except
bad acting. He remained idiotically cheerful and irresponsible,
spending what money his supporters raised on acquiring fresh
girls for the Concubinate, which had been disagreeably depleted by the Prince Harrier.

Even more serious than these untimely frivolities was the influence of his eunuchs. With hardly credible folly he gave his
confidence to a certain Ma Shih-ying, his Chief Eunuch, a
rascal who had belonged to the faction of the notorious Wei.
This deplorable fellow, jealous of the high esteem in which
Shih was held, contrived to block the supplies which should
have gone urgently to the army and even persuaded the Em-

peror to allow him to pass orders about matters which fell within the province of the General.

In the spring of 1645, when a Ch'ing offensive was expected any moment, Shih was obliged to memorialize his Emperor in such blunt terms that, had he not been indispensable, he must have been cashiered.

'While Your Majesty is banqueting on rare foods', he wrote, 'and drinking toasts from jade cups, you forget that your soldiers are starving in the line. If, in spite of his efforts, the late Emperor was unable to avoid disaster, how much more should you, inferior to him in ability, tremble as one who stands on the brink of a precipice. Perform your duties with zeal and maybe your Imperial Ancestors will intercede with God and your heritage be regained. But if you remain lolling in Nanking, rewarding sycophants and forgetful of your troops, if you shout our secret plans from the housetops and detect no difference between loyalty and treason, then your Ancestors will not bestir themselves to help you and your final destruction is absolutely inevitable.'

The course of Chinese history is sprinkled with strong letters addressed to Emperors by Censors, but I do not recall one from a general quite so refreshingly blunt as this. It had, however, no effect at all. Indeed it was suppressed by the Chief Eunuch, who became only the more persuaded that so independent a man as Shih must not be allowed to win a victory. Efforts were made to prove him incompetent by depriving him of the means to prove that he was not. By March 1645 these intrigues had seriously impaired the efficiency of his army. The Manchus, under the command of Prince Yü, younger brother of the Regent, had launched the offensive when Shih submitted a last despairing memorial.

'Since the catastrophe of last year your Ancestors' graves have been left untended,' he begins. 'Chaos reigns throughout your Empire. Not a blow has been struck in its defence. It was absurd to suppose that unless you took the offensive you would be allowed to remain at Nanking in peace. When you came to the throne your troops were eager for battle. But today all is changed: the army is starving, while your Court daily dines extravagantly. I can hold out no hopes. My spies report that the flower of the Manchu army is advancing. All north of the Yellow River has been irrevocably lost, and here I sit by the Huai, disabled for want of supplies.'

'How can we march without food?' he asks. 'Words alone are not enough to inspire valour. Send us the money you now spend on entertainments. Exercise thrift even in the Rites. Avoid the seraglio and the banquet. Rise early, retire late. Keep only proven men about you. So may Heaven relent and lend us countenance.'

But it was all too late. The Manchu cavalry swept south-wards and Shih had to fall back on Yang-chao, forty miles from the capital. A herald from Prince Yü came to demand his surrender. Shih was cursing him from the wall, when he shouted back: 'The fame of your Excellency's loyal and eminent services is spread throughout China, yet the Ming Emperor does not give you his confidence. Why, then, not gain a name and a reward by joining the Ch'ing?'

Shih drew a bolt on him.

It seems that Prince Yü, like his brother, the Regent, had a genuine admiration for Shih and was sincerely anxious that so brave a man should not die in so bad a cause. He sent again to beg him to reconsider his refusal, delaying the assault in the hope of a parley. We have a vivid pen-picture of this Yü from the hand of a Yang-chao gentleman, who saw him pass a few days later:

'A young man of about thirty, wearing a Manchu hat, red clothes and black satin boots, came riding by. He had a breast-plate of the finest mail; his horse was beautifully caparisoned and he was attended by a large suite. His features, though Tartar, were exceedingly handsome; he had a strong chin and a high forehead.'

At that date there was something fresh and chivalrous about the Manchu aristocracy.

Yang-chao had a population of a million. The circumference of its walls was four miles. The houses were packed closely in narrow streets. Shih had not more than 40,000 soldiers. He billeted them in private houses, but their discipline was bad. The retreat, their privations and lack of pay had taken all the spirit out of them.

The assault began. For ten days and nights there was fierce fighting on the walls, Shih rallying his men in person, and directing the defence. He had some cannon founded by Jesuits which was superior to the besiegers' guns. The citizens began to hope that the enemy might be repelled. 'But one evening,' writes a witness, 'while we were having quite a lively party in our house, orders from the Commander-in-Chief were suddenly brought to Colonel Yang, who was quartered with us. He read the note, turned deadly pale and hurried to the city wall. Our party broke up, everyone afraid bad news had come.'

Next morning they were reassured by a proclamation of General Shih's, but in the afternoon it was rumoured that Manchu troops were in the city. The witness already quoted left his house to enquire. He reports:

'On reaching the main street, I met crowds of men, women and children, many of them barefooted and half-naked, all rushing wildly along. To my questions they could make no clear replies, all muttering or gasping incoherently. Next I observed a small party of horsemen desperately galloping towards the South Gate. They passed like a torrent in flood, but I had time to notice that the person they were escorting was General Shih himself. The General was wounded. Next I saw one of his subordinate generals riding northwards, evidently intending to surrender to the enemy. His face wore a look of misery such as I hope never to see again. By this time the troops on the wall had begun to throw away their weapons.'

The rumour was true. The Manchus had breached the northern wall and were pouring into the city. It seems that at this desperate moment Shih had called one of his staff and said:

'The city is lost. Be good enough to kill me.'

The officer took a sword, but in his agitation the stroke went wide and Shih, seizing the weapon, wounded himself in the throat. When they saw this, others of his officers intervened and, putting him on a horse, took him to the South Gate in an attempt to gain the Nanking road. But they were met and stopped by a force of Manchus.

'I am a Grand Secretary. Take me to your Commander-in-Chief,' Shih told them in a loud voice.

They took him before Prince Yü, who spoke to him warmly: 'You have made a gallant defence. Before the siege began I sent several letters to your Excellency and you refused to negotiate. Now that you have done all that duty could dictate, I am happy to offer you a high post. You shall be our Imperial Commissioner for the pacification of Nanking Province.'

Shih replied: 'I will accept no favour except one—death.'

The Prince persevered, pointing out that another of the Grand Secretaries had made his peace and been rewarded by an appointment. Shih denounced him. 'How can you expect me to imitate the behaviour of a traitor?' he asked.

As Prince Yü could not shake him, he gave orders for him to be confined. For two days they pressed him to submit. He continued to refuse and was decapitated on the third day.

By acting in this manner Shih followed tradition. He might, while refusing to serve the Ch'ing, have bowed to circumstances and retired into private life. The Prince would certainly have met him along these lines. But in China there existed a rule of conduct, then two thousand years old, which was more extreme than any which has obtained in Europe. It has never been incumbent upon our captured generals to demand death: Shih was bound to demand it if he desired to be called a man of honour in the strictest sense. The code he followed had been built up from the interpretations which centuries of Chinese gentlemen had given to the original maxims of Confucius. Like the code of the English gentleman, it was not a religion. A Ming grandee of the type of Shih would not generally have had any religion beyond the formal deism implicit in the classics. Neither Buddhism nor Taoism was patronized by the scholar class of that period, as they had been on occasion in earlier dynasties. The ecstatic vision of the one and the impish transcendentalism of the other had ceased to be an inspiration for men of letters, and both religions had sunk to the level of popular cults. Even if this had not been so and it had still been the fashion for scholars to dabble in their esoteric side, neither would have guided Shih in his determination to die rather than make concession to the enemies of his dynasty, for neither put a value on that sort of behaviour.

The conception of virtue for which Shih thought it worth dying had therefore no other sanction than tradition, the long belief that it was proper to act in that way. And, indeed, if ever there was a time when it was proper to die for such an ideal, it was then. The neglect of it in public life had been the ruin of the Ming. The Court should have been the centre from which respect for the classic virtues radiated throughout the administration. On the contrary, as we have seen, both Court and administration in their practice had abandoned these virtues. The capital would never have been taken by Li nor the Empire by the Manchus if officials generally had been living up to them. That is the significance of Shih's death. That is why the Manchu nobles, who were also Confucians, admired him. He died to show his abhorrence of the evils which had rotted the body politic, to demonstrate by his death that the code he followed was of supreme value. No Chinese has ever thought the extremity of his devotion excessive or odd. He remains one of China's great worthies.

# IX

## *The Flight into Burma*

The fall of Yang-chao was followed by the capture of Nan-king and the death of the Emperor Hung Kuang. Curiously enough, this did not put an end to Ming resistance. Damaged though its reputation was, the dynasty could still command support. The explanation is the enormous extent of China. Its adherents retreated at once to Fu-chao, 400 miles further south. There another Emperor was set up, Lung Wu, who was cap-tured a year later and executed by the Manchus. Still the Mings were not done. They retreated 400 miles again, and at Canton, the centre of great provinces in the south-west, set up yet an-other member of the House, Prince Kuei, with the reign title of Yung Li. His father had been a brother of the Emperor T'ien Chi and so a son of the Emperor Wan Li. He was there-fore in the direct descent, and claimed to be the legal successor of Ch'ung Chên, because the Heir Apparent, who impru-dently left his hiding place, had been apprehended by the Ch'ing Government and executed after trial. The protracted Ming resistance had hardened the Regent's heart. He was no longer ready to give their princes court appointments.

Yung Li was the last of the Ming family to bear an imperial title. For thirteen years he held out against the Ch'ing until in 1659, as stated at the beginning of this narrative, he was obliged to flee into Burma.

The Ming Court at Canton in 1646 was much more modest than their Court at Nanking two years earlier. Nor was time given it to organize its resources, for the Regent sent an army and in 1647 Yung Li was obliged to retreat still further westward and cross into Kwang-si, which adjoins Indo-China. In the immensities of that remote province, he made a stand. In 1649 the Regent died and for a moment prospects were better. But by the following year Yung Li was retreating again. The disorders resulting from Li's rebellion had not been entirely suppressed in these distant regions, and now by an irony of fate he found that the best source of recruits for his diminishing army was the gangs of ruffians who had once followed the Prince Harrier. In this way he upheld as best he could his claim to be rightful Son of Heaven, though beginning to look more like a bandit than an Emperor.

By a further ironic chance our old friend, General (now Prince) Wu, was living not far away. When he had finished the work set him by the Regent of breaking Li's power, he retired to the fief which had been conferred on him as a reward. This fief consisted of the provinces of Yunnan and Kwei-chao, on the north border of Kwang-si, where Yung Li was maintaining himself. Thus the scene was set for the last act of the drama.

Wu's capital was the city of Yunnan-fu, now called Kun-ming, from which the road to Burma now starts. In his palace he maintained imperial state, that is to say, he had a Court, a Concubinate, Eunuchs and Ministers, housed in an inner city of halls and pavilions modelled upon the Forbidden City. And there were his gardens, the 'Park of Peaceful Prosperity', and his lake pavilion, 'Beside the Crystal Wave', in which was his library—all the standard classics.

We have a description of what he looked like at this period of his life. From being the commander of an army, the son of a Minister, the romantic lover of a noted beauty, he had become a great lord, Prince of territories larger than France, a man with the power of life and death over millions, and his appearance had grown correspondingly formidable. His aquiline nose was fiercer, as fierce now as Li's. The bridge was somewhat mis-shapen, and on it was a black birthmark which would swell and turn purple before he broke into a rage, a warning of which his officials availed themselves to withdraw, as they also did when they heard him snort, a further token of rising anger. His face at this date was clean-shaven, his ears, always enormous, seemed larger than when he wore a beard, and his habitual expression was extremely forbidding. As for his prose style—in completing the picture of a Chinese grandee one should always mention his style—it was noted for its vituperative force, and was seen at its best in military proclamations, a characteristic it was to share with General Bonaparte's. Of these proclamations the most famous was the one in which, when Li came marching to the frontier, he hallooed his troops against that 'puny hobgoblin', as he dubs him in the exordium. 'Wolves and jackals,' he roars, 'infest our capital, dogs and swine squat in its Halls. They have driven his most sacred Majesty to suicide, they have put to the sword our scholars and gentlemen; they have massacred our people, have looted the Great Within. High Heaven echoes with the bitter plaint of the Ancestors. In the Yellow Springs our illustrious Ancestors weep tears of blood.'

It was a noble harangue, and now in 1655, eleven years afterwards, he received orders from Peking to hunt down Yung Li, his rightful Emperor, the cousin of his late most sacred Majesty.

The hunt lasted four years. Yung Li had enlisted a notable body of cut-throats, and was not easy to catch. His camp—for the capital of the Ming was now a moving camp—was a Court in miniature, for he carried with him his Empresses, his concubines and his officials. His Chief Eunuch was a person called P'an Achilles and a devout Catholic, but of that we shall have more to say lower down. Yung Li himself was a man of thirty at this date. In appearance he strongly resembled his grandfather, Wan Li, having a round face, protuberant forehead and thick beard. He was fond of reading and a student of the classics. One feels that during the rough and tumble of this present life he cannot have had much opportunity for indulging such tastes. The fact that he had them and, though surrounded by the sort of soldiers whom Wu had described as wolves and jackals, that he maintained the etiquette and rites of the Forbidden City, evokes a picture which is quaint and touching, and which suggests that not even at the most hopeless moments did he view himself as a mere leader of desperadoes. His army might have come to resemble Li's, but he was no rebel. He was always the Emperor, the Son of Heaven, ruling only a fraction of the Ming Empire, but refus-ing to concede any title to the Ch'ing.

In the course of his efforts to resist Prince Wu, he was driven from Kwang-si to Kwei-chao and from there westwards into Yunnan, where he managed to establish himself for a time not far from the Burmese border. At last, in 1659, he was brought to battle at Têngyüeh and there suffered his final defeat. To avoid capture by Wu, he fled with his Court and about 700 guardsmen down the road to Bhamo, a Shan principality within the boundaries of Burma, and asked its Sawbwa or Prince to transmit a present of 365 pounds' weight of gold to his King, with a letter asking permission to come to Ava, the capital. This permission was granted and the whole party de-scended the Irrawaddy by barge, their horses going overland. At Ava, which is some 250 miles south of Bhamo, they were received by the King, whose reign title was Pindalé, and sent by him to live across the river at Sagaing.

On the first page of this narrative I wrote that I also had lived in Sagaing. Two hundred and seventy years had elapsed since Yung Li was there, but it cannot, I think, have changed much in the time. Country places in Burma do not change. Bullock-carts creak through the dusty night; at dawn the bazaar is full of voices; a procession passes at dusk to the pagoda. In June the ploughing, in December the reaping, from January to May the rustic festivals. That is the immemorial pattern.

Sagaing was enclosed by brick walls in the seventeenth cen-tury, sections of which are still to be seen. The houses then as now were of wood and thatch. Beyond the walls were some famous pagodas. The best of these was the Kaunghmu-daw or Royal Offering, which had been built only a few years before Yung Li's arrival by King Pindalé's father. In it they kept what

68

was held to be the most important relic of the Buddha, his tooth, though a story existed that it was not an original, the real tooth having been captured by the Portuguese in Ceylon, and ground to powder by the Inquisition of Goa. Whatever the truth, the relic's authenticity was certainly not questioned in Sagaing or in Ava. The pagoda was designed to be worthy of its treasure. The entrances were guarded by gigantic lions, the great solid dome was gilt and the eight hundred boundary pillars each held an oil light. On the other side of the town is a range of hills crowded to the top with monastic buildings. Day long bells are tinkling and the sweet sound of gongs throbs in the hot sun. The scene all through is richly Buddhist, not the Mahayana Buddhism of China, but that other quieter sort, the Hinayana, where piety is simple and narrow, and doctrine primitive in the sense of pure. For a man like Yung Li it must have seemed like the end of the world.

He would not, however, have preferred to live in Ava. To have had to associate with the Burmese Court would have been an utter weariness. He was better across the river, lonely and dull though it was, with the few scholars who had come with him. The courtiers of Ava were Outer Barbarians. They had not read the classics. They were not gentlemen.

Such a verdict was, of course, too severe: no other class in the world except the Ming gentry would have pronounced it at that date. The Court of Burma was brilliant enough. The reigning Toungoo Dynasty was enjoying a second period of prosperity. Its first capital had been Pegu in the southern portion of the country. When Caesar Frederick, a notable merchant of Venice, visited it in 1569, he thought it a very splendid city, as did Ralph Fitch of London in 1587. Both of these business men were much impressed by the crocodile moat, the walls and watch/towers, the profusion of rubies, the wealth of the shrines. The former, describing the King in his Palace, wrote:

'He sitteth up aloft in a great hall, on a tribunal seat, and lower under him sit all his barons round about; then those who demand audience enter into a great court before the king, and there set them down on the ground forty paces from the king's person . . . with their supplications in their hands. Then come the secretaries down to read these supplications. . . . He hath not any power by sea, but in the land, for people, dominions, gold and silver he far exceeds the power of the Great Turk.'

Between the time of these two men and of Yung Li, the Toun-goo Dynasty had suffered vicissitudes and the capital had been transferred from Pegu to Ava. If Ava was not quite so rich as Pegu, we may be sure that King Pindalé did not admit this, and that he kept the same state as his predecessors, or said he did. He may have had no crocodiles in his moat, for crocodiles are not found in the higher reaches of the Irrawaddy, but he cer-tainly possessed plenty of elephants, unlimited rubies and glittering shrines.

Though the layout of a Burmese palace-city, with its queens, concubines, officials and ministers, had a certain resemblance to the Forbidden City, the culture of Burma was no provincial copy of the Chinese. Her literature and art reflected a distinct ethos. The Court ceremonial derived from both Hindu and Buddhist sources; it had no connexion whatever with Con-fucianism. The official outlook was more unbalanced, less in-tellectual. Though bright and gay the Court lacked sophistica-tion. It was not educated in the sense that word bore in Peking. So we can understand why Yung Li could not have taken it seriously. Occupied with religious duties, bizarre or popular, debating events of narrow interest, wholly ignorant of the only literature of value, its courtiers and officials would have bored him painfully, for unlike an educated man of today he had no interest in ethnology, nor can the quaint and exotic have attracted him.

On the other hand, living in Sagaing was hardly diverting. A stockaded wooden palace of sorts had been built, where his ministers and officials tried to maintain the ceremonial. Kung Yi, President of the Board of Rites, was perhaps the most dis-tinguished scholar in his depleted train. I have mentioned that

his Chief Eunuch was called P'an Achilles, and the paradoxical fact that he was a Catholic. The reader may well ask
how this could be. The explanation is curious.

During the reign of his grandfather, Wan Li, a Jesuit called
Matteo Ricci was sent to China by the Society. The Portuguese held then as now a concession at Macao, in the vicinity
of Canton. It was a depot for goods to be exported to Europe.
The Chinese Government had granted the concession strictly
on the understanding that the Portuguese should keep within
its boundaries. Trespass beyond was punishable by death, for
the Portuguese were regarded as pirates and ruffians, as, indeed,
many of them were. Ricci, who was an Italian gentleman of
charm and intelligence, had large ideas and chafed at this
restriction. For centuries no Christian missionaries had entered
China: his ambition was to accomplish this difficult feat. He
solved the difficulty by learning Mandarin, not only how to
speak, but also how to write it, and made as thorough a study
of the classics as a member of the official class. Thus distinguished, he obtained permission to leave Macao, and by making friends with people in high positions worked his way up
from Nanking to the capital.

Ricci's reception in Peking and the full significance of his
labours will be discussed in a later chapter. Suffice it to say here
that as a result of his popularity a number of Jesuits were able
to enter China. After the fall of Peking and Nanking, when
the Ming Court was at Canton, a German Jesuit named
Andrew Xavier Koffler was attached to it. The consolations
of religion which in that time of trouble he was able to offer
proved so attractive to the ladies of Yung Li's household that
the Empress Dowager, his mother, and his two Empresses, the
Empress Consort and the Empress Mother, were baptized.
Their example was followed by many of the secondary consorts or concubines and by several eunuchs, among them P'an,
who took the Christian name of Achilles, the three afore-
mentioned *grandes dames* calling themselves respectively Helen,
Anne and Mary. Their conversion made no difference, of

course, to the way of life of any of these personages, who continued as before in their stations as consort, concubine or eunuch.

So it came about that at Sagaing in 1659 there lived a Helen, an Anne and a Mary, preceding by two hundred and twenty-six years the many other Helens, Annes and Marys who began to live there after 1885, when upper Burma was annexed by the British.

The conversion of these three Chinese Empresses to Christianity was the greatest triumph ever won by the Jesuits or by any missionary society before or since. Father Koffler was naturally proud of his achievement and thought it would do him no harm—indeed, that it should do him a great deal of good—if the matter were brought to the notice of the Pope. Accordingly, he induced the Empress Dowager to address a letter to Innocent X. It was sent by special envoy and presented to him in 1655. The Vatican archives contain a multitude of rare letters, but this one from Yung Li's mother must surely rank as one of the most unique. Yet more curious, perhaps, was the letter which accompanied it, not for its contents (neither letter contained more than a message of goodwill), but because it was written by P'an Achilles. It is said there have been eunuchs in the Vatican choir, but P'an Achilles as Superintendent of an Imperial Concubinate was surely an unusual correspondent for the Holy Father. At first sight, Achilles is hardly the name one would select for a eunuch, but it seems that it was given him for good reason because, in addition to his other work, he held the position of Captain of the Imperial Guard and at one time was even Commander-in-Chief.

These conversions, with other amiable eccentricities which followed them, must have occurred with Yung Li's knowledge, and the fact that he raised no objection may be taken as proof of what has already been stated, that they amounted in practice to nothing at all. Women and eunuchs always dabbled in some religion when times were bad, the future uncertain. Since the reign of his grandfather Christianity had been fashionable.

His ladies naturally preferred it for that reason. In some ways it was much less *outré* than Mahayana Buddhism. So bland, in- deed, was his attitude that Koffler believed him to be at heart a Catholic. But the Jesuits were prone to be over-sanguine. Those at the Court of India, for instance, wrote home that they had converted the Emperor Akbar.

# X

## *Wu again*

We must now relate the tragic sequel to the flight into Burma. It will be recalled that when Yung Li was fighting in Kwang-si and Yunnan, he was assisted by the bandits who had been infesting those regions. His defeat at Têngyüeh by Wu did not mean the destruction of all the forces of disorder. There remained several bandit leaders at the head of large followings. When Wu turned his attention to these, a number of them crossed the Burmese border in strength and proceeded to ravage the northern districts. King Pindalé was a man of irresolute character and the army, which, in the days of the earlier kings of the dynasty had been strong enough to invade neighbouring countries, was now too weak to protect its own. The bandits looted at pleasure, even carrying their depreda-tions to the gates of Ava. It appears probable that Yung Li saw in this a chance of bettering his position and that he got into touch with the marauders, some of them men who had served him before, and discussed the project or, at least, the possi-bility, of combining to make an attack on Wu. But this does not seem to have led to any concrete arrangement. The bandits were already lucratively employed, and Wu, moreover, had already proved himself too strong for them.

The news that these negotiations had taken place reached Wu in due course. When Yung Li fled into Burma, he had made no demand for him to the King, but now decided it was neces-sary to do so. Even in remote Sagaing the Ming was evidently still a danger. Accordingly he wrote to the King, threatening that if he were not surrendered he would come and fetch him.

# Wu again

A revolution had recently taken place in Ava. Pindalé's inability to stay the invasion of the Chinese bandits had so alienated the grandees that they invited his brother, Pyé, to seize the throne. This he did in 1661, and sewing Pindalé in a velvet sack had him thrown into the river. Wu's letter was, therefore, addressed to Pyé. The new King did not take any immediate steps to comply, though he seems to have allowed Yung Li to know of the demand for his extradition. The Ming was much alarmed and decided to write to Wu, appealing to his better feelings. The letter is dated 1662.

'Your Excellency has deserved right well of the present Dynasty, but once you were a bulwark of our own,' he began. 'Unhappily the Ming fell upon evil days; the rebel bandit Li laid waste the land and marched on our capital. Our tutelary altars were destroyed, so that his late Majesty felt that suicide was his duty.

'At that time', he continues, 'Your Excellency had not lost all right and natural feeling; you wept at the thought of the Dynasty's plight, and at the head of an avenging host marched to its aid in mourning robes.'

We know that this is far from an exact description of Wu's tortuous behaviour on the frontier eighteen years previously, but it suits Yung Li's argument and, moreover, is a phrase with a classical pedigree. That Yung Li did not mean it literally is clear from the next sentences:

'How comes it, then, that since that day you have staked your fortunes upon those of the Ch'ing? You pretended a loyal desire to take vengeance on our enemies and all the time you were the humble obedient servant of the Manchus.'

The Emperor then recalls how the throne was re-established at Nanking, how Hung Kuang perished there in battle, and how his successor, Lung Wu, was executed at Foochao. 'Facing these swift-footed disasters, I, all unworthy, had but little desire to live; what thought had I to spare for our dynastic altars? Nevertheless, my Ministers forced the throne upon me and I was induced against my wishes to assume the burden of inheritance. Since then fifteen years have passed.'

Again and again he had had to flee in confusion, he says, before the advancing Manchus until at last he reached Yunnan. 'There I had hoped to be left in peace by my ruthless enemies, to be allowed to remain in possession of that remote and worthless corner of my ancestors' patrimony. But your Excellency had forgotten the benefits which my ancestors bestowed upon you. You led your armies against me, destroying my nest of peaceful retreat. I had to cross a desert barrier and now I look for my protection to Burmese hospitality. In this distant region joy and I have long been strangers; tears are my daily meat and drink. Yet, though lost is the glorious heritage won by my ancestors after such efforts, doubtless I am fortunate to be alive at all, nor should I complain of the wretchedness of my lot in having to live among these barbarians of the south.

'But', he complains, 'Your Excellency, unappeased, pursues me to the end. You have now asked your Sovereign's permission to invade Burma and hunt me down, a sad and lonely wanderer and an exile. Is not the whole Empire wide enough for your ambitions? Is there to be no resting place for me anywhere? Can you, I wonder, bear to repeat the poem?—"Oh, owl, owl, you have robbed me of my young, have you the heart to rob me also of my nest?" If you do not desist from your merciless pursuit of a fallen prince, what name will Your Excellency leave in history, what manner of man will you be called by posterity?'

Yung Li then seems to break down altogether:

'Today I appeal to Your Excellency. I am left with scarcely a soldier to defend me, like an orphan solitary in a hostile world. My life, humble and worthless, is in Your Excellency's hands. If you must have my head, it is forfeit to you. I am not afraid of death, were my bones to be left to whiten. I do not expect Your Excellency to spare me. Yet why should you exclude me from the protection which the Ch'ing extend to all under Heaven?'

He ends the letter with a final appeal to Wu as a Confucian gentleman. 'It is now for your Excellency to decide. Faithful servant of the new Dynasty though you be, you cannot forget the favours bestowed on you by his late Majesty nor fail to cherish the memory of his illustrious Ancestors. I must leave you to think out this matter for yourself.'

But Wu was not a Confucian gentleman, he was not guided by the rules of the Master's Code. Though in his library were the classics, he gave them no more than lip service. A man who had written as he had written to his father, was unlikely to heed a fallen Emperor's plea. His reply was to send King Pyé an angry reminder that he would come and fetch his guest, if he were not immediately surrendered.

Meanwhile an unpleasant incident had occurred. The King, who was a less easy-going man than Pindalé, had decided that what with Yung Li's *pourparlers* with the bandits and Wu's peremptory letter, it would be better to split up the Imperial Guard, which consisted of seven hundred men, by sending them in small parties to different villages. For him to deliver Yung Li to Wu was hardly consistent with his dignity, but by disarming him completely he hoped to satisfy the tiresome Prince of Yunnan. Planting in villages soldiers taken in war was a recognized practice. At the time groups of Portuguese prisoners were living in various hamlets of the locality. Accordingly, he summoned the Guardsmen to the Tupayon Pagoda near Sagaing, going there himself with his Musketeers, a regiment composed chiefly of Portuguese mercenaries. He would cause the Chinese to swear an oath of allegiance and then send them under escort to the destinations he had chosen.

When the Guardsmen were informed that they were to be separated from their Emperor and placed in separate villages, they raised an outcry. Whereupon the King ordered his Musketeers to open fire, and many of them fell killed or wounded. The rest were immediately despatched where they stood. By this stroke Pyé relieved himself of an embarrassment and complied, he hoped, with what was essential in Wu's requirements, without himself having lost face. At the same time, feeling that the slaughter of the Guard was inconsistent with the good rela-

tions which he still desired to maintain with the Ming personally, he sent him that evening from his table some choice dishes
and wine, with a message, half apologetic, that he had been
obliged to fire on the Guard because the men had resisted. This
message was a great relief to Yung Li, for when the news of
what had happened reached him he had feared that a general
massacre would follow. So alarmed had been some of the
Court ladies that they had committed suicide.

Soon after this incident Wu's final reminder was received. It
was backed up by the despatch of troops, which penetrated
some distance into Burmese territory. King Pyé had no alter-
native but to make up his mind: he must either fight Wu or
deliver Yung Li. The Council was summoned.

The question was more delicate than might appear at this
distance. After the thirteenth century when the Emperor Kublai
Khan took Pagan, the then Burmese capital, the Chinese Government had claimed Burma to be a feudatory state. This had
been acknowledged by a tribute in the form of presents which
was sent, not regularly, but sufficiently often to keep Burma's
subservient status alive. Only a few years previously had this
degrading payment been discontinued. Pyé was not one of
Burma's more distinguished kings. He knew that well enough,
he knew he owed his position to the unpopularity incurred by
his weak brother. Now he feared that if he complied with Wu's
rude demand, made all the ruder by his sending troops to en-
force it, his critics would allege—and who could say how many
they might be?—that he was again acknowledging Burma's
feudatory status, the mere suspicion of which might easily be the
ruin of him, for nothing would more hurt Burmese pride of race.

The Council was well aware of these considerations. But—
what to advise? They were in a dilemma. If the army had made
little headway against bandits, it had no chance at all against
regular troops, and yet if they agreed to Wu's demand, the
result might be as serious as a defeat in the field. There was,
however, a way out. On the King demanding an opinion a
Councillor submitted that in matters of this kind one must pro-

ceed by precedent, and that if there should be precedents—there were and he would quote them—which covered the surrender of political refugees by *both* sides of the present dispute, then by applying such precedents Yung Li could be handed back without giving even to the most ill-disposed the opportunity of raising the question of Burma's sovereign status.

The precedents were then quoted. In 1446 the Burmese Government had surrendered to the Ming the Shan Sawbwa of Maw, who was a Chinese subject, and in 1601 the Ming had surrendered the Sawbwa of Bhamo, who was a Burmese subject. No one could, therefore, say that if they now surrendered Yung Li they were doing more than comply with a mutual arrangement between the two governments. King Pyé accepted this solution and signed the order for his arrest. Shortly afterwards Yung Li and his Court were handed over to envoys sent to take them away.

Wu met them at the frontier. It is not recorded what transpired between him and the Ming, but a code of manners governed such delicate occasions. We know that Wu produced a sedan-chair and invited Yung Li to take his seat in it. 'All along the route to Yunnan-fu the people crowded to see him,' writes a contemporary observer. ' "This is the former Son of Heaven," they said to each other, and hardly a man but shed tears at so melancholy a sight. He bore himself with the true majesty of his rank.'

On arrival at Yunnan-fu he was assigned a residence pending orders from Peking. These orders would probably have been his indefinite detention had it not been that he became involved in a plot. His extradition had shocked a number of people in Yunnan-fu. So much harshness against the representative of a Royal House, which once had shown Wu such favour, was held to be conduct unbecoming to a gentleman. Wu had gone far beyond his duty, they contended. After the destruction of the Imperial Guard he might very well have left Yung Li undisturbed without failing in his loyalty to the Ch'ing. He had shown such vindictiveness only because Yung

79

Li had evaded him for so long, or because he was over-ambitious and sought further honours.

With these arguments and with money the malcontents won over some of Wu's household troops, big stalwart fellows and noted sportsmen. But the plot miscarried. When the persons concerned had been executed, Wu sent despatches to Peking, asking for revised instructions about his prisoner. Yung Li was confined more closely. He must have realized that his life was forfeit.

Kung Yi, his President of the Board of Rites, who had been with him at Sagaing and had accompanied him to Yunnan-fu, seems to have thought that he might now welcome an opportunity to commit suicide. At any rate, the Minister knew what he himself must do. He therefore took food and wine and went to Yung Li's door. The gaolers were for turning him away, but he begged to see his Emperor once more, and they allowed him to enter for a consideration.

Telling his master that he had brought food and wine so that they might dine a last time together, he spread out what he had brought on a table in the main room, and inviting him to take his seat on the dais and face south in the old ceremonial way, he began to serve him on his knees. Presently kotowing he presented a cup of wine. Yung Li divined what was in the cup; he wept bitterly, but he would not drink. The Minister prostrated himself and urged him a second time. He moistened his lips, and passed back the cup, when the other drained it and fell dying.

In April 1663, three months after the arrival at Yunnan-fu, instructions were received from Peking authorizing Wu to execute Yung Li. Accordingly, he invited him to a chess party at the Treasury and there had him bowstringed. The Ming was in his thirty-ninth year and in the seventeenth of his reign. His son, a boy of fourteen, was also strangled. His mother later committed suicide, but his Consorts were neither ill-treated nor did they take their lives, being sent to Peking, where they lived in retirement.

# Wu again

The drama which here ends was, as we have perceived, set in motion by Li. To round it off, I must now mention two incidents, for they relate it back to the dynamic bandit. One of them concerns Shun Chih, the ward of the Regent Jui, who assumed the duties of Ch'ing Emperor in 1650 at the age of twelve; the other tells of Wu in his old age.

In 1661, when Yung Li was at Sagaing, Shun Chih's heart was broken by the death of Lady Tung, a lesser Consort, who was a stylist and a beauty. Unable to bear his pain in the world, he retreated into a Buddhist monastery, much to the scandal [1] of the Court, and remained there till his death in 1670. Thus Li and Shun Chih, rivals for the throne of China, became brothers of the Robe, the first because he had lost everything to the second, and the second because, though he had won everything which the first valued, had lost everything which he valued.

Wu also followed Li's example, but in a different way. In 1674, eleven years after he had shown such zeal for the Ch'ing Dynasty and the same year that Li died, he turned rebel, declared himself Emperor, setting up his own Dynasty, which he called the Chou. His reason was that K'ang Hsi, the successor of Shun Chih, issued a decree extending to the provinces over which Wu ruled the ordinary provincial administration, the effect of which was to transform him from a feudal Prince into a mere Viceroy. He died four years later of paralysis while in the early stages of his campaign against the Ch'ing.

Thus Wu in old age became the very thing the destruction of which in youth had made him all he was. His sole excuse for forsaking the Ming had been that he was saving China by serving the Ch'ing. By forsaking the Ch'ing and becoming a second Li, he nullified that excuse and proved that his prime interest had never been China but always himself.

[1] So much so that rather than admit it Sun Chih was officially declared to have died.

XI

# Last Meeting

The Emperor K'ang Hsi reigned for sixty years and was suc,
ceeded by Yung Cheng. By that time the Ming Dynasty was
no more than a memory. But there were descendants of the
family, the surname of which was Chu. These Chus had long
since ceased to regard themselves as pretenders to the throne,
and were loyal supporters of the new dispensation. It seems that
from 1644 to 1723, the period of Shun Chih and K'ang Hsi,
the thirteen tombs of the Ming Dynasty, which lie a few miles
north-west of Peking, had lain neglected, the Ch'ing Govern,
ment not having appointed an official to look after them nor to
perform the customary sacrificial rites. Yung Cheng's attention
was drawn to this omission, and since, as I say, the Ming descendants were now his loyal subjects he thought it fitting to
appoint the most worthy of them Superintendent of the Ming
Tombs, making his action the more magnanimous by confer-
ring on his nominee the title of Marquis of Extended Grace, a
delicate way of expressing the gracious notice he extended to the
family which his ancestors had ruined. No emoluments were
attached to the appointment beyond payment of the expenses
incidental to the annual journey and the celebration of the
sacrifices.

The post was hereditary and continued to be filled by a descendant of the first Marquis during the rest of the eighteenth
and the whole of the nineteenth century. The Ch'ing Dynasty
reached its maturity, declined, and, in 1912, fell, when the last
Emperor of the line, Hsüan T'ung, a boy of six, abdicated in
favour of a republican form of government. By the terms of his

abdication, while losing all executive power, he retained the right to continue living in part of the Forbidden City as Emperor under his reign title and was provided with sufficient funds to maintain the Court, its rituals and ceremonials, as heretofore.

In this twilight state, which was between that of a reigning and a deposed sovereign, he grew up, his principal tutor being an Englishman, Mr. Reginald Johnston.

In 1924 Hsüan T'ung still resided in the Forbidden City, though his twilight was to pass that year into night, and he was to take refuge in the British concession at Tien-tsin and be known to the world under his personal title, P'u Yi, prefixed rather oddly by the name Henry. Mr. Johnston relates that in the *Court Gazette* of August 1924 he noticed the following announcements: 'The Marquis Chu on this day set out on his journey to the Ming Tombs to offer sacrifice,' and, 'The Marquess of Extended Grace having duly fulfilled his mission to the Ming Tombs returned thanks for the Imperial bounty,' and, knowing who the Marquis was, thought it would be a fitting and dramatic turn, if this representative of the defunct Ming Dynasty should be brought face to face with Hsüan T'ung, Emperor of the Ch'ing which was also dead. Accordingly he spoke of the matter to the Emperor, not, we presume, enlarging on its dramatic aspect, but presenting it as an act of courtesy, for no notice had ever been taken of the Marquis, whose very existence was known to few beside the official responsible for disbursing his travelling allowance. The Emperor took up the the suggestion and on 7th September received the Marquis in private audience.

'On the afternoon of the same day', writes Mr. Johnston, 'I happened to be at home in my own house North of Prospect Hill when a visitor's card was brought in. On the card was written: "Chu Yu-hsün, descendant of the Imperial Ming House, Marquis of Extended Grace, bearing the additional personal name of Ping-nan and residing in Yang-kuan Road, Little Street, North of the Tung-chih Gate".'

# The Ruin of the Great Ming

The Marquis was ushered in. He was a stoutly built man, with an amiable, rather stolid, expression, and was dressed in a dark silk coat reaching below the knee, the full sleeves concealing his hands, his hat conical like the cover of a Chinese vase— the prescribed costume for an imperial audience. He came forward with the apology that his intrusion would have been unpardonable had not His Majesty, from whom he had just come, commanded him to call.

'I found him a very quiet and unassuming man,' says Mr. Johnston, 'obviously without much booklearning, but by no means unintelligent. He told me he was fortythree years of age and had two sons, aged nine and four. He assured me, deprecatingly, that they were both contemptible little brats.'

When he was about to go, Mr. Johnston told him he would like to return his call, but 'he besought me most earnestly not to do so as he lived in a hovel and had no guestroom.' 'You must not think', he went on, 'that the official coat and hat I am wearing are my own. I borrowed them for the audience.' So saying, he stood and opened his coat, to show me the poor and wellworn garments underneath. He was evidently sincere in his desire that I should not return his call, for after leaving me he spoke privately to my servants, begging them to dissuade me from visiting him, and pointing out that the borrowed garments had to be handed back to their owner that day.'

A little later Mr. Johnston sent him a present. The bearer on return reported that the house was, in fact, no more than a hovel and that he had 'found the Marquis sitting in rags on a broken bench'.

So we take leave of this very last of the Mings, in rags and seated on a broken bench. Mr. Johnston here raises an interesting point. The Manchus in origin, as we know, were foreigners trom outside the Wall and when the Republicans caused Hsüan T'ung to abdicate, they justified their action by the argument, among others, that they had replaced a foreign by a native government. To mark this event Sun Yat Sen, the President, made in 1912 a ceremonial visit to the tomb of the first Ming

Emperor and there, dressed in a frock-coat and top hat, informed the Illustrious Ancestor of the fall of the usurping
House. But neither the Marquis nor any other descendant of the
Mings was summoned to be present. Mr. Johnston opines that
the reason for this omission was that no regard was felt for the
Ming Dynasty except in the narrow sense that it was a native
dynasty. Its sovereigns had been notoriously less distinguished
than K'ang Hsi and Ch'ien Lung, the great Emperors of the
Ch'ing, so that for the Government now to treat its descendants
with special consideration would only have been thought eccen-
tric. This explains the abject poverty of the Marquis, who otherwise might now have expected a reasonable pension. In fact,
after the flight of Hsüan T'ung to Tien-tsin at the end of 1924,
the Republic refused to recognize his Marquisate.

One last touch to top this tragi-comedy. The Marquis, who,
as Mr. Johnston asserts, was essentially a gentleman, both in the
Confucian and the English sense, on hearing that the Emperor
had become a refugee borrowed enough for his train fare to
Tien-tsin and there, respectfully kneeling before the representative of the House which had ruined his own and which was
ruined in its turn, so that its descendants might one day even sit
in rags on a broken bench, he thanked him for his immense
condescension in receiving him in audience, observing in his
prostrations and style of phrase the full etiquette of The Great
Within.

# PART II

## The Great Ch'ing's Opportunity

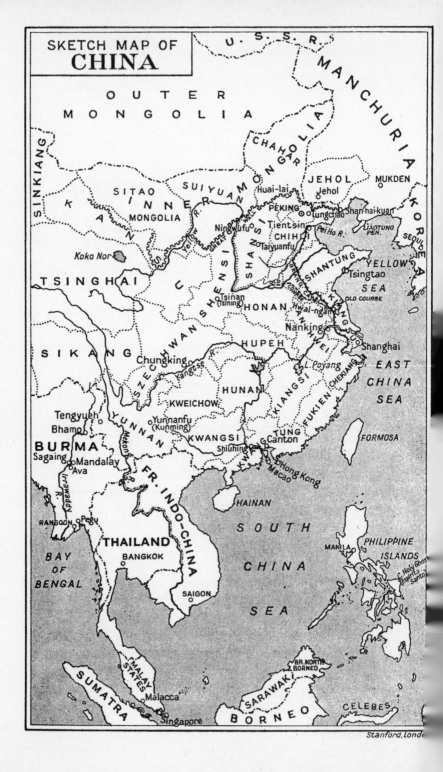

SKETCH MAP OF
CHINA

U. S. S. R.

MANCHURIA

OUTER
MONGOLIA

SINKIANG

CHAHAR

JEHOL
Jehol

MUKDEN

SITAO
MONGOLIA

SUIYUAN

INNER

Huai-lai

PEKING

Lungchao Shan-hai-kuan

KOREA

K A N S U

YELLOW R.

Ningwufu

Tientsin

Pei Ho R.

LIAOTUNG
PEN.

SEOUL

Koko Nor

Taiyuanfu

CHIHLI

SHANSI

GREAT WALL

SHANTUNG

Tsingtao

YELLOW
SEA

TSINGHAI

SZECHWAN

SHENSI

Tsinan
(Tsining)

HONAN

Hwai-ngan

OLD COURSE

KIANGSU

SIKANG

Chungking

Yangtse R.

HUPEH

Nanking

ANHWEI

Shanghai

EAST
CHINA
SEA

Yangtse R.

L. Poyang

KWEICHOW

HUNAN

KIANGSI

CHEKIANG

Tengyueh

YUNNAN

Yunnanfu
(Kunming)

KWANGSI

FUKIEN

FORMOSA

Bhamo

KWANGTUNG

Canton

Shiuhing

Macao

Hong Kong

BURMA

Sagaing
Mandalay
Ava

FR. INDO-CHINA

Irrawaddy R.

Mekong R.

HAINAN

SOUTH

PHILIPPINE
ISLANDS

MANILA

RANGOON
Pegu

THAILAND

BANGKOK

CHINA

Holy Ghost
Espiritu Santo

BAY
OF
BENGAL

SAIGON

SEA

MALAY
STATES

BR. NORTH
BORNEO

SUMATRA

Malacca

Singapore

SARAWAK

BORNEO

CELEBES

Stanford, Londo

# I

# The Mandate of Heaven is transferred to the Ch'ing

In the preceding pages the cause of the Ming Dynasty's fall has been ascribed to the breakdown of the administration: at the centre persons of disreputable character had usurped the authority of the Grand Council and the six Boards; in the provinces their nominees in the Civil Service and in the army were corrupt and incompetent. Conditions were such that a common bandit could sack the capital, and a small nation on the border enter the country and seize the Dragon Seat.

As Confucianism was essentially a philosophy of practical life, it was greatly concerned with the preservation of good government on a basis of honesty, fairness and moderation. That the later Ming should have been distinguished by the absence of these qualities was tantamount to their abandonment in practice of the state religion. By this most execrable of all acts they were believed to have destroyed the harmony between heaven and earth.

Such was the view taken by the Manchu leaders. The behaviour of the Ming had been so abominable that, in the old Chinese phrase, their Mandate from Heaven was exhausted. The Manchus had adopted Confucianism some fifty years earlier. They had built up their state in accordance with its principles. It was that which now gave them the right to sit on the Dragon Throne. Heaven had transferred its Mandate to them. With them now lay the power to balance heaven and earth. More, it was their bounden duty to do so. The Ming had been deaf to the ancestral voices; they would listen to and obey them. China would be led back to its pristine grandeur by an insistence on the classical virtues. The Ming had once been the most Confucian of dynasties, had taken every step in accord/ ance with precedent. Well, they had failed to maintain that high level. The grand estate inherited by its last rulers had been grievously maladministered; by following tradition it could be restored. No change of other sort was required. Clearly, change must be for the worse, for the old system had an absolute validity. By as absolute a conservatism they would be guided.

This belief in Confucianism as a panacea was supported by the plain facts of the situation. If the Manchus had tried to in/ troduce innovations, they would have set the most worthy and intelligent part of Chinese society against them, the Civil Service and the retired Civil Servants. By restoring to that service the position and dignity which was its right under a true Confucian government, and of which it had been deprived by the eunuch government of Ch'ung Chên, they were able to undertake at once the direct administration of the greater part of the empire, a feat they could not have attempted without such collaboration.

This brings us to our first point. Though they could not know it, the Manchus' resolve to re/establish the traditional form of Chinese government in its narrowest and most orthodox form was a great misfortune for China, because that system was out of date. This was not so from the general administrative point of view, where it was even in advance of its time. A Sovereign bound to follow the advice of his Council as long as that advice was founded on precedent, and a Civil Service, composed of men of the highest attainments and drawn from all ranks of life, which administered a written code of law without interference by a church or an aristocracy, ensured (if only in theory) an administration of the first class. Where the system was out of date was in the assumption, which was the essence of later Con/ fucianism, that China was the only civilized country in the world, and that therefore it had nothing of importance to learn from any other. This view of the absolute superiority of the Chinese, buttressed as it was by the figment that their Emperor was the Son of Heaven in the sense of being the sole interpreter on earth of the unknown power which swayed the universe, did not take into account the possibility that among the races classified as outer barbarians and therefore inferior to those governed in the perfect way, there might arise one or more whose theory and practice of life, if not superior, could not be ignored because they yielded, at least on the practical plane, results more potent than any achieved in China.

And here is the second point. Several countries in Europe, having broken away at and after the Renaissance from a system of thought and government as static and absolute as Confucianism, had by 1644 made discoveries of so novel a kind that they were intellectually ahead of the rest of the world. Unless China were prepared to modify her system as soon as she became aware of these advances, she was bound to fall behind, and the more this happened the more she exposed herself later on to grave risks. To maintain herself, she would have to extend her studies beyond her own classics. That sounds a small thing, but in China it would have meant a fundamental revolution in thought. The last persons to undertake such a revolution were the Manchus.

# II

# The Dutch visit The Great Within

One of the discoveries which it was incumbent upon China to appraise at its true value was the discovery of herself by the West. Europe, of course, had known of China since Roman times, and in the thirteenth century Marco Polo's book had provided a mass of information. But it was not until the sixteenth century, when Europeans began to go by ship to the East, that China was really discovered. The arrival of Europeans there in numbers, which increased steadily during the last reigns of the Ming, was an event of capital importance. Its results are still working themselves out. Had the nations of Europe stayed in their own territories, China might have continued as a museum in which was preserved an antique way of life. The Manchus' belief in the sovereign efficacy of the classics would have been sound enough. But the nature of Europeans, the conditions of their life, the new ideas which began to fill their minds from the sixteenth century onwards, made it inevitable that they would go East and West in search of wealth. When sure enough they appeared on the coast of China, that country should have made it its business to find out all about them, to grade their importance not from a Chinese literary point of view (that was the normal Chinese method of valuation—you had or had not read the classics), but by an intellectual and objective scrutiny.

The most interesting way to illustrate this clash of thought will be to examine at some length the account which has come down to us of the first visit by modern Europeans to Peking. This occurred in 1655, eleven years after the fall of the Ming. The visitors were a body of Dutchmen, and the object of their visit was to induce the Chinese government to come into line, in the matter of trade, with the custom of the modern world. Between the date of the mediaeval Polo and the modern Dutch, no Euro-peans had been to Peking except a few Jesuits and an occasional Portuguese. The latter were not modern Europeans in the sense that they had not imbibed the new spirit which had grown up in parts of Europe during the sixteenth century. The Jesuits, how-ever, were moderns in some important respects; their significance will be treated in the next chapter.

Before describing the Dutch visit it is necessary to recall a few facts and dates. The Portuguese were the first Europeans to reach China by sea, but as they were more representative of the medi-aeval than the modern age, their appearance in the East did not pose the same problem to the Chinese as did the coming of the Dutch.

Their Eastern adventures began in 1497 when Vasco da Gama reached India. Being stronger on the sea than the govern-ments of the Indian littoral and the Malay islands, they gradually acquired by force a number of key points, from Ormuz on the Persian Gulf to Malacca near the present Singapore, on which they built fortresses and from which they controlled the trade which was one of the objects of their voyages. As early as 1517 they sent ships to China. There for the first time they met a powerful Asiatic government, and though, more in the manner of pirates than merchants, they managed to get cargoes at certain small ports, the Chinese authorities had no great difficulty in driving them off. In 1557, however, they were allowed by the local Government of Canton, on consideration of a payment of money, to erect sheds on a barren spot at the mouth of the Canton estuary called Amakau, the later Macao, and to unload and take on cargoes there. By the end of the century the sheds had become a considerable town of brick and stone buildings, and the con-sideration a large annual fee payable to the Magistrate of the Chinese District in which Macao was situated. This contract was their permission to reside; but it gave them no extra-territorial position. The town was administered by the Chinese Civil

Service under the Chinese code like any other town in the Empire. The most that the Portuguese ever obtained was the recognition of their Council as a body competent, under the general supervision of the Chinese Magistrate, to administer the municipal rules and by-laws. In all important respects they were subject to Chinese law and procedure. They had not, however, the privileges of Chinese subjects, but were regarded as barbarians from oversea and outcasts from decent society, being forbidden on pain of death to go beyond the limits of Macao. It was to this port that the Jesuits came, and from whence they were permitted to travel into China for the reasons shortly mentioned in Part I.

In 1580 Portugal was annexed by Spain. Till that date the other nations of Europe had been able to buy from Portugal what Asiatic products they required. The Spaniards, however, closed the Lisbon market to the Dutch and the English. The Dutch, a nation about to enter upon its great creative period, thereupon decided to go East and get at the source what was refused them by the middlemen. Backed by their democratic States General and breathing the strong national air that was already beginning to nourish a galaxy of artists which contains, among many others, the names of Rembrandt and Vermeer, they stormed eastwards and during the first half of the seventeenth century took most of the important Portuguese fortresses in the Indian seas and developed a highly lucrative trade.

Direct trade with China, however, was what they most desired because there could be obtained tea, silk and porcelain, three commodities for which there was a growing demand in Europe. Accordingly they sent ships to Canton, the great southern port, and asked to be given the same privileges as the Portuguese. But the Ming refused to grant them any facilities whatsoever. It was a cardinal point in their policy not to allow foreign ships to enter their ports, because they were not persuaded that it was worth their while. A closed and self-sufficient China was their conception of sound government. They had made a partial exception in the case of the Portuguese and after some difficulty had transformed them from near pirates into obedient merchants.

But they had no desire to undertake such responsibilities again. It did not cross their minds that international trade might become necessary for national progress. They had, indeed, no desire for progress. Their ambition was to maintain things as they were, in accordance with a narrow interpretation of Confucian doctrine. They believed, too, that China had no need of European products. The coasting trade carried on by their own ships brought them what Asiatic products they required. There was therefore no reason except charity why they should oblige these new barbarians who had come to make demands on them. In return for such kindness they would get nothing but trouble. Europeans were ignorant of their laws, and notoriously turbulent, disrespectful and unreasonable. Their vessels, moreover, were armed with cannon and once in port were a source of disquiet. Such were what appeared solid reasons for their refusal.

Over a course of years the Dutch attempted to induce the Ming Government to change its mind, but without success. In 1644, as we know, that dynasty fell, and ten years later, by which time the chief provinces had been pacified, they decided to try their luck with the new government and send to Peking an embassy with a letter to the Ch'ing Emperor, whom we have already met as the young, impressionable Shun Chih. Sending an embassy was in accordance with Chinese precedent. For thousands of years the outer barbarians of Asia had been allowed to approach the Dragon with a letter and presents from their sovereigns. Such embassies were called tribute embassies, and there were volumes of regulations on how they should comport themselves. In Ming times they formed an exception to the general rule that foreigners were not permitted to enter China, but the members were conducted to the capital under a military guard. No modern European state having sent such an embassy, the peculiar meaning attached in China to that word was not understood in Europe. The Dutch thought that if they approached the throne direct they might get a concession, and accordingly adopted the established procedure of an embassy. For the Chinese the projected visit could be no more than another case of a barbarian state which was anxious to pay its respects to the Son of Heaven. One must beware of attributing to the Chinese a ludi-crous self-complacency at this date. It was indisputably true that in early periods they had had a great civilization when none existed elsewhere, and that in later centuries their civilization remained superior to any other. What they did not realize was that by the seventeenth century parts of Europe had made sudden and enormous progress and that, though the nations there had not in general reached their level, in some important ways they not only equalled but even surpassed them.

Coming as it did when the period known as the Enlighten-ment had begun in Europe, this Dutch Embassy of the year 1655 had particular significance. There existed no reliable popular accounts of China except Marco Polo's volume, which had been published three and a half centuries before. The book which was afterwards written about the Embassy's adventures and observa-tions was destined to be the first of a spate of such books and to create quite an extraordinary interest. China, wrapped in its con-servatism, was not interested in the West and had no idea that in her lack of interest she was guilty of a mistake. Europe, on the contrary, now full of intellectual curiosity, was intelligent enough to see that she had much to learn from China. This anxiety to learn demonstrated her vitality, and it was this vitality which eventually became such a danger to China. At first the theory of Chinese government and society aroused admiration; and some of the less important aspects of Chinese art made a great impres-sion. But Europe was able to digest all these exotic ideas and progress rapidly on her own lines. The time came when her power was greater than China's. Then her admiration turned to contempt. Meanwhile China had stood still. The Manchus had not carried her an inch on her way, and from being the mentor of Europe she became its victim.

The book[1] on the Dutch Embassy was written by John Niev-hoff, steward to the Ambassadors. A translation of it was pub-

[1] *An Embassy from the East India Company of the United Provinces to the Grand Tartar Cham, Emperour of China.*

lished in London in the year 1669, in the ninth year of Charles II's reign, by one John Ogilby, Esq., Master of His Majesty's Revels in the Kingdom of Ireland, a well-known scholar who had already published translations of Homer and Virgil, and whose prose is a good example of the strong vivid style for which the reign is noted. An engraving of his portrait by Lely is extant. Translated by so prominent a man the book was widely read in London society. It was profusely illustrated by engravings pur porting to be from sketches made by Nievhoff on the spot. Among its contents is printed a letter from a Jesuit resident of Peking who, as a supporter of the Portuguese, opposed the Embassy; and there are extracts from a work called *Antiquities of China*, composed about the same time by Athanasius Kircher, the famous Jesuit who invented the magic lantern. Altogether the volume pro vided a quantity of news about China, much of it incorrect when it touched history or religion, but so novel and interesting that it set all seventeenth-century Europe talking. Selections from it will still have interest for us and will supplement the narrative of the first part of this volume. Their relevance to our main argument will appear by degrees. The reader will not have forgotten that in 1655 Prince Jui had been dead six years and that Shun Chih was about eighteen years of age. Yung Li was fighting in the wilds of Kwang-si, Li was in his monastery and Wu on his feudal throne. Except Shun Chih we shall not directly meet these people again, but through having known them we are qualified to savour to the full what the author tells us, far more than could have the readers of his own time. In particular, his impressions of the Manchus after their great conquest will answer questions which must already have occurred to us.

The Embassy was not sent by the Dutch Government but, after obtaining their permission, by General Maatzuiker, the President of their East India Company, whose headquarters in the East was at Batavia in Java. The names of the Ambassadors were Their Excellencies Peter de Goyer and Jacob de Keyzer. They set sail from Batavia on June 14, 1655, their party consist ing of four merchants, six servants, the steward Nievhoff, a secretary called Baron, a doctor, two interpreters, a trumpeter and a drummer. They carried letters from the President addressed to the Emperor and to the Viceroy of Canton, together with a quantity of presents. On July 18 their ship anchored in the harbour of Heytamoon inside the Canton estuary, at a distance by river of some eighty miles from the city. They had passed close to Macao, but had been careful not to enter that port, as the last people they wished to meet were the Portuguese.

The local officials of Heytamoon came aboard and, after a protracted examination of the visitors, sent word to the Viceroy of Canton that a tribute embassy had arrived and wished to come up the river. In a day or so some senior officials appeared in 'several Vessels, very handsomely set off with Silk Flags and Pennons' and 'with great civility' invited the Ambassadors, their secretary and four servants to accompany them to Canton.

Canton was a walled city of over a million inhabitants, the residence of a Viceroy, and was administered under him by a Governor. The chief military officer was called the Tartar General, who was of equal standing to the Viceroy. Besides these high officers, there was a Senior Magistrate and a great number of subordinate officials, the majority of whom were Chinese, the Manchus having interfered as little as possible with the cadre of the Civil Service. At the time of the embassy the Viceroy and the Tartar General were Manchus.

The Ambassadors arrived in due course at the landing stage and were conducted by the officials across the open space of about four hundred yards which lay between the river bank and the wall. At the gate they were told to wait while the officials entered the city to report. A couple of hours passed before a mandarin returned and took them back to a lodging outside the walls. A guard was set by the Commissioner of Police.

Next morning a member of the Governor's Council called. He proceeded to examine them, filling in a form with such information as their names, ages, whether married or single, their last employment and the nature of their business. He expressed surprise that they had no copy of their letter to the Emperor and the hope that the letter itself (which was sealed in its case) was on paper of a better quality than that on which was written their letter to the Viceroy. Then he entered their nationality and the name of their sovereign. After a number of further questions he turned to consult his subordinates. 'They seemed to Mutter, and be displeased at the slight fashion of the Credentials.' When the Ambassadors ventured to ask for an official audience with the Viceroy, they were informed that this was out of the question until instructions were received from the Emperor, to whom a report had been sent announcing their arrival. Meanwhile the Viceroy might call unofficially to view the presents. With that the Mandarin took his departure.

The presents were on board the ship at Heytamoon, which was now allowed to come up the river. On August 4 it let go its anchor in front of the city. 'After our devotions', says Nievhoff, who had remained on board, 'we went that day a Shore to the Embassadours, whom we found lodged in a Stately Edifice, situated upon the River side (over against which lay our Yacht). The Vice-Roy had ordered two Mandorins that they should guard with a good number of Souldiers the Gates for our security.'

The authorities now changed their minds and told the Ambassadors to re-embark, stating that until sanction was received from the capital the Viceroy had no power to allow them to stay on land. Accordingly, much against their will, they all returned to their vessel. Peking was over fifteen hundred miles away by river and canal, and they knew they had a long wait until the Viceroy received an answer to his letter. For three weeks they remained lying in the stream with nothing to do but look at the immense city and the people entering and leaving the gates. 'Daily there were at least five or six Men crowded to death in passing through the Gates,' writes Nievhoff. He had read an account by a Jesuit called Martini of the Manchu expedition against Yung Li at the time he was established in Canton about eight years previously. It was the old story. The Manchus in-duced a traitor to open the gates. When they burst in, 'the place

99

was soon turned to a Map of misery,' Nievhoff says, 'for everyone began to tear, break, carry away whatsoever he could lay hands on. The cry of Women, Children and Aged People was so great that it exceeded all noise of such loud distractions.' The sack continued for nineteen days, when the Manchu General restored order. A hundred thousand people were said to have been massacred. 'And although this City was thus lamentably laid waste, yet through the great care of the Viceroys, it was in a few years after restored to her former lustre.' Nievhoff could detect no traces of the damage. Perfect order prevailed, there was no outward sign of animosity between the Chinese and their conquerors, and there was evidence on all hands of great wealth and prosperity. It seemed to him an impregnable place. And for exactly two hundred and two years it remained impregnable, when it was stormed by an English army.

At the end of three weeks the Ambassadors were allowed to land again, 'and were most nobly received in their former lodg-ings; but yet were so narrowly guarded by a number of Foot-Souldiers, that they were not permitted to go into the Streets'. It seems, however, that no orders had yet come from the capital and that in bringing them ashore the officials' object was to squeeze them, for two days later a Mandarin called and suggested that if they wanted their mission to be a success it would be good policy to buy the goodwill both of the Imperial Council and of the Council at Canton. He named an outrageous sum. The Am-bassadors agreed to give about one-twentieth of what was asked. The Mandarin pretended to be indignant, but when he saw that he could get no more he accepted it with surprising civility. The sum paid was about £40, then worth quite six times as much as today. It was sufficient to put the authorities into an excellent humour, for next day the Ambassadors received an invitation from the Viceroy to a dinner, not at his residence, but on the open space beside the river. Until the Emperor had accepted them as tribute-bearing envoys he could not ask them into the city.

Tents were erected on this open piece of ground. The Viceroy

Festin des Vice-Rois
Pres des murs de Kanton.
't Koninchlijck Banequet
voor de muur van kanten.

Convivium
proregum ante
Muros Cantonis.

A. Le vieux Vice-Roy.
B. Le ieune Vice-Roy.
C. Le Tutang.
D. Les deux Ambassadeurs.
E. Les deux Mandarins.
F. Les Musiciens.
G. Cinq Porte parasls.

A. Den ouden ouder Koninck.
B. Den jongen onder Koninck.
C. Den Tou-tang.
D. De twee Ambassadeur.
E. twee . Mandarijns.
F. 's Konings Musikanten.
G. Vijf Koninchlijcke Sonne Schermen.

ENTERTAINMENT OF THE DUTCH AMBASSADORS BY THE
VICEROY OF CANTON ON SEPTEMBER 19, 1655
*From Nievhoff's 'Embassy'*

and the Tartar General sat in a circular Mongol tent facing south, the direction in which authority always faces in China. The Ambassadors and their staff were conducted from their house in procession, two mandarins with wands leading the way, while a servant held a parasol over their Excellencies. The tent where they were to sit was on the Viceroy's right, a side less honourable in China than the left. There a band was playing so loudly 'that there was no hearing one another speak'.

From their tent the Ambassadors were led up before the Viceroy and the Tartar General. This was the first time they had seen them. It was September 19, so that two months had passed since their arrival in the estuary. But this was nothing to the delays they would later have to bear. 'After some Complements passed between them, they were reconducted to their tents by the same Mandorines.'

In the meantime the Viceroy's Steward 'came crowding through the people', who had collected in large numbers to see the dinner given to the foreign devils. 'He had a brave Sky-colour Silk Coat, richly embroidered with Gold and Silver Dragons, and about his neck hung a Chain of best Corral. This Steward gave immediately order to two of his Attendants to serve the Meat up.'

The Ambassadors dined at the table in their tent. It was 'heaped with several sorts of Dishes and Sweet-Meats, most delicately ordered to please the Palate; upon each table stood about forty Chargers, all of Massie Silver, some whereof were very Artificially wrought, and in each Dish were several sorts of Viands'. The band played, and to show that they, too, understood music 'the Embassadours caused one of their Followers to give the Viceroys' (the Dutch called the Tartar General also Viceroy) 'a lesson upon their own Harpsical, which exceedingly pleased them'. In this the Ambassadors were no doubt flattering themselves, for Asiatics cannot abide European music. It is, moreover, laid down in the classical books that on no account is barbarian music to be played on state occasions. 'At the beginning of the Dinner', explains Nievhoff, 'there were several bottles of Thé or Tea served to the Table', and goes on to explain that this was drunk with milk and salt. As we know, the Chinese never add milk to their tea, while the Mongols do or drink buttered tea. It may be, therefore, that our practice of using milk in tea is derived from the Manchu practice.

A certain amount of conversation was carried on between the two tables by means of interpreters, the Viceroy asking for particulars about Holland. Then followed toasts, the Viceroy and Tartar General drinking often to their guests in the rice wine which was laid on. The Ambassadors had brought a case of Port with them, and presently asked their hosts to sample it, which they did, continuing to drink it in place of their own liquor.

Though this was only an *al fresco* meal, the Dutch were astounded at the magnificence of the appointments and the quiet expedition of the service. They also admired their hosts' children, who were dining in a tent of their own, and who, says Nievhoff, 'were so civilly Educated, that I never saw any in Europe better brought up. A little before the Dinner was ended, they rose from the Table, and as they passed by the Tent of the Vice-Roys, fell upon their knees, and bowed with their faces thrice to the ground.'

To relish this remark to the full one should be able to call to mind Frans Hals' great 'Family Group' in the National Gallery, which had been painted five years before the Ambassadors went to China.

The answer from Peking did not arrive until February 1656. During their weary wait, in November, they saw the Tartar General depart for Kwang-si province at the head of his troops. Yung Li and the Ming forces were then in that region, as we know, and he was setting out against them or their sympathizers. The Ambassadors were invited to witness his departure, which was by water, up the Si-Kiang, a great river whose source is in far Yunnan. Tents had been pitched on the river bank 'on purpose to accomodate there at a Treatment the Vice-Roy and the Noblemen of the Court'.

Nievhoff then gives a description of the Tartar General, which may stand for that of any Manchu field officer who fought against the Ming or who now was in command of one of the Manchu armies stationed at key positions throughout China. This is how he pitches it in the bold language of the translation: 'As he rid to the Waterside, this young King was mounted upon a Dapple Gray Horse, with his Quiver of Arrows fastened about his middle, and his Hanger by his side, as is to be seen in the annexed Print taken from the life. The coat he had on was lined with Sables, and the wrong side out/ward: He wore a Red Cap lined with Sables, and behind (which declared the Royal Dignity, for no ordinary person is suffered to wear the like) hung the end of a Peacocks Tail: The Saddle/Cloth was Gold Tissue embroidered, and about (the horse's) Neck hung three great Tassels which touched the ground. Thus richly Accoutred he rid to the Great *Jonck* to take his leave there, which was performed with much state and Hilarity. The Grandees were treated in several Tents; the Em/bassadours had also a tent provided for them, where they were most nobly Caressed.'

The Dutch had some notion of recent events in China. They did not know them in the detail given in the first part of this book, but in Chapter 18 of his account of the Embassy Niev/hoff provides a sketch of Chinese history, and when he is deal/ing with the fall of the Ming he has hold of essentials. For in/stance, referring to Li's rebellion being the first cause of the disaster, he says: 'This noble and flourishing Empire had that Viper hatching within its bowels, that would work its con/fusion, and was the only cause of its overthrow.' After describ/ing Li's life as a bandit, he says: 'Licungzus in the year 1641 marched his Army out of the Province of Xensi, after he had wholly Plundered and Destroyed its chiefest Cities,' and that he began to reduce the fortresses on the way to the capital. Then 'he took upon himself the Title of Emperour, by the name of Theinxun, which signifies Obedient to Heaven; for by Pre/text of this glorious name, which he used for a Cloak of his

Villany, he gave out in speeches, and so made his Souldiers believe, that it was concluded in Heaven that he should ascend the Throne, and deliver the oppressed Subjects out of the covetous hands of the present Emperor, to inflict punishment on the corrupt Governours of Provinces who had over-burthened the People with intolerable taxes.'

A detailed account follows of Li's advance on Peking and the manner in which he induced traitors to open the gates. Then comes the description of Ch'ung Chên's suicide, after 'Licung-zus with the Prime of his Army was gotten through the second Gate'.

'When he was first told of the Enemies being within his Court, he was astonished with admiration at the unexpected hearing of such direful news; but after a small Pause, seeing there was no hopes to escape, he took his Pen, and writing a Letter with his own Blood accuses his Officers therein of most horrid Treason. . . . Having finished this Letter, as a Man Dis-tracted he kills his Daughter in his Chamber, being a young Virgin of seventeen or eighteen years of Age, that she should not be mishandled or abused by the Rogues; and then with a settled resolution not to survive this dismal misfortune, going into the Garden, with one of his Garters he Hanged himself upon a Plum-Tree. This was the miserable catastrophe of the Emperour Zungchinius.'

Then we have Li seated on the Dragon Throne and 'sum-moning the chiefest Persons of the Empire to a meeting; . . . Whither they no sooner come, but a company of the basest fel-lows, were turned in upon them.' Nievhoff had also heard about old Wu and his son, General Wu San-Kuei, whom he calls Us and Usanguejus. He even gives one of old Wu's letters, or some-thing like it, and his son's frigid reply: 'I shall never owne him for my Father who will not be true and faithful to his Sovereign.'

The part Wu played in bringing in Prince Jui is also related. 'The *Cham* who had long been waiting for such a convenient opportunity, readily accepted his offer.' And the story is rounded off with a few vivid touches about Li's flight, which are worth

Jonge Onder-Kooning.
Iunior Prorex

THE TARTAR GENERAL
From Nieuhoff's 'Embassy'

quoting not only as showing how much Londoners learnt of this startling drama two hundred and seventy-three years ago, but also because the language is strangely evocative, not of China but of old England. 'As a testimony of the greatness of the Treasure that was carried out of Peking by this flying Tyrant and his Followers, it is most certain that 7 or 8 days were spent wholly about the loading of Waggons and Horses with the same; and yet they left great store of riches behind them, being surprised with fear at the sudden coming of the Tartars. And thus were the infinite riches of Gold, Silver, Jewels and costly Furniture, which sixteen Emperours of the Race of Taminga had been scraping together for the space of 280 years, destroyed and carried away: But he had not yet gotten into Harbour with his Booty; for in his flight he was set upon by the Tartar, who recovered from him all that mass of Wealth which he had so traiterously stoln. . . . What became of Licungzus is not certainly known, for his Forces were most of them kill'd upon the place by Usanguejus; and therefore some are of opinion that he fell into the Slaughter amongst the rest, for he never was heard of after that Battel.'

This Latinizing of Chinese names was usual in the seventeenth century. We have only retained it in two cases, that of Confucius and of Mencius.

Nievhoff had plenty of time to collect historical information of this kind and to make his sketches, because, as related, the Emperor's letter was only received in February 1656, seven months after the first arrival of the Dutch. The contents, as communicated to them by the Viceroy, were to the effect that the Ambassadors and their immediate staff had sanction to come up to the capital as tribute-bearing Envoys. The Emperor was also pleased to give permission that their ships (they had two) might take cargoes. This was in accordance with normal precedent. Tribute-envoys were always allowed to trade on the occasion of their visit. The Dutch, however, took the permission to be a sure sign that the request they intended to make to the Emperor for open trade between Holland and China would be granted.

They were much cheered and applied to the Viceroy for leave to set off at once. The journey to Peking meant traversing the whole length of China. At the rate of twenty miles a day it would take three months, but four months was the more usual time. All the arrangements were in the hands of the Viceroy. His subordinates would conduct them and bring them back.

Before they left, the Viceroy asked them to dinner at his palace inside the walls. They were conducted on horseback through the streets. The interior of the palace struck them as very splen⁄did. 'The Galleries, Courts, Halls and other places of this Court were very artificially and Curiously built, and most richly fur⁄nished with Pictures, Silk Hangings and costly Carpets.' The Mandarins had all been invited. The Viceroy, in a lemon⁄coloured robe embroidered with dragons and with a peacock feather in his hat, sat by himself on a carpet thrown over a square daïs. On his right thumb was an archer's ring, as was the custom of the Manchus. 'During Dinner, which was ordered in great Pomp and Solemnity, the Viceroy toyed with his Children, who were instructed with childish questions and taught wanton reparties.' Near him were seated 'several young and beautiful Ladies', whom the Ambassadors would certainly not have seen had it been a Chinese dinner party. 'The Entertainment being ended and the Embassadours highly Caressed in solemn man⁄ner, they took their leaves and departed to their lodgings.'

Throughout Nievhoff's account it is clear that the Dutch were generally very satisfied with their reception and rarely had any⁄thing but admiration for the Manchus and Chinese. Although the East was stranger to these seventeenth⁄century travellers than to us, there seems not to have been the gulf between Europeans and Orientals which became so marked in the nineteenth century.

A last party took place before the Dutch started for Peking. The Tartar General was away on his expedition, but had left word with his secretary that the Ambassadors were to be in⁄vited to his house. The entertainment there was less formal. 'Besides the variety and store of well condimented dishes, they were presented with a farce of various Entries, Masquerades,

Dancing in shapes of Lions, Tygers and Leopards, and other strange Creatures of their Country, to the extraordinary satis-faction of his Guests.' These animal dances are to this day a feature of the Courts of the Shan Sawbwas, where I have seen them, and are Mongolian not Chinese in taste. This Mongolian or Manchu atmosphere was further emphasized by the Tartar General's mother, who came from time to time to have a look at the company. 'She was very neatly and richly dressed after the Tartar fashion, middle sized, slender, of a brown com-plexion, of a pleasing and taking countenance.' Her chair of state was near the drawing-room door and to it, though she was not seated there, 'in honour of that great Lady, we humbly paid our respects'. No doubt they were told to do this, for it was the custom in China to prostrate yourself before the empty chair of a royal or viceregal personage.

The long journey began on 17th March. The Ambassadors were accommodated 'on a very brave Vessel', with fifty boats for their staff and servants, the presents, the Mandarins and the soldiers who escorted them. The expenses were paid by the Chinese Government. Their route was wholly by water, except for the crossing of two watersheds on foot, and lay first to Nanking on the Yang-tse, thereafter through the Middle King-dom on the Grand Canal to the Yellow River and Tien-tsin, and from thence the odd hundred miles into Peking. They had no misadventures, for complete peace reigned in those vast expanses of the Empire. Nievhoff industriously made his sketches of every place of importance. They show him to have been an excellent artist whose style seems to partake more of Claude Lorrain's (1600–82) than of the Dutch landscape school, the masters of which were in 1655 mostly under thirty. But in some of them appears a Chinese technique, as if they were renderings of Chinese pictures.

At the principal towns the Magistrates and local gentry seem to have received the Ambassadors with honour. They gave them dinners, offered them presents, showed them the Buddhist temples and fired cannon on their departure. Later European envoys found the journey far more tedious; they were rarely allowed on shore, and the Mandarins were stiff and the people impertinent. The Dutch, however, got on well with everyone. They were easy, did not stand on their dignity. In the smaller towns the inhabitants, though friendly, were inclined to be timid. At Yu-kon, a little place on Lake Po-yang, 'we were no sooner come to Anchor, but the news of the arrival of the Hollanders filled the whole city with joy, so that both old and young came running to shore to view us and our Vessels, who beheld us with great admiration, and fain would have been talking to us, if the difference of Language had not hindered: We caused our Trumpets to sound that old Tune of William of Nassau, supposing to have delighted them; but on the contrary they were so much affrighted with their Brazen voice, that they ran roaring with full speed to shelter in the City.'

That is a true Chinese rustic scene, as is the following, which took place thirty miles further on, where there were rocks and a dangerous wind which sometimes blew suddenly out of the mountains. 'When the Chinese Pilots saw our Cook going to make a fire to dress Dinner, they came into the Cabin to the Embassadours, fell down upon their knees, and earnestly entreated that they would forbid any such thing to be done, for that (as they said) there was a certain Spirit who kept himself under water about this Pool, and appeared in the shape of a Dragon, or great Fish, and had the command over this Countrey, and whose nature and constitution was such that he could not endure the scent in his Nose of Roasted Poultry, Boyled Bacon or other savory smells; for so soon as he was sensible of any such thing, he immediately raised a storm, which did infalliby cast away the Vessel. The Embassadours at their earnest entreaty sent word to the Cook that they would be contented with a cold Dinner for that day. During the discourse, there appeared playing in the Water two or three Tunny Fishes, which put the poor Chineses into no little affright, in regard they imagined that the Water-Spirit had already given order for the casting away of their Vessel.'

The Ambassadors reached Nanking shortly after this episode, more than half their journey being thus accomplished. Here, eleven years before, the Ming, Hung Kuang, had set up his Court and here, after his General, Shih K'o-fa, the great Confucian, had been overcome by the Manchus at Yang-chao, he was killed and the city sacked. It had not wholly recovered from this catastrophe, for the Imperial Palace was still in ruins. But on the whole it was in a very flourishing condition. The three chief officials were Manchus. In the house of one of them, where the Ambassadors called, there was more the air of a tent on the steppe than of a Governor's drawing-room in the richest and most cultivated provincial capital in China. The Governor could not even speak Chinese. His wife, in a manner quite shocking to Chinese notions of female propriety, came bustling in, began asking questions about Holland, pulled out the Ambassadors' swords and discharged their pistols through the window. Then tea was served, both in the Mongol and the Chinese manner, with and without milk, in wooden bowls and in porcelain cups. But the young people of the family seemed to have acquired a tincture of Chinese manners. Their mother's bluff hearty presence reminds us of our own hunting and shooting women. In a generation or two such ways were abandoned. Manchu women gave up field sports and became as fragile and retiring as Chinese ladies of the traditional type.

The wife of the Governor was not the only Manchu lady whom the Ambassadors met. They came across another, even more free. The description of her is the best I know of that formidable, good-hearted, refreshing type, which is still to be met with on the north and western frontiers among the Mongolian aristocracies. 'As we were riding out one day to take the Air, and to view the City,' says Nievhoff, 'we passed by the Gate of the old Imperial Court, where sat a great Tartar Lady, with her servants waiting upon her, about forty years of Age: She very civilly sent to our Interpreter to invite the Embassadours into her House; Jacob de Keyzer hereupon lighted, and the Lady then made towards him: She was very debonair and

free, looked upon our Swords, and much admired their bend-
ing without breaking; she took the Embassadours Hat, and put
it on her own Head, and unbutton'd his Doublet almost down
to his Waste: Afterwards she led the way into the house, and
desired him to follow, appointing one of her Attendants to
conduct him, who brought us into her apartment, where we
found her standing with her Daughter about half her age,
waiting our coming, in great state.

'The Daughter was clothed in a Violet-coloured Damask
Gown, and the Mother in Black Damask, and had both of
them their Ears hung with Rings; their Hair braided and
twisted about their Heads with strings of Pearls, but over their
Hair they wore little Caps made of Reed, with a Tassle upon
the crown of Red Silk. Their Cloths reached down to their
Heels, tyed about the middle with a broad Ribbon, and but-
toned down from the Neck to the Waste: Their Shooes were of
Black Leather, their faces unmask'd without any Painting.
They had us into a large withdrawing room unfurnished, only
a few Benches covered with Silk, upon which they desired us
to sit: They drank to us several times in their liquor made of
Beans, which is very strong, but agrees wondrous well with
their constitutions. They set before us also some of their Sweet-
meats, much entreating us to Eat, excusing the meanness of the
Entertainment, her Husband being absent.'

Such were the wives of the men who overthrew the Ming,
such were their mothers and the robust cheerfulness of their
homes. There were many of them in Nanking, for the Manchu
garrison, says Nievhoff, numbered forty thousand. Though the
Manchus later on adopted the etiquette of Chinese life, they
always remained a separate caste and were not allowed to marry
outside it. Seen by the Dutch only twelve years after their incursion, one might have expected them to be less civilized than
already they clearly were. The Mongols who conquered China
in the thirteenth century had been savage barbarians at the first.
The Manchus in origin were even more primitive than the
Mongols. But for over fifty years before they crossed the border

their virgin minds had been influenced by Chinese thought, so that after the conquest they were prepared and, indeed, eager to become the pupils of the conquered and to graduate in their studies.

The Ambassadors spent a fortnight in Nanking, leaving on May 18 in fresh barges placed at their disposal by imperial order. 'These Vessels were very large and commodious, all Guilded and Painted with Dragons that had open Mouths and fierce Claws: At one end of these Imperial bottoms was a place for Musick.'

To get to the entrance of the Grand Canal they had to sail down the Yang-tse for some distance. On the night of the 20th they anchored at a small town not far from it and there had an experience of Chinese beggars, who carried their pertinacity to a macabre extreme. 'Here came several Beggars aboard us to shew their Tricks; among the rest there were two, who knocked their heads with so much force one against another, that we looked every moment to see them fall down dead upon the place; and in this gesture they continued till the Company had bestowed their charity upon them; for unless they give some-thing, they never cease rancountring heads, till they kill each other, which has often hapned. I saw likewise in this City an-other Beggar lying upon his knees, who seemed to mutter something to himself; afterwards he struck his naked head against a black stone, with so much force and violence that he made the Earth to shake under him: several other such Feats they use to win remorse from Strangers.' Just as saints have used austerities to rouse God's pity that He grant them bliss, so did these beggars mortify themselves till charity awarded them the paradise of a coin.

Next morning the Embassy turned into the Grand Canal, Kublai Khan's greatest engineering work. The Dutch, always glad to see any canal, were much delighted. 'Well may this Channel bear the name of the Royal Water,' exclaims Niev-hoff, 'since there is nothing so pleasant to be seen in all the world, both sides of the Aqueduct having not only smooth large Banks, but planted also with stately and shady Trees. On the West and East of this Royal Channel (for it reaches from South to North) we saw rich Pastures and delightful Woods, the like not to be seen in all Asia; thick sowed with wealthy Towns, Villages, Pleasant Seats and Dwellings opulent and stately; insomuch that nothing can be more delightful, as if Art and Nature had strove to please the Passenger upon his way through this famous Channel.' This rich plain was the site of the ancient state of Lu, where two thousand two hundred and seven years previously Confucius had been born, where his tomb was situated, and where his descendants, still bearing his surname, K'ung, continued to live.

We cannot pause to note here the many interesting towns that were passed, except to say that on May 24 they anchored at 'the brave City of Yang-chao', where eleven years before had been enacted the classical scene between General Shih and Prince Yü, the handsome commander of the Manchu army. It had recovered from the sack and massacre, stood now 'in as great Splendour as it was at first'.

At Hwai-ngan, fifty miles further on, they came across a Jesuit, Father Gascomer, who was so delighted to see Euro-peans that he forgot he was a Catholic and the Dutch Pro-testants and that they were trying to break the Portuguese trade monopoly. 'He seemed a very open hearted person,' writes Nievhoff. After the Ambassadors had entertained him 'he gave them darkly to understand, that upon their request and desire for free Trade in China, or any thing else, they would meet with great opposition at Peking from the Portuguesses, who would do their utmost to hinder it.' The Ambassadors thanked him for the hint and became thoughtful.

Continuing up the Grand Canal they reached the Yellow River. 'This River is called by some the Saffron from the Yellowness of the Water; at a distance it seems to be a thick Morish Plash.' At that time it flowed into the sea in the latitude of Hwai-ngan, over two hundred miles south of its present mouth. To reach the upper section of the Grand Canal the

Dutch had to ascend the river to Tsing-ho and, crossing there, enter the lock gate. From that point it was about 450 miles to Peking, a long journey still, but full of interest. They saw tame cormorants used for fishing, they saw 'rough white Cats, not unlike the Malteeza Dogs, with long Ears, which are there the Ladies Foysting Hounds or Play-fellows; they will catch no mice, being too much made of', and at Hokien they tried to visit a huge bronze lion which stood in the market-place, 'but the Chineses, when they saw us coming, shut their Gates upon us, being struck with terrour for fear of the Hollanders'. At last on July 16, four months after leaving Canton, they reached Tung-chao, which is twelve miles from Peking. There travellers disembark and go the rest of the way by road.

Since the Dutch had first anchored in the Canton estuary a year had elapsed, and now at last they were about to come to close quarters with the Chinese Government and get to the business which had brought them all that way. They had had plenty of time to reckon their chances. They knew that they were officially regarded as a tribute-bearing Embassy and that the regulations for such Embassies laid down that they should be received in audience by the Emperor, when their letter and presents would be accepted. They also knew that the etiquette of the Court, which was very different from the etiquette of European Courts, would have to be followed. This require-ment does not seem to have bothered them. It entailed the elaborate ceremony of the kotow, it meant that they would have to acknowledge that the Emperor of China was also Lord of the World and that Holland was one of the tributary states on his borders. But as such an acknowledgment did not correspond with the facts, was, indeed, so far removed from the truth that in no conceivable circumstances could it embarrass Holland, they appear to have come to the conclusion that it might harm-lessly be made, and that the audience with all its attendant pro-strations should be regarded as a ceremonial without signifi-cance. If compliance with it was necessary in order to obtain the imperial permission to send ships annually to Canton, they must certainly comply. Business came first. Punctilio must not be allowed to interfere. During the year in China, moreover, they had met with a great deal of politeness from the authorities. It was a wonderful country and its Emperor was truly a very great personage. The obligation to treat him with greater marks of respect than they would have accorded to the head of their own Government was tempered by these considerations. They landed from their state barge full of hope and good spirits.

Officials were there to meet them, for word had been sent ahead. Horses were ready for the Ambassadors and their staff, and a quantity of wagons for the presents and luggage. A pro-cession was formed. 'Two Trumpeters rid at a distance before, then followed the Standard Bearer with the Prince of Oranges Blazenry; next to him the Embassadours, accompanied with several Tartar Lords and Gentlemen, well mounted. The Cap-tain and Souldiers who had thus far conducted the Embas-sadours, and were about fifty in number, came after in good order, with the Emperours Presents, and the Embassadours goods.'

In this guise modern Europe presented itself for the first time at 'that incomparable Imperial City'.

'We past through two highly eminent Gates,' continues Nievhoff, 'and lighted at a very famous Temple,' where they were served with refreshments. The Tung-chao road enters the outer or Tartar City on its eastern side by the Ch'i Hua Men, which must have been one of the 'eminent Gates' referred to. While they rested at the temple a Manchu official from the Court, 'who carried a Falcon upon his hand,' arrived to conduct them to the house where they were to lodge, which was in the Imperial City, the second enceinte, in the centre of which was the For-bidden City. The house had a walled courtyard and soldiers were posted at its gates. When they lay down to sleep that night they could hear the gongs beating from the towers of The Great Within.

Early next morning one of the Grand Secretaries called. He was Chinese and was accompanied by two Manchu military officers and other high officials of the Board of Rites. This Grandee formally bade the Ambassadors welcome and, proceeding to business, asked for a list of the presents. There were ninety-three items. It will be interesting to note some of them. They were divided into four classes, those for the Emperor, for the Empress, the Empress Dowager, and again for the Emperor, in this last case being personal presents from the two Ambassadors. The Jesuits had made their way at the Court of Peking by presents of clocks, mechanical contrivances, and by themselves supplying scientific information about astronomy and the founding of cannon. Most of the Dutch presents were not of this kind, and for that reason were less aptly chosen. It is true that items (1), (2) and (23) on the Emperor's list were 'A Suit of Armour Embossed with Gold', 'twenty three Guns of several sorts and sizes, all richly and curiously wrought', and 'a silver Optick Tube'. No doubt these were acceptable, but the other items such as cloves, nutmegs, broad cloth, cinnamon, carpets, beads, quilts, a parrot, were not likely to impress a sovereign who had a vast superfluity of such articles. The presents for the Empresses were selected with more art. They included looking-glasses, scent, furniture, tapestry, velvet and pictures. Seven rosaries were for the Dowager, a curious gift from Protestants to a person who was not a Catholic. Her name was Bonjikitu, and she was a woman of spirit, was mad on hunting and a dead shot. *Seven* rosaries appear excessive. Moreover, she was only thirty-six.

The Grand Secretary passed the presents and went on to make certain enquiries about Holland. Was there such a place? Was it not rather a fact that the Dutch were really sea-rovers without a country, living on their ships and only landing to plunder? The Ambassadors, who guessed that the Portuguese were responsible for this story, produced a map and pointed to Holland. The Grand Secretary appeared satisfied and began to ask questions about their government. It was not easy to explain the constitution of the United Provinces, which were governed by a Council presided over by the Prince of Orange.

Indeed, how difficult such an explanation must have been at that date will be understood by those who are acquainted with the cosmographical conceptions in the theory of Chinese sovereignty. These conceptions gave the Dragon Seat a middle place in a philosophical doctrine which joined Heaven and Earth. The Grand Secretary was therefore not at all impressed by the constitutional theory explained by Their Excellencies. It appeared wholly unsound, founded upon nothing, with no astronomical or astrological justification, in other words with no justification at all. It made him revert again to his former question—was there, in fact, such a place as Holland? Once more the Ambassadors produced the map. The Grand Secretary then declared that, though he did not propose to argue further about the existence of their country, he would be unable to advise the Emperor that it had a stable form of government.

This critical attitude, though no doubt in the main characteristic of the official outlook, may have been influenced by what the Jesuits had been saying at Court. The Fathers had strong reasons for opposing the Dutch. In the first place the latter were Protestants. Secondly, they were the enemies of Spain and Portugal, having broken away from the dominion of Catholic Philip II and seized so many Portuguese possessions in Asia. Their object in coming to Peking could therefore be interpreted as part of a design to destroy utterly the Portuguese empire. That would seriously have endangered the position of the Jesuits, who had vast schemes far wider than the mere making of converts.

How far they had attempted to turn the Emperor against the Dutch may be gathered from a report on the Embassy written by an anonymous Jesuit, which is included in Ogilby's volume. This man quotes a letter written by another Jesuit called John Valleat, who is recorded as stating that on the 13th of February 1656, five months before the embassy arrived, he was with the Emperor, 'who being pleased (according to his wont) to honour me with familiar discourse', asked about the

Hollanders. This gave Father Valleat the opportunity of declaring that they were the rebellious subjects of Spain, that their country was not really theirs but had 'Trayterously been usurped from their lawful Sovereign', and that they were no better than 'Vagabonds of the Sea, seeking Rapine there from all people, to furnish themselves for maintenance of their Rebellion at home'. So was described the great fight for liberty which Motley has immortalized for us in his *Rise of the Dutch Republic*, but the Jesuits stood well at Court and the Chinese Government was so indifferent at that period to the importance of acquiring reliable information about the rise, ambitions and power of new states, that though the charges were insufficient to cause the Emperor to cancel the permission he had given the Dutch to come up, they must have inclined him to use every caution.

Father Valleat goes on to relate that he was called in to advise when the Grand Secretary was examining the presents, and that he told him most of them were of Indian manufacture and did not come from Holland as pretended. The suggestion here was that that country was too backward to produce such articles and that they represented plunder taken in Asia. 'But a Messenger coming for me from the Emperour, I was forced to break off,' he says, and adds with some complacency: 'when I arose to go out, they all stood up and the two Captains (i.e. the Ambassadors) proffered me their utmost service.'

When he came to the Emperor's presence, 'I approached near', he writes, 'as if I had some secret to whisper to him and said that if the Hollanders ever get a footing, upon pretence of Commerce in any place, immediately they raise a Fortress and plant Guns (wherein they are most expert) and so appropriate a Title to their possessions.' The Emperor giving him all his attention, he went on to say that just as the Formosan pirate, Coxinga, had established himself on an island near the mouth of the Yang-tse and had been driven away with great difficulty, so might the Dutch attempt to establish themselves. 'If they should there build a Castle, they would command that passage, and be capable of all supplies from Sea, in despite of this whole Countrey.'

These words, though uttered in malice, showed an extra-ordinary grasp of the elements of a situation which was after-wards to dominate the future of China. It would hardly be an exaggeration to say that hidden in them was the most important warning ever given to a Chinese Emperor. Going beyond what the Jesuit could have consciously imagined, far beyond the possible dangers of that date, they hinted at the power which command of the sea gave to European nations. As this nar-rative proceeds it will become abundantly clear that the arrival of the Dutch Embassy at Peking in 1656 marked the beginning of an era of changes which eventually were to dissolve the ancient Chinese Empire. The Dutch, or what they stood for, were potentially a formidable danger, greater than had been to the Ming either Li or Prince Jui. Yet, on the page where the Jesuit unveils for an instant this danger, he also suggests, not to the Emperor but as a reflection of his own, the remedy which, had it been adopted, would have preserved China from a cen-tury of troubles. The Dutch, he says, made a mistake in the choice of their presents, most of which were useless and un-likely to bring them reputation. What they should have brought were 'some Engineers and Officers to train up and exercise Souldiers'. Engineering, science, modern ordnance and arms, that was what China really needed and what the Jesuit Order, for their own ulterior reasons, wished to give her and did offer her as far as they could. Had she accepted them, she would have been able to strengthen herself long before the distant phantom of an armed West approached over the sea and seized her in its mailed paws.

The Grand Secretary having made his report on the presents, the Ambassadors were ordered to deliver them to the Board of Rites for transmission to the Emperor. When the order came, it was pouring wet and they asked for a postponement, but this was not granted and they were obliged to proceed forthwith to the Board Chamber, where the members were awaiting them.

Sitting in the place of honour beside the President, who was a Manchu, they saw the famous Jesuit, Adam Schall, 'Shaved and Clothed after the Tartar Fashion, a very comely old Man with a long Beard'.

In spite of the advice which his Order had been giving the Emperor, the Father was very civil, came and saluted them and asked after certain Roman Catholics who lived in Amsterdam. The President, who had not yet seen the presents, now took them out of the boxes. 'As often as he took out any thing that was very rare, Father Adam fetched a deep sigh.' The Dutch suspected well enough that he was no friend of theirs. The President specially commended the arms, saying they would be very acceptable to His Majesty.

While some Mandarins 'were as busy as Porters to help away the Chests and Cases', the President 'found himself hungry, and sent for a piece of Pork to satisfy his Appetite, which was half-raw, whereof he did eat most heartily, in a slovenly manner, that he looked more like a Butcher than a Prince'.

This is a revealing touch. The Ch'ing dynasty was twelve years old, but the Manchus had not yet reformed their table manners. Even in the shadow of The Great Within they still ate like the Nomads of the steppe. We may assume that the President was a tough old soldier, and that he did not care what the Chinese thought of him.

'No sooner had he stayed his Stomack with this Collation,' continues Nievhoff, 'but he ordered the son of the old Canton Vice-King, who had his residence in this Court, to provide an entertainment for the Embassadours, which he accordingly performed in some better fashion and order than the former.'

Apparently the President regarded his pork chop as a mere snack, for 'when Dinner was brought up, his Highness and the rest of the Tartar Lords fell on again as greedily, as if they had eat nothing all day; but neither the Ambassadours, nor Father Adam, could eat of their Cookery, most of the Meat being raw; which his Highness perceiving, caused the Dishes to be taken off, and a Banquet of Fruit and Sweetmeats to be set upon the Table, earnestly urging the Embassadours to send home to their Lodgings whatsoever was left, which they civilly refused.'

During the dinner Father Adam depressed the Dutch (on purpose) by telling them that a Russian Embassy had been in Peking for the last four months, having made to the Throne, without success so far, the very request for yearly trade the Dutch were making. This was the Baikoff Embassy, which was never received in audience because Baikoff refused to conform to its etiquette. What that was in detail we shall see directly, for now that their presents had been sent in, the Dutch could expect an audience any day.

The dinner at the Board of Rites lasted till nightfall. When it broke up the Ambassadors did not fail to notice that Father Schall was carried away 'by four Men in a Palakin or Sedan, attended by several considerable persons on Horse-back'. He was a Mandarin of the highest rank and engaged, as we shall see later on, on public work of great importance.

On July 31 the Emperor issued a Mandate formally granting audience to the Ambassadors. This encouraged them to believe that a successful issue was assured. Though Father Adam might be working against them, there was no sign that he had got his way with the Emperor. With their presents accepted and an audience sanctioned, they were within sight of a grant to trade. But news now reached them that though the Manchu members of the Board favoured the grant, the Chinese were opposed to it on the ground of precedent, and further argued that if the Dutch were allowed into Canton, the English would attempt to follow, or might attempt to pass themselves off as Dutch. At that date the Chinese Government considered the English the most desperate of all the Western barbarians because nineteen years before, in 1637, a Captain Weddell had burst into the Canton river, silenced a fort with his broadsides and seized prisoners in a manner which to Chinese eyes was indistinguish-able from piracy. Disturbed by these rumours that the Council was less well disposed towards them than they had hoped, the

Ambassadors spent anxious days waiting for the audience, the exact date of which had not been mentioned in the Imperial Mandate.

On August 22 things began to move: they were given a lesson in the etiquette of audience. Mandarins conducted them to a library inside the Forbidden City, where the Imperial Seal of China was kept. In the courtyard of this building they were lined up facing in the direction of the Seal, and a herald explained through an interpreter that on words of command shouted by him they should kneel, then touch the ground three separate times with their foreheads, and at a last command get on to their feet again. This had to be done three times. About a hundred officials who were consulting books in the library came out to watch. The herald duly shouted the words of command, and the Ambassadors knelt, touched the ground as ordered and got up. This was the famous kotow, the ceremonial salute which all persons received in audience by the Son of Heaven invariably gave. The Dutch knew that the Russian Ambassador, Baikoff, had refused to give it because to do so, in his opinion, would have implied that his sovereign, the White Czar, was a feudatory of the Emperor of China. That was the reason his mission was hanging fire. They also knew that the kotow was meant to have that implication. But since they had no king, were not even representing the government of the United Provinces, but only the East India Company, they saw no official objection to performing it. As stout Republicans it was disagreeable to have to do so, but as merchants they conceived it to be good business. Unless they performed it, there was no hope of an audience. All the Grandees of the Kingdom had to do it. How could they, officially described as barbarian tribute-bearers, hope to escape? These were the very practical considerations which induced them to comply (as gracefully as their Western clothes and tall hats permitted) with the herald's shouted orders of command. The Mandarins responsible for the rehearsal were quite satisfied. The 2nd of September was fixed for the audience.

From time immemorial the hour of an Imperial Audience was dawn. As the sun rose, the Son of Heaven showed himself to his people. His presence was as important as the sun's. Seated in the centre of The Great Within he radiated his light upon the whole world. The inhabitants of the Middle King, dom and the barbarians of countries, named and unnamed, nearer or more distant, discovered or unknown, lying in con, centric circles that extended to the last confines, looked to him to reconcile them to the macrocosmos. In this conception, astronomy and astrology combined in the metaphysical system which lay at the root of Confucianism. An Imperial audience had therefore something of the nature of a Communion or of a scene in epic drama. The Manchus had adopted it in all its antique detail.

Those to be received were obliged to take up their stations while it was still dark. In summer this was no matter: and the first week of September is still warm in Peking. Mid,winter audiences were more trying. A ninth,century poet, Po Chü,i, has left a description of one held at that season in Ch'ang,an, the then capital, or rather of his getting to the Palace and the wait outside till the bell went.

> At Ch'ang,an—a full foot of snow;
> A levée at dawn—to bestow congratulations on the Emperor.
> Just as I was nearing the Gate of the Silver Terrace,
> After I had left the suburb of Hsin,Ch'ang
> On the high causeway my horse's foot slipped;
> In the middle of the journey my lantern suddenly went out.
> Ten leagues' riding, always facing to the North;
> The cold wind almost blew off my ears.
> I waited for the bell outside the Five Gates;
> I waited for the summons inside the Triple Hall.
> My hair and beard were frozen and covered with icicles;
> My coat and robe—chilly like water.
> Suddenly I thought of Hsien,yu Valley
> And secretly envied Ch'ēn Chü,shih,

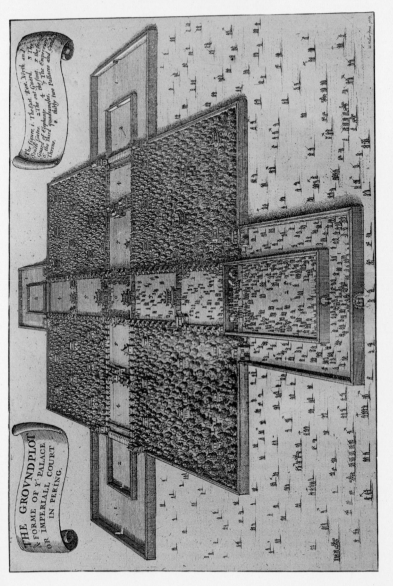

GROUND PLAN OF THE GREAT WITHIN

*From Nievhoff's 'Embassy'*

## The Dutch visit The Great Within

In warm bed-socks dozing beneath the rugs
And not getting up till the sun has mounted the sky.[1]

The officials responsible for bringing the Dutch arrived with
lanterns at their lodgings as early as two o'clock in the morning,
and took them to The Great Within by the southern approach
through the Wu Mên or Meridian Gate, whose name is an
allusion to the analogy between the Emperor and the sun at
noon. Beyond this gate is a large quadrangle, at the north side
of which is the Gate of Supreme Harmony, the name here a
reference to the even balance between heaven and earth, which
it was the office of the Son of Heaven to secure: The Great
Within was a sort of temple. To the left of this gate they were
halted and told to wait till dawn. No less than three other
parties of envoys joined them there; the most splendidly dressed
being from the Court of Shah Jehan, the Mogul Emperor of
India, who was then building the Taj Mahal; the most curiously, from the Court of the Dalai Lama at Lhassa, in yellow
robes and hats 'much like a Cardinal's'; the roughest, Mongols
from a state near the Great Wall, the leader of which looked
'more like a Souldier than an Embassadour'. The Dutch wore
wide cloaks over doublets, knee breeches, hose and heavy
shoes, a high crowned hat with feathers, their hair falling to
their shoulders.

Seated together on the blue stone pavement, they made an
incongruous group, these various envoys, waiting patiently for
the dawn. When at last it was light enough, they saw three
black elephants posted like sentinels at the three ports under the
gate. Detachments of the Imperial Guard stood to arms and a
crowd of officials and courtiers loitered near by. These now had
the distraction of looking at the envoys. Nievhoff says they
stared at the Dutch 'as if we had been some strange Afrik
Monsters', yet withal so politely that they gave no offence.

Then came the sound of a bell and the Mandarins who were
in charge of the Dutch led them through the gate into another

[1] Arthur Waley's translation.

123

courtyard, and from there into a second and yet a third, till passing under the Gate of Heavenly Purity, which is the very centre of the Great Within, they entered the courtyard in front of the Ch'ien-ch'ing Kung, the Palace of Heavenly Purity, in which was the Dragon Throne or that particular one which it was customary for the Emperor to use in audiences of the present kind.

Behind the throne-hall and invisible to the Dutch was the Chiao-t'ai Tien, the Hall of the Blending of Heaven and Earth, where rituals symbolizing the harmonious interchange of forces, supernal and terrestrial, were performed. Fronting the east and west sides of the courtyard were various buildings, such as the Hall of Industrious Energy, which was to be used in the following reign as the Imperial Study. Reproduced here is Wencelaus Hollar's etching of this courtyard or quadrangle. That famous artist never visited Peking, but at the time the book on the Dutch Embassy was published he was resident in England and no doubt was given a plan by Nievhoff. His picture is therefore no more than a reconstruction, yet must have satisfied those who were there as the impression which the place left in their memories. It was the first picture of The Great Within ever seen in London, though it belongs rather to chinoiserie than to the realm of actual fact.

When the Ambassadors entered the courtyard, the throne inside the Palace of Heavenly Purity was not yet occupied by the Emperor. They had plenty of time to look about them, saw the Imperial Bodyguard in coats of crimson satin drawn up at the foot of the buildings to right and left, saw on each side of the throne-room standard-bearers in black hats with yellow feathers, and Grandees each holding a yellow parasol. Near these were court attendants bearing insignia, gilded radiant circles denoting the sun and moon, and others who supported the Imperial Banner emblazoned with a five-clawed dragon in clouds.

The quadrangle had been much damaged by the fire at the time of the bandit Li's departure, and the repairs and rebuild-

Interior aulæ Imperatoriæ facies.
'T KEYSERS HOF van binnen

1 *Exhibitum in quo Imperatoris solium continetur.*
2 *Legati Batacorum.*
3 *Igoana Majoris Majestic.*
4 *Pavillion oblongatus equi.*
5 *Gerbæsai cum servicio inferiorum.*
6 *Tecticula.*
7 *Imperatoris Somatophylaces.*

8 *Palepsiluir i Keysers Throom in staat.*
9 *De vier Nederlandse Ambassadeurs.*
3 *Een Ambasssdeur aan den Grootten Segel neefft hoom wille Pandes.*
11 *Een Tectiengeite een luer Wooffungh.*
12 *Een Storiad.*
13 *Keysers Lifwaehten.*

THE CH'IEN-CH'ING KUNG OR PALACE OF HEAVENLY PURITY
IN THE CENTRE OF THE GREAT WITHIN
*From Nievhoff's 'Embassy'*

ing had only recently been completed. Nievhoff states that one of the reasons why they were kept waiting for the audience was the presence of workmen in the throne-room. So the Dutch had the good fortune to see the redecorated palace at its freshest and best. It struck them as very magnificent. 'All the Edifices are most richly adorned with Galleries, Balconies and carved Imagery, to the admiration of all that ever saw them.' Most of the timber visible on the outside of the buildings was lacquered and gilt, making them 'Shine and Glisten like Looking-glasses'. The roofs were covered with yellow glazed tiles, which as the sun rose higher shone 'brighter than Gold, which has made some believe and report that the Roof of this Royal Palace was covered with pure Gold'. Though they did not understand half that they saw, and had seen no more than a fraction of the whole nor ever had the chance of a peep at the remainder of the vast accumulation of works of art inside the buildings, the Dutch were convinced that The Great Within 'far exceeds all Royal Palaces in Europe for Splendour, Art, Wealth and Pleasure'.

But now they heard 'the noise and jingling of a little Bell, sweet sounding and delightful to the Ear'. This was the signal for a preliminary ceremonial, the kotow in the direction of the Throne before the Emperor sat upon it. First, the Grand Secretaries, the Presidents of the Boards, the noblemen of the Council advanced to numbers engraved on the flagstones of the courtyard which denoted their proper stations, and there each in his right place, gracefully, humbly and yet in great state, their bright silks spread about them, made the grand obeisance towards the empty throne, their rising and falling, the movements of their arms and hands, seeming to chime with the ritual music, 'both Vocal and Instrumental', played as an accompaniment.

When all the officials of the Court and the other envoys had completed the kotow it was the turn of the Dutch Ambassadors. They were conducted by an official whom they called the 'Chancellour' to a flagstone marked with the number ten.

Nine was the lowest rank in the official hierarchy, so the Ambassadors were graded below the most subordinate official. The herald was waiting for them, and put them through the motions of the kotow as they had rehearsed them before the Imperial Seal.

The whole company was now invited by the ushers to enter the throne-room of the Palace of Heavenly Purity, which stood above them on a platform. They mounted the steps and each took his appointed place in the pillared hall. The Dutch were accommodated thirty yards from the Dragon Seat, which was situated in the middle of the back wall. It was still empty. Tea with milk was then served.

Presently the approach of the Emperor in the Imperial Sedan from his apartments behind was signalled by the playing of a particular ritual air of great antiquity. The instruments were bells, gongs, drums and sounding stones, bell-chimes, bowl-gongs, tongued bells and gong-chimes, such as were used at the state rituals in the Temple of Confucius. There were singers also who chanted a liturgy. The company was kneeling, with eyes cast down, so that it was not easy for the Dutch to see what happened; moreover, forty Lifeguards stood close about the throne. But presently they became aware that a figure was seated there, and 'for as much as they could discern of him, he was young and of fair complexion, of middle stature and well proportioned, clothed and shining all in clinquant Gold'. Thus did Shun Chih appear to them. His sweetheart, the Lady Tung, was somewhere in the buildings behind, as may have been the Buddhist monks who five years later were to persuade him to renounce his glory.

'For a quarter of an hour', says Nievhoff, 'this Mighty Prince sat thus in Magnificent State,' silent, hieratic, unsmiling, motionless, as he faced south and magically induced God's blessing and peace on all the world. Then he rose, still without a word, and, when already turned to depart, looked back at the Dutch Ambassadors, so that it seemed to Jacob de Keyzer that for an instant their eyes met. What was it that prompted

The Supreame
MONARCH
of the CHINA-TARTARIAN Empire.

SHUN CHIH, THE FIRST MANCHU EMPEROR OF CHINA
*From Nievhoff's 'Embassy'*

him to give them that glance? Curiosity, no doubt; they were the most strangely garbed in that assembly; and standing up he had a clear view. Yet with what much greater attention would he have regarded them could he have divined the real signifi, cance of their coming! Not all his intuition could have told him that secret, which was hidden deep in the folds of time. It is curious that his astrologers had divined something of the truth, for, records Nievhoff, there was current 'an old Pro, phesie that a strange Nation, Fair of Complexion and Clothed all over, should come thither from a far remote Country to Con, quer the Kingdom of China and possess it as their own'.[1] What Shun Chih saw before his eyes that 2nd of September 1656 was the vanguard of a civilization, whose power was to lie in the application of science to arms, a civilization which had already entered upon the Americas and would possess them in due time, which had its teeth into India, would devour that empire, and Africa, too, and Australia and the Islands, until in 1840 its fair, complexioned troops would defeat his Manchus, in 1860 burn his Summer Palace and in 1900 sack the For, bidden City itself. Nor was that all, for the modern spirit, of which it was the exponent, would infect the Chinese them, selves, so that they would rise and destroy his dynasty; would enable his neighbours, the Japanese, to construct mechanisms strong enough to give them mastery over the richest of his pro, vinces; and eventually would appear so essential to the new Government (for only so could it rid itself of the Japanese), that it would largely abandon Confucianism, as he understood it, and adopt in its place a cosmopolitan culture, till it might be said that old China had, indeed, been overcome and pos, sessed by the West.

No, we may be sure that Shun Chih saw not a glimmer of

[1] The Seigneur Michael Baudier, who wrote a book called *The History of the Court of the King of China*, a translation of which was published in London in 1635, mentions this prophecy. 'One of their Prophesies threatens their tranquillitie with troubles in this sense: that a day will come when they shall be subject to men who have long Beards, Aquilin Noses, and great Eyes like unto Cats eyes.'

all this as he glanced curiously at the Dutch, even if he remembered what Father Valleat had said to him the previous February. Yet it was a pregnant rencounter, big with consequences which are not yet worked out. I shall return to it in a later place.

With the departure of the Emperor, the audience was at an end and the Dutch returned to their lodgings. They might now expect an answer to their letter asking for the right to trade. With that in their pocket they would start for home at once. They were anxious to get away, for their six weeks' stay in Peking had been very dull. 'We were continually kept close in our Lodgings as Recluses in their Cells, without once stirring abroad to take our pleasure,' says Nievhoff, though he admits that in all other respects they were treated with the greatest consideration. Their rations were lavish. Each member had an allowance according to his rank. The Ambassadors' table was loaded with food. Daily for the use of these two men alone were sent 8 lbs. of meat, one goose, two fowls, 3 ozs. of tea and of salt, 5 lbs. of flour, two fishes, with vegetables, spices, oil, fruit and fuel in abundance. They were also supplied with ample drink. But this did not make up for being confined without exercise or amusement. A merchant fraternity of Peking was so sorry for them that it sent an invitation to dinner, but this they were not allowed to accept, 'which made them disconsolate and despairing,' writes the anonymous Jesuit with evident satisfaction.

It was the custom, however, for the Government to give Ambassadors a dinner after audience, and on the afternoon of their reception the Dutch were entertained by the President of the Board of Rites at his own house, along with the Mogul, Tibetan and Mongol Envoys. Being an official dinner the guests were all expected before they sat down to kotow towards the north, the direction of the Emperor. The officials present and the servants were Manchus, and the mixture of splendour and country manners was highly typical of Manchu society at this early date. The Comptroller of the Imperial Household, who represented the Emperor, 'sat alone upon a broad sideboard with his Legs across, like a Taylour on his Shop-board'.

The waiters were dressed in cloth of gold. The Dutch Ambassadors, with two of their staff, had a table to themselves which
was 'covered with thirty Silver Dishes, full of rare Fruits and
Sweet-meats'. These were the first course, the second being
huge quantities of roast beef and mutton, as underdone as was
usual with Manchu cookery. Towards the end of dinner, when
they had eaten to repletion, the Dutch saw the Comptroller take
up a rib of roast camel, 'of which he eat so heartily, as if he had
been fasting all that day'. There was the usual distribution of
the food that remained to the guests before they returned home.
The description of this is one of the best passages in Nievhoff's
book, a splendid example, in the translation, of what English
prose could do at the time of the Restoration. 'This brave high
Treatment finished, the Embassadours, according to the custom
of the Countrey, were to put up what they left into their Pockets
to carry home. It was a very pleasant sight to see how these
greazy Tartars stuffed their Pockets and Leather Drawers of
their Breeches with fat Meat, that the liquor dropt from them as
they went along the Streets; so greedy were they in eating and
carrying away, that they were more like Peasants than Courtiers.' These were the Riders of the Steppe, the conquerors of
China, the successors of those formidable mounted archers who
in the thirteenth century had won battles from Peking to the
Baltic, had never been worsted except by the Mamelukes. Their
physique, their digestions, their teeth were still superb. It was
their brains that were mediocre. They did not know what to do
with their conquest. They had the chance of modernizing
China, and instead made it more old-fashioned than ever.
These hearty simple fellows going home with the grease drip-
ping down their trousers were soon to become as correct and
formal as the members of the Han-lin Academy.

The Ambassadors had to wait six weeks, till October 16,
before they obtained the Imperial Mandate and their leave to
depart. First they were summoned to receive the return presents.
No one was forgotten. In addition to the presents for General
Maatzuyker, head of the East India Company at Batavia, each

member of the embassy received a sum of money and some rolls of silk, the money varying from £30 for an Ambassador to £5 for a follower. Even the soldiers who had conducted them from Canton were remembered, twenty of them getting a coat of black and blue silk damask. All this care, the official dinner, the elaborate details of the reception at Court, proved that the welcome of visiting envoys was governed by a well-established procedure. It was the considered policy to treat envoys with condescension and to send them home dazzled and instructed. If they made stupid requests, these were politely refused. It was all admirably done, admirably suited to the past, when the Court of China was without equal or rival. But the world was changing rapidly; the Western part of it was advancing with great strides; and the procedure, when applied to the Dutch envoys, contained already an element of the ludicrous.

On the 16th at one o'clock the Ambassadors went to the Council Chamber of the Board of Rites to receive the Emperor's Mandate. They had been given no opportunity of discussing business with any official during their stay, nor were they given that opportunity now. The Mandate was on a table covered with a yellow carpet, a gilt-edged scroll emblazoned with dragons. A Councillor read it out to the kneeling Ambassadors. It was bland, polite, sympathetic, but—crushing.

Here is the substance of it: 'The distance which divides Holland from China is so great that regular intercourse between the two countries is hardly practicable. Indeed, there is no record of any previous Dutch embassy. Aware of the long and arduous journey of the present Ambassadors, WE were happy to give them audience and receive their tribute-presents. In earnest of our goodwill WE returned them gifts of suitable value. But when WE think of the danger of storm and shipwreck that besets the passage hither, WE are too solicitous of the welfare of the Dutch people to do more than permit them to send ships to China once in eight years, what time they may sell four cargoes and bring presents to OUR Court.'

The reading of the Mandate, which in effect was a blank

refusal of the Dutch demand, disconcerted the Ambassadors, whose hopes had remained high, in spite of the influences known to be working against them. However, there was nothing to be done. The President of the Board of Rites was not in the Council Chamber or they might have tried a last appeal. Nor was there opportunity for any protest, for immediately officials directed them to approach and kneel again that the Mandate might be presented to them. When they had complied and received it 'with all humility and respect' it was taken from them and bound on the back of an interpreter, who led them out of the building and from the Forbidden City, the central gate of the Wu Mên being 'set open on purpose to make way for this Imperial Missive'. On reaching their house they were told that they should leave at once, 'so that we were necessitated to depart at noon out of this Imperial City of Peking, and had no time to take a view of the circumference of the place, or of any thing else that was rare and worth the notice'.

The long journey back to Canton began, where they arrived on the 28th of January 1657, being three months and twelve days on the way. There they had a nasty experience, quite the most unpleasant of their whole trip. To begin with, the Viceroy and Tartar General were very civil and sympathized when they were told of the unsatisfactory contents of the Emperor's Mandate, politely putting it down to Portuguese intrigues. It became evident, however, that both of them expected a New Year present, for the Chinese New Year falls in February. This was awkward, because the Ambassadors had not provided for such a contingency and were now short of cash. However, they scraped together what they could, bought the presents and went to offer them. The two lords gave them audience at once, but on examining the presents, considered them inadequate and, much offended, put forward the demand that the Dutch should pay the expenses of those of the Viceroy's servants who had been ordered to accompany them to Peking and, more outrageous still, money they had promised to give if their application for free trade were granted. The total sum amounted to no less than £1,600. The Ambassadors refused to comply, but when they found that the common people had been incited to insult them in the streets and when their interpreter died in suspicious circumstances, they took fright, paid the money by some means unspecified, and only then were given a pass to board their ship.

They sailed on February 22, but before they were clear of the city there occurred a last incident, highly typical of the Orient. The ship was held up in the river by a contrary wind, when they saw rowing down to them the viceregal stewards, together with the Mandarins who had accompanied them to Peking. The Viceroy and the Tartar General had both refused to receive the Ambassadors when they called to say a formal fare-well. Now their subordinates came cheerfully aboard, bringing with them a case of the Viceroy's brandy, and insisted on treat-ing them in the name of their masters. 'After some Healths had gone about, they took leave and went back to Canton,' says Nievhoff, without further comment on this revealing incident. Those who are conversant with the ways of officialdom in the East will know precisely what it did reveal. On second thoughts the Viceroy and his colleague thought it risky to let the Ambas-sadors go away angry. Supposing on their way down the river they set fire to a village! The Emperor would hear of it, if they did, and he might learn the reason why. There were always informers ready to carry tales. Both officials knew they could be dismissed for less. So they sent their stewards with a dozen of brandy.

On March 31 the Embassy reached Batavia and made their report. It was not a bright one. Summed up, the account was as follows: they had laid out on presents, tips and general expenses the total sum of £9,883 1s. 6d., and against that expenditure they could put nothing 'but that the Hollanders were received as Friends by the Emperour in China, and might return eight years hence to salute his Imperial Majesty'.

As they believed the fiasco to be due largely to the Portuguese desire to maintain their monopoly and to the influence of the Jesuits at Court, it was some consolation for them to learn on arrival that a Dutch force had just taken Colombo from the Portuguese, thereby gaining for Holland the great island of Ceylon.

But the Ambassadors probably exaggerated the malific influence of the Jesuits. The Emperor had given orders in accordance with precedent. Throughout the Ming dynasty China had been a closed country to foreigners. Shun Chih was merely continuing that policy. Half the members of the Grand Council were Chinese. They advised as might have been expected. The Manchu half could have pressed for a new departure, had they had new grounds to advance in support. But originality was never a Manchu strong point.

Yet we cannot blame Shun Chih, as we shall be able to blame his successors, because he did not understand. It was all too novel. Modern Europe was knocking at the door. In the person of the Dutch it was making a sensible and straightforward proposition. Trade by sea between East and West had begun. Would not the Chinese join in it? The West was the scene of great intellectual activity. Surely China would be well advised to exchange ideas? Western nations, or some of them, were under effective governments. An arrangement with such governments was perfectly feasible. It was true that the Portuguese and the Dutch, followed in a small way by the English, had seized by force and without right strategic positions throughout the Eastern oceans. All the more reason that the Chinese should meet them man to man, as they were able to do, and while preventing them from menacing China, give them by reasonable trade concessions sound reasons for remaining on good terms with her government.

But these conceptions of the balanced relationship of one state with another were too modern. They had no place whatever in Ming theory. The Ch'ing were given the great opportunity of conducting China steadily and surely into the modern world. Again and again its Emperors had pointed out to them what they should do. As the years passed the truth became more and more obvious. But they never saw until it was too late.

# III

# Ricci's Attempt to Convert the Son of Heaven

The great exhibition of Chinese art at Burlington House in 1936 had the effect of focusing public attention on the Taoist and Buddhist aspects of Chinese culture. This was largely due to the fact that early Chinese painting and sculpture could not be understood without some knowledge of them. Attention was so concentrated in this novel direction that the importance of Confucianism, which in the seventeenth and eighteenth centuries had interested Europe to the exclusion of all else from China, tended to be forgotten. Tao and the Mahayana now seemed the essence of China, her real message to the West. In comparison, the doctrines of Confucius appeared uninspiring, no more than a level common sense. The bronze ritual vessels, the scholar's desk and the examples of calligraphy, three out-standing Confucian exhibits at the exhibition, though not ignored, were looked at, the first, archaeologically, the second as a piece of furnishing, and the third only in its relation to painting. The more direct significance of these objects was found less absorbing: that the bronze vessels belonged to the ancient state cult, which Confucius found in abeyance, sought to re-establish, and which was re-established some centuries later; that the desk was the place where every Chinese gentle-man sat to study the Confucian classics and to execute the calligraphy which was considered the surest proof of his superior character.

The reader of this book has heard nothing of Taoism and

little of Buddhism, for a society which was interested in neither has been its subject. But he has seen Confucianism in its various workings and, more by implication than directly, has perceived how it dominated the Court and the administration. The time has now come to examine it rather more closely, for we are about to make a comparison between the state of knowledge in China and in Europe during the first half of the seventeenth century. The knowledge current in any country depends largely on what is taught to young people, the subjects which are set them in examinations. A glance at the Civil Service examinations under the Ming will show that in China Confucianism was co-terminous with knowledge.

In the Civil Service regulations the prescribed books were, firstly, the five edited or traditionally supposed to have been edited by Confucius in the fifth century B.C.—the *Book of History*, the *Book of Changes*, the *Book of Songs*, the *Book of Rites* and the *Spring and Autumn Annals*; secondly, the four compiled after his death and which recorded his views—the *Analects*, the *Great Learning*, the *Doctrine of the Mean* and *Mencius*. These nine books were called the *Classics*. The student might be asked to write an essay on any subject arising out of them. He might also have to quote passages, so that he was advised to memorize the text. Along with these books he was expected to read a number of their commentaries, the official histories of the previous dynasties, certain collections of laws and edicts, manuals on rites and on comportment during ceremonies. It was further laid down that he should practise writing in conformity with the principles of the ancient calligraphists, for his examination papers would be judged not only for their accuracy and content, but also by the degree of elegance shown in the formation of the ideographs. There followed a regulation apparently less easy for us to appreciate: he must practise archery once a fortnight, following the classic ritual of that art or pastime. The substitution of the word cricket for archery will help us to a conception of his duties under this rule.

The student's course was thus analogous to that of the School of Literae Humaniores at the University of Oxford. Archery or cricket is not specifically included in the syllabus of that School, but the latter is generally practised by those who take it, nor is any detail of its classic ritual omitted.

The last of the Chinese student's subjects was a non-classical one, Arithmetic, though it had to be studied in a minor classical book, the *Chin-chang suan-shu*, a work which was burnt in 213 B.C. when all the major classics were burnt, and was, like them, reconstructed afterwards, but, it is stated, with greater difficulty because the number of those who had learned it by heart were few and scattered. However, reconstructed it was, and in Ming times, seventeen centuries later, was not only still read, but was the only volume on mathematics prescribed by the Board of Civil Office. No doubt the work was sound and good in its way, but it had become very old-fashioned. The examiners, indeed, never failed a man because he did not qualify in it, if his other answers were satisfactory. One may say, therefore, that the examination was wholly literary.

If it had a resemblance to the School of Literae Humaniores at Oxford, it was of much greater importance, for while the Oxford School is one of many, there being in particular a number of mathematical and scientific courses of study of equal weight and dignity, in China there was no other. Candidates for the Civil Service could only take classics. It followed that the whole bureaucracy from top to bottom, and in China that meant the greater part of the literate public, all the most influential men in the Empire, was ignorant of any subject outside the classics or, shall we say, if its members took up other studies later they approached them in the amateur frame of mind of the classical scholar.

It would be an error to suppose, however, that the Ming curriculum did not provide a good education. It provided a splendid education for men whose bent was literature and art. Nor could any other have prepared them so well for an ordinary post in the administration. It had been drawn up on the assumption that China need never change, that the secret of the good life had been discovered and that all she required to do was to live it, to go on living it for ever. But China was not the world: that was the potential danger in an educational system which was impervious to new ideas, to new knowledge.

Yet the young men who passed the Civil Service examina-tion had acquired the elements of a charming culture. When they took up their first appointments, as deputy assistant Magis-trate or the like in some provincial town, they had a lively per-ception of the great mechanism of which they were a part. The ideal aim of the government they had joined was to reproduce on earth the Way of Heaven. This Way was known, for the legendary Emperors of China, shadowy figures like the Yellow Emperor, and Yao and Shun and Yü, who, according to tradition, reigned as far back as the twenty-fifth century B.C., had found the Way. They were Sages, Philosopher Kings, whose reigns had been the Golden Age, because they knew how to interpret the Way of Heaven, so that peace, virtue and happiness flourished undisturbed. Thanks to Confucius, who lived in a troubled cruel period of war and famine and poverty and lies, and who yearned for the far days when such evils did not exist, some record of the old Emperors had been preserved. What could be more moving, more inspiring in its noble simplicity, than, for instance, the anecdote recorded in the classics of the Emperor Yü? 'Once when Yü met a criminal, he immediately alighted from his chariot and weeping asked him the story of his crime. When his Minister remonstrated with him, Yü explained that he wept because his virtue, unlike Yao's and Shun's, was not sufficient to influence the hearts of the people and so dissuade them from committing wicked acts.'

That was the whole secret—'government by goodness', as it was phrased in the classics. Heaven had entrusted its Mandate to the sovereign so that under his rule earth might become like heaven. It was only necessary for him to be virtuous that his officials should be moved to copy him. If they were virtuous, the people would follow their example, the inferior would obey his superior, the son his father. Everyone would go about his business with propriety. Human nature was naturally good. It could only become bad if thrown out of equilibrium by the ruler's failure to put into practice the Way of Heaven.

The young assistant deputy Magistrate as he looked round at his colleagues might not find that their acts always agreed with the classic principles which they admired, but the Chinese Civil Service could not have existed for two thousand years unless on the whole its conduct had remained inspired by a high ideal. One can understand how iniquitous the later Ming Court must have seemed to all that was best in the bureaucracy.

The Chinese classics had far greater authority than Europe has ever accorded to its classics. On that account they have been called scriptures. Yet they differed from the ordinary conception of a scripture, for they did not deal in revelation or miracles. Their contents were mundane, clear and precise. Supernatural beings did not figure in them. Much of them was mellow comment upon right behaviour for rulers and gentlemen. To give a taste of their flavour and show how excellently they served their educational purpose, the training of government officials, we may select a few passages from the *Analects of Confucius*.[1]

'Of Tzu-Ch'an, a certain Minister, the Master said that in him were to be found four of the virtues that belong to the Way of the true gentleman. In his private conduct he was courteous, in serving his master he was punctilious, in providing for the needs of the people he gave them even more than their due, in exacting service from the people he was just.' Book V. 15.

Or in a lighter vein: 'The Master said, Gentlemen never compete. You will say that in archery they do so. But even then they bow and make way for one another when they are going up to the archery-ground, when they are coming down and at the subsequent drinking-bout. Thus even when competing, they still remain gentlemen.' Book III. 7.

The *dicta* are often very shrewd: 'The Master said, when

[1] Translated by Arthur Waley.

everyone dislikes a man, enquiry is necessary; when everyone likes a man, enquiry is necessary.' Book XV. 27.

They are sometimes universal: 'Tzu-kung asked, Is there any single saying that you can act upon all day and every day? The Master said, Perhaps the saying about consideration: "Never do to others what you would not like them to do to you." ' Book XV. 23.

They have a dry humour: 'Chi Wên Tzu used to think thrice before acting. The Master hearing of it said, Twice is quite enough.' Book V. 19.

And are robust: 'The Master said, Having to conceal one's indignation and keep on friendly terms with the people against whom one feels it, I am incapable of stooping to such conduct.' Book V. 24.

And human: 'In his leisure hours the Master's manner was very free-and-easy, and his expression alert and cheerful.' Book VII. 4.

And noble: 'The Master said, A Divine Sage I cannot hope ever to meet; the most I can hope for is to meet a true gentle-man.' Book VII. 25.

And sportsmanlike: 'The Master fished with a line but not with a net; when fowling he did not aim at a roosting bird.' Book VII. 26.

And profound: 'The Master said, Is Goodness indeed so far away? If we really wanted Goodness, we should find that it was at our very side.' Book VII. 29.

And humble: 'The Master said, As to being a Divine Sage or even a Good Man, far be it from me to make any such claim.' Book VII. 33.

Confucius' own manner was a model for all those in autho-rity: 'The Master's manner was affable yet firm, commanding but not harsh, polite but easy.' Book VII. 37.

He could not stand bullies: 'There are three things that a gentleman, in following the Way, places above all the rest: from every attitude, every gesture that he employs he must re-move all trace of violence or arrogance; every look that he com-poses in his face must betoken good faith; from every word that he utters, from every intonation, he must remove all trace of coarseness or impropriety.' Book VIII. 4.

He had a dreaming earnestness: 'Once when the Master was standing by a stream, he said, Could one but go on and on like this, never ceasing day or night!' He meant, never ceasing to strive for goodness. Book IX. 16.

He loved music because it inspired Goodness. After hearing on one occasion an old ritual air called the Succession, he did not know what he was eating for three months. 'I did not picture to myself that any music existed which could reach such perfection as this,' he said.

The propriety of his conversations at Court was a model for all time: 'At Court when conversing with the Under Ministers his attitude is friendly and affable; when conversing with the Upper Ministers, it is restrained and formal. When the ruler is present, it is wary but not cramped.' Book X. 2.

His lofty ideals did not conceal from him the realities of government, the true strength of states: 'Tzu-kung asked about government. The Master said, Sufficient food, sufficient weapons, and the confidence of the common people. Tzu-kung said, Suppose you had no choice but to dispense with one of these three, which would you forgo? The Master said, Weapons. Tzu-kung said, Suppose you were forced to dispense with one of the two that were left, which would you forgo? The Master said, Food.' Danger of enemies, danger of starvation, such were recurrent perils and which could be overcome if confidence were unshaken. But once let confidence go, neither arms nor food could save the country.

One might continue to quote with profit. But these short extracts are sufficient to show that the Chinese possessed a splendid public tradition. Anyone might become a gentleman in the Confucian sense provided that to sufficient character he added sufficient culture. Culture meant an education based on the classics. All officials were gentlemen in so far as they acted in accordance with what they had been taught. With such really superior men in charge of affairs it was argued that good government was certain. Good government, a reflection as it was of heavenly government, had a magical force. It converted the people to a good life. When working perfectly it would convert even burglars, says Confucius in another place.

Needless to say no government in China was able to put into practice all the Master had enjoined. But what he declared to be right, was believed to be right. His teachings were the estab-lished cult. No government openly disregarded them. The worst governments paid them lip service. All the dynastic histories were written from the Confucian angle, praise and blame being distributed according to classic principles: all Censors memorialized from that standpoint.

The above sketch of what a student aiming at an admini-strative post under the Ming would have to read is not intended to do more than suggest the sort of education available at the time. It should be recalled that the Master died in 479 B.C., and that two thousand years had elapsed since that event. His doctrines had had their vicissitudes; they were even prescribed for a short period; they were amended, changed, extended, mis-interpreted. Buddhism and Taoism at times threatened them. Men of letters put new meanings into them. But in spite of the corroding power of two millenniums they remained a living force, their message fresh for each generation. Even under the late Ming, when the Court disregarded them in practice, they continued, as the first part of this book shows, to inspire among many the utmost loyalty and heroism. But devotion to any system of ideas tends to endow them with an absolute value. And when a system is regarded as absolute, pedants and ex-treme conservatives rule policy. It is an irony of history that the philosophy which carried China safely from remote antiquity into modern times should by the very weight of its excellence and authority have prevented her from adapting herself to the modern age and, so, have been the cause of terrible mis-fortunes.

Let us now turn to the European scene at the beginning of

the seventeenth century and note some of the dynamic elements there, which when later brought to China's notice were to set up a discord not yet resolved.

The medieval Church was a closed system analogous to the Confucian. In the thirteenth century, the century before the Ming received the Mandate of Heaven, the Dominican, Thomas Aquinas, wrote his *Summa*, in which he reconciled all existing knowledge with the dogmas of the Catholic Church. By accepting his *Summa* the Church put a ban on further speculation and assumed that a static condition of knowledge had been reached from which it would never be necessary to advance. Ideas were therefore fixed. Education, which was controlled by the Church, amounted to no more than the inculcation of those fixed ideas. It would be idle to pronounce whether the standard was higher or lower than in China. Both systems were self-sufficient and mutually incompatible, for the Chinese Emperor was as much a Pontiff as was the Pope.

But unlike China Europe did not stand still. It had the great good fortune in the fifteenth century to receive a powerful mental stimulus from its own past. Ancient Greek civilization contained certain elements which in the objective domain of reason were what we call modern. In that tiny country contemporaries of Confucius had turned their attention not only, like him, to the problems of good government and behaviour, but also to experimental science, the deductions of untrammelled reason from observed facts. This ancient dynamic European culture remained three-quarters buried until the fifteenth century, when it was rediscovered in its entirety. The excitement of the find revivified Europe. The Ming, then reigning, had no such good fortune. Their ancient culture had never been buried. No cache of ideas existed in their continent. At the moment when Europe began to see the world with fresh eyes, China drew over hers a further veil.

Europe now began to think, to observe objects directly. The Church, clinging to the *Summa* of Thomas Aquinas, saw in this mental renaissance the most serious threat to her authority that had ever been made. Her enormous influence was directed against its spread. But when the mind is stirred ideas burst into it. No one has ever discovered how to stop that incursion. It is as invincible as the onrush of madness. Men of genius appeared. Men of genius tend to appear just before and during such periods of general mental disturbance. No men of genius appeared under the Ming.

In Europe the great names began with da Vinci (1452–1519), the artist whose scientific curiosity was insatiable. His sure vision of what was ineluctably coming swept forward four hundred years and gave him a glimpse of the greatest, the most terrible and perhaps the ultimate triumph of applied mathematics—and he designed the first aeroplane.

The next capital name is that of Copernicus, the Pole. In 1543, as he lay dying, was published his *De Revolutionibus Orbium Coelestium*, wherein the theory advanced by Pythagoras that the sun, not the earth, was the centre of our system, was convincingly argued. Giordano Bruno (1548–1600) added elaboration to the same revolutionary thought. These two were theorists; Tycho Brahe (1546–1601) and Kepler (1571–1630) supported their theories by direct observation and by mathematics. Galileo, the inventor of the telescope, the founder of modern physics, the investigator of the laws of motion, the formulator of the principles of the pulley and the cogwheel, died in 1642, two years before Li entered The Great Within.

In 1645 the Royal Society was founded in London to review the new discoveries in physics, anatomy, geometry and astronomy, navigation and mechanics, and to discuss specific problems like the weight of the air and the improvement of telescopes. Divinity and politics were barred from their meetings. They had at their disposal the logarithms invented by Napier (1614) and the algebraic formulae used by Descartes (1596–1650) to summarize Euclid's geometry. Newton at that date was three years old; Boyle was eighteen, the Boyle whose investigation of gases prepared the way for the invention of the steam engine; and Huygens, the perfector of the pendulum clock and watch balance, was sixteen. To sum up, we can say that on that summer day when Li's myrmidons were kicking the Confucian scholars in the neck as they kotowed before the Dragon Seat, there already existed in Europe all the elements of that extraordinary movement which, by using scientific know-ledge for practical purposes, instead of, as in the past, to attain occult power, changed the whole face of the world in the course of three centuries.

And here is the curious paradox. These discoveries, more potent than the claimed powers of all the elixirs, were brought to the notice of the Chinese, as they became known, by Jesuit emissaries of the Catholic Church. The explanation of how this came about reveals one of the major ironies of history.

The Society of Jesus was founded in 1534 by Loyola. It had several aims, but the one which became predominant was to assist the Catholic Church to combat the movement, human-istic, religious and scientific, which threatened to undermine the *Summa* of Aquinas. The Society planned to do this, not by coercion, in the manner of the Dominican Inquisition, which used punishments to reinforce its arguments, but by a great intellectual effort, which mastering all these new ideas would restate them in a grand synthesis, a new *Summa*, in conformity with the dogmas of Rome. This ambition, tremendous enough, was further enlarged by a design to persuade the uncounted millions of Asia and America, countries discovered or redis-covered only a few decades earlier, to become Catholics, thereby bringing the whole world under the spiritual jurisdic-tion of the Holy Father.

To achieve these ends it was necessary to recruit a body of clever young men and give them a more advanced education than that provided in the universities. A college at Rome was founded for that purpose, and there the Jesuits received instruc-tion in all the science of the day and in a philosophy which reconciled science with theology. The men received into the Society were extremely talented. They had to be, for their duty would be to meet the greatest intellectuals in open argument and convince them with a logic which could not be refuted that the new knowledge was not incompatible with Catholicism.

The curriculum of the Collegio Romano towards the end of the sixteenth century is extant, and may be compared with that followed by Chinese scholars of the same period. It was a three-year course. During the first, besides theology and other purely Catholic studies, the young Jesuits had to learn Euclid, arithmetic and the principles of astronomy as then understood. This meant Greek or Ptolemaic astronomy, for though Copernicus had published his great work in 1543, the theories it propounded were not known outside a small circle till after the end of the century. In the second year the theory of music and optics were taught. The chief subject for the third year was an advanced course in astronomy and mathematics, the latter being applied to the mechanics of clocks. The contrast with the Chinese curriculum was thus very marked.

In the year 1576 a young Italian called Matteo Ricci was one of the senior students at the Collegio Romano. He was a man of all-round ability and a natural mathematician. At the time, a Father Clavius was lecturer in astronomy. Ricci was his best pupil, though on leaving the college he still had much to learn about that difficult science. The General of the Society selected him for service overseas, and he arrived at Macao, the Portuguese trading post near Canton, in 1582, in the ninth year of the reign of the Emperor Wan Li, the grandfather of Ch'ung Chên, the last ruling sovereign of the Ming.

His sole object in going to China was to convert the Chinese to Catholicism. This book is not directly concerned with his object: Christian missions lie beyond its scope. But it is concerned with the means he adopted to achieve his object. These were very novel, quite unlike the procedure of previous missionaries, though in keeping with the policy of the Society in Europe. There, as we have noted, the Jesuits sought to combat the assault of the new thought by mastering it and then, through sheer skill in logic, out-arguing those who attacked the Church's dogmas by showing how the scientific knowledge of the day could be harmonized with sacred philosophy. Ricci decided to apply these principles in China. The intellectual leaders of that country could be treated on the same plane as the new philosophers and scientists of Europe. He would master their philosophy, whatever it was, their language, their literature, their whole way of thinking, and then by superior intellectual power convince them of their errors or by a bold synthesis, a more ambitious *Summa* than that attempted by Aquinas, oblige them to admit the force of his arguments and so bring them willingly into the fold. The project was enormously difficult. In the first place no foreigners were allowed to enter China. To put it into effect he had to get permission to leave Macao and, more difficult still, reside in Peking, for it was the Government he sought to convince, the Confucians of the capital, not the provincials or the people. Moreover, he must learn Chinese, not merely how to speak it well enough to explain his mission with elegance, but how to write it like a scholar, like a man who had passed the Civil Service Examination, like—was it possible?—a man of letters. He had, therefore, to become more than a sinologue at a time when sinologues did not exist in Europe.

Excellent accounts have been published describing how Ricci mastered literary Chinese and how, largely on the ground that he was now a Chinese gentleman, he was permitted to enter China. He now made a discovery of the greatest importance to his future plans. Had he not made it, but proceeded according to his original project to argue with the *literati*, it is certain that he would not have got very far. What he discovered was that his European mathematics and such knowledge of astronomy and mechanics as he possessed were of great interest to certain Chinese of rank.

The result of this discovery was paradoxical. He had mastered the Chinese language and literature so as to be able to present his religious faith in a manner acceptable to learned society. He now perceived that society to be so eager to hear what he could tell them about science that they would listen to nothing else. Only by turning lecturer in mathematics, pure and applied, could he hope to secure their attention and sup-port. Reflecting that it was a means to an end, that if they came to respect him for the knowledge he had brought from the West, one day they would accept the Western faith, he gave up his time almost wholly to teaching mathematics, astronomy and clockmaking, the three subjects in which he had matriculated at Rome. The officials he met, having had the literary education already described, were amazed at the profundity of his know-ledge. Knowing his own limitations, that he was no more than a versatile amateur, he found his success almost laughable. In his *Opere Storiche*, referring to the literary circles at Nanking and other provincial capitals, he says: 'Their studies are in moral philosophy and their chief occupation is the cultivation of style. They are persuaded that I am a phenomenon of scien-tific knowledge and that no one like me has ever come from Europe, which causes me no little amusement.'

It may seem curious that classical scholars should take an interest in mathematics. The explanation here must be that in China, as everywhere else, a proportion of the educated class had not literary but mathematical aptitudes. To make their way in the world they had had to take classics, and probably it had been a struggle, as they had no real interest in them. When such persons were introduced to Euclid it seemed the most fascinating mental exercise. Such a man was Ch'ü T'ai-su. 'He seemed quite insatiable,' wrote Ricci, 'passing day and night in study.' Later he published Chinese translations of some of Ricci's books. This Mandarin, writing to Ricci on May 19, 1596, says that at Nan-ch'ang one day, while telling the scholars of the place about him, he met a man who was study-ing for the Civil Service and wanted to give up classics and, instead, take lessons in mathematics. 'I dissuaded him', says Ch'ü T'ai-su, 'because his mother was old. He successfully passed the examination and now has an appointment in Kuang-tung.' This is most revealing. It was impossible for a man, unless he had private means and renounced a career in the public service—and the Chinese Civil Service was a unique career, offering money, rank and authority—to make a study of mathematics in youth.

Ricci, in spite of his reputation and popularity among the gentry of the chief provincial cities, did not succeed for many years in obtaining a permit to visit Peking. But his increasing knowledge of the inner working of the Chinese system allowed him to make a further discovery which eventually was to open the way. This discovery was the great importance attached to the Calendar by the Chinese.

In Europe the reform of the Julian Calendar had been introduced by Gregory XIII about the time of Ricci's departure for the East, and was promulgated in Goa on November 14, 1583, when he was staying there *en route* to Macao. He therefore used it privately for his calculations in China. In 1592 he was introduced to the President of the Nanking Board of Rites, who, knowing that he had mathematical information not generally available, hinted that the Chinese Calendar was not wholly reliable and that he might be called upon to give certain advice.

Nothing more came of this at the time. In 1598, when he had settled in Nanking, the first city after the capital, he came into contact with its Bureau of Mathematics. In view of what has been said about the ignorance of mathematics which prevailed among the official class, it may be a surprise to hear that such a bureau existed. Its members, however, were not really mathematicians, but a special body of men whose duty it was to draw up or assist in drawing up the Calendar, not by direct calculation but by means of tables which could be manipulated by rule of thumb. One day these people called on Ricci and when he went to return their call and had climbed the hill within the city walls on which was situated their office, he was astonished to find on a terrace near by a number of large and massive astronomical instruments. 'We certainly had never seen or read of anything in Europe like them,' he wrote. It was the year 1600 and Tycho Brahe (who died the next year) had already revolutionized the technique of astronomical observations in his Uraniborg observatory, but Ricci, who had been out of Europe for twenty years, did not know this.

He examined the instruments on the terrace and observed a Celestial Sphere, six feet in diameter, longitude and latitude being marked, the equator in its place, the ecliptic indicated, there being a contrivance to measure the orbit of the moon. The second instrument was an armillary sphere, representing the firmament, the third a gnomon for recording the shadow at the solstices and equinoxes, and the fourth an instrument having the appearance of four monstrous astrolabes in juxtaposition.

Ricci's astonishment increased when on entering the office of the Bureau of Mathematics he was informed that these instruments were not in use, because—it had to be admitted—no-one knew how to use them. How did they make their calculations, then, for the Calendar? By means of the tables filed in the office.

The explanation of this has a strong bearing on the argument I am developing. The instruments had been constructed in the thirteenth century by Kuo Shon-ching, an astronomer of the Mongol dynasty, styled Yuan. The Mongols under Genghis Khan and his successors conquered most of Eurasia, including a part of the Islamic world. The Arabs had taken over and developed the Ptolemaic system of astronomy. This was adopted by the Mongols, who introduced it into China, as the ancient Chinese astronomy was less exact. The Mongols were interested in mathematics; they had, moreover, a different outlook on world affairs from the native Chinese dynasties. Their post-roads connected them with the Middle East and the Mediterranean. Foreigners were able to come and go, as we know very well from Polo's memoirs. The atmosphere of the Court was liberal and tolerant. During the eighty-eight years of the Yuan dynasty China kept abreast of world ideas, was, even, more modern than the rest of the world. The Ming represented a nationalist restoration. The policy of their predecessors was largely reversed. China became a closed country. Anything un-Chinese was weeded out. The examinations were narrowed down to the classics. As for the Yuan Calendar they first sub-stituted ephemerides calculated in accordance with the ancient Chinese rules called the *Ta t'ung-li*. This not proving a suc-cess, they staffed a new bureau with Mohammedans, who were supposed to understand the Arab system, but lacking outside advice were not able to grasp the meaning of those Yuan records which had survived the period of transition. Certain tables, however, were found, and these they followed blindly. And they made a gross mistake. The instruments which Ricci saw had a polar elevation of 36°, for they had been designed for use at P'ing-yang in Shansi, where there was a Mongol college which had that elevation. The Ming astronomers, un-aware of this, moved them to Nanking, which is in latitude $32\frac{1}{4}°$. Thus, even had they known how to use them, their calculations would have been incorrect. By Ricci's time the instruments had been standing idle on the terrace for two hundred years, but so well had they been made that though 'exposed to the rain, the snow and all other inclemencies of the weather,' as he wrote, 'the bronze was untarnished and as if new'.

Ricci understood well enough how calculations were made with them. It is important to note the reason. Europe had also acquired its preliminary knowledge of the Ptolemaic system through the Arabs, and at about the same date as did the Mongols. Unlike the Ming, she did not lose that knowledge. On the contrary, she added to it at the time of the Renaissance. Ricci had not seen such good instruments, but he had seen instruments of the kind. At the Collegio Romano he had made calculations with them. As has been stated, he was not a pro-fessional astronomer, but he knew a great deal more than did the Nanking Bureau of Mathematics. But he did not know more, even theoretically more, than did the Yuan, for the latest developments of European astronomy were only then taking shape. Thus, the armillary sphere, representing the earth in the centre of the firmament, the sun and stars fixed in their solid spheres, the whole revolving round the earth, appeared to him a representation of fact. What he was qualified to do, therefore, was approximately to give the Chinese back the astronomical knowledge they had possessed in the thirteenth century. He, himself, did not, of course, know precisely what they had possessed or, if the instruments at Nanking suggested to him what knowledge might have been lost, he did not know all the facts of the case.

The meaning of the hint given by the President of the Nanking Board of Rites was now clear. Ricci began to study the question of the Chinese Calendar, so as to be prepared if asked to advise. At this time its full significance became clear to him. The Calendar was an integral part of the Confucian structure: its importance was more astrological than practical. It fitted into the immemorial theory that the Way of Heaven could be made to prevail on earth, if earth and heaven were kept in harmony by the right action of the Emperor-Pontiff. The Great Within, the residence on earth of the Son of Heaven, was the correlative of the Pole Star in the sky, literally the link between heaven and earth. The first duty of the Son of Heaven was to indicate to the people how this link operated. He did so by means of a Calendar. This was not primarily a compilation marking the divisions of time for general convenience, but a guide to the harmonious working of the cosmos. It therefore contained tables giving the dates when all the most important actions of everyday life could harmoniously be undertaken, dates for ploughing and reaping, for marriages and journeys, for litigation and changes of domicile or occupation. If the Emperor neglected the Calendar or if the dates were incorrect, the whole population would find itself doing on the wrong dates all those things upon which the national prosperity depended. The wrong dates were the inharmonious dates, the dates that clashed with the Way of Heaven. When that happened, all went awry; there occurred famines, droughts, floods and deaths, ending in rebellion and the fall of the dynasty, from which Heaven had withdrawn its Mandate. For a Minister to advise wrongly about the Calendar or to attempt to substitute another Calendar was a capital offence. In sum, the Calendar was a state document whose importance was inestimable.

The Chinese themselves had become aware that the accuracy of the Calendar was probably not absolute, because when eclipses occurred there was always some discrepancy with the predicted minute. Those who had studied with Ricci had a general idea in what the error lay, and since they were in full accord with the long-established view of the Calendar's place in their system, they became anxious that the central Government should take Ricci's advice. This offered him the opportunity which now for eighteen years he had been awaiting. If he were appointed by the Emperor to revise the Calendar, he would become one of the most important men in China. Resident in Peking, working on a matter of the most vital national importance, in close contact with the Court, with the Emperor himself, he would have an opportunity, far better than any he could have imagined possible, of bringing to the attention of all the leading men the truths of Catholicism. In such a situation it would not be too optimistic to hope for the conversion, first, of the Government and, subsequently, by example or decree of the whole population. China's millions would look to Rome. What a triumph for the Society of Jesus!

There was, however, another side to these projects, which must have occurred to Ricci. By correcting the Calendar he would be fortifying the very system which he desired to destroy. When the calculations were accurate, the balance between heaven and earth would be restored. Even if he himself did not believe that the rectifications would have any such effect, he was aware that everyone else in China would believe it. Would it not therefore be more difficult for him subsequently to explain that, though with such acclaim he had removed the errors which perturbed the Government, in fact these had not the occult weight supposed, because the belief that the Emperor was the link between heaven and earth was a false belief, the truth being that the Pope had approximately that position, though for totally different reasons? Yes, that was a question for grave consideration. But perhaps it was looking too far ahead. When the time came he would think how to answer it. There was also a more particular objection. Might it not be alleged that by reforming the Calendar and so giving the astrologers a firm basis upon which to calculate their lucky days, for such in reality were the tables of dates in the Calendar, that he would be himself dabbling in astrology, the study of which was forbidden to members of the Society? Such an allegation would have some substance. As adviser on the Central Bureau of Mathematics, which might equally be called a bureau of astrology, he would be an official of the first rank whose bounden duty it was to serve the government which employed him. In that capacity he would unquestionably be working, in appearance at least, to strengthen astrologically a politico-metaphysical system inherently pagan. Yet if that should be the only manner in which he could obtain the influence essential for his real task, he would be justified as soon as the whole tale was told. When, a friend of the Emperor, of the Court officials, of—it might well be—the astrologers, he at last unfolded the great synthesis which would convince these personages that their beliefs allowed in logic of a merger with Catholicism, who then would criticize his method of labouring for the devil so as to open the way to God?

Opponents of the Jesuits have sometimes called arguments of this sort casuistical. But we are not here concerned with such judgments. Our task is solely to explain how it came about that the scientific knowledge of Europe began to be offered to China. It is a curious story, not easy to understand. With all its implications it has never been objectively stated.

Immediately confronting Ricci was one difficulty. He was not, he felt, personally competent to make the calculations for a reformed Chinese Calendar. This was not the view of his Chinese friends; they had the utmost confidence in him, for they had seen him predict more accurately than the Nanking Bureau of Mathematics a number of eclipses. But he was aware of lack of experience as an astronomer. Nor had he with him all the books required. He therefore took the precaution of writing home to ask for the latest publications and also that a skilled astronomer be sent out, at the same time explaining the great opportunity which appeared to be presenting itself of spreading the gospel.

It was not, however, until 1601, nineteen years after his arrival at Macao, that the road to Peking was opened to him. In 1598 he had been there for a few days in the train of a Nan-king Mandarin, who was his friend. But the moment was not propitious, for the Japanese were attacking Korea and all for-eigners were suspected of espionage. He left hurriedly, his stay being long enough, however, to permit him to note the differ-ence between Peking and Nanking. In the southern town many of the officials were men of character, independent and honest, while at the capital the eunuchs had begun to usurp the functions of the Civil Service. the fatal course which was to destroy the Ming within fifty years.

The way in which Ricci entered Peking and his relations with the Emperor Wan Li have been described in a number of books, but generally in a fanciful manner. For instance, Fülöp-Miller, in his *The Power and Secret of the Jesuits* (1930), a book which purports to be written from original authorities and has been widely read, tells no more than a silly tale. It was not until three years ago that a full and sound historical narrative was published. I refer to Henri Bernard's *Le Père Matthieu Ricci et la société chinoise de son temps*. Henri Bernard is a Jesuit and a sinologue. His account of Ricci's entry into the Forbidden City is not only reliable, but far more interesting than Fülöp-Miller's cheap and tiresome pseudo-drama. But his book was published at Tien-tsin and has not been translated into English. In conse-quence the true adventures of Ricci are hardly known in Eng-land. These are sufficient excuses for repeating some part of them here. The reader will find, moreover, that they serve as a commentary on the fall of the Ming and on the Dutch Embassy of 1656.

Ricci's main reason for wishing to reach the capital has already been stated. He had also a subsidiary reason. It was against the law for a foreigner to travel or settle in Ming China. Though he had been able to evade that law thanks to his influential friends among the provincial Mandarinate, he knew that his position was not secure. It was only necessary that some adverse report should reach the central Government for him to be arrested or deported to Macao. He was now advised that his best course was to conform to the rule relating to foreign envoys. He should petition the Board of Rites, which dealt with such matters, and state that he desired to make gifts to the throne. His Chinese friends in Nanking would help him to get as far as Tien-tsin at the head of the Grand Canal, where he could await the Imperial Order. They would also give him introductions to important people in the capital.

He decided to adopt this advice, and after raising certain funds in Macao selected his presents. The most important of these were two clocks. Ricci's clocks had already aroused much interest. The European clock represented the beginning of that application of mathematics to practical life which led on to the mechanical age. The Chinese measured time by the water-clock or by other non-mechanical contrivances. A mechanical clock was therefore a startling novelty. And as in it was the nucleus of so much else to come, it was potentially a gift of serious value. The other presents included a clavichord, some religious pictures, crosses and relics. Ricci was such an intellectual and his whole policy was to address himself to intellectuals, that at first sight it is surprising to hear that he thought it good policy immediately to present Wan Li with objects of Catholic worship. The explanation must be that he hoped they would arouse the Emperor's curiosity and, so, that he would be asked to explain their import, thereby opening for himself unobtrusively a way for later preaching. He refers to them tactfully in the petition, which he now drew up for transmission to the Emperor. Only incomplete versions of this petition have been published in English. I give it in full, for it is a document which can be understood and enjoyed in the light of the information already supplied. It was written in the Chinese classical manner with the help of his Mandarin friends, and was strictly in accordance with the procedure laid down for such petitions from foreigners.

'Your humble servant,' it begins, 'who has come from Europe, respectfully begs permission to present Your Majesty with some presents, of a kind which have not heretofore been seen in China. Far away though his country lies, news reached him of the profound learning and good government which obtain under Your Majesty's benign rule. He long desired to share in such blessings and to become one of Your Majesty's subjects. In the belief that he would not be entirely useless, he dared to make the tremendous journey. On his first arrival he was like a dumb man, for he did not know how to speak the language; so renting a house he applied himself to its study. For fifteen years he remained in the cities of Shiuhing and Shoochow. During that time he made acquaintance with the doctrines of the Sages, read the Nine Classics and their com-mentaries, committing parts of them to memory, and, as far as his poor capacity allowed, was able to master their lofty mean-ing. Thereafter, he crossed the mountains and came to Nan-king, where he remained for the space of five years.

'The extreme benevolence shown by the Great Ming to-wards strangers has encouraged him to approach the Dragon Seat. The gifts which he desires to present, if of small value, may perhaps be regarded as rare and curious, coming as they do from the far West. Like the water-cress and the sun-rays offered by the simple villager in the story, may Your Majesty be pleased to accept them as the token of a humble veneration.

'From childhood your petitioner has sought to cultivate virtue. Now he has passed the meridian of his life. Having no wife or family, he has no favour to ask, his whole desire being that the sacred objects, which are among the presents offered, may serve to prolong Your Majesty's life and invoke upon your Person and Kingdom peace and the blessing of the Master of Heaven.

'Your petitioner begs that Your Majesty's high compassion be extended to him, a wanderer come to bow beneath the August Law, a poor pilgrim bearing gifts. Unbounded will be his gratitude for such infinite complacence; unending his endeavour to repay such goodness; single and unswerving his lasting affection.

'As for his qualifications, such as they are, he graduated in his own country, honours were bestowed upon him. He thoroughly understands the celestial sphere, geography and geometry and the mathematics. He can make calculations with the astrolabe and the gnomon by methods which, needless to say, are in accordance with Chinese precedent. If Your Majesty will deign to accept the services of so inconsiderable a scholar, his endeavours will only be exceeded by his happiness in working for the Sovereign Lord of the World. Awaiting a Mandate.'

Armed with a passport issued by the Nanking Board of Rites, Ricci accompanied by another Father called Pantoja and two Brothers, all dressed in Chinese costume, left the southern capital in May 1600 on board one of six boats which a eunuch, whose name is given in the Europeanized form of Leupusie, was taking laden with silk to the Court. The route was the usual one by the Grand Canal. Traffic was very dense, and the population so thick that along most of the way there was an unbroken line of houses on both banks. At Tsining a very high official, whose son had met Ricci at Nanking, came to call in state. On returning the call next day Ricci was received by the family with the greatest kindness. The Mandarin's 'amiability was so exquisite', he writes, 'that one seemed to be among Christian friends and intimates rather than at the other end of the world in a gentile's house.'

But at Lintsing, where the Grand Canal joins the Yun-ho river, 250 miles from Tien-tsin, his troubles began. This was a customs-station and the Superintendent was a eunuch by the name of Ma-t'ang, for the deplorable practice of appointing eunuchs to Civil Service posts had already begun. This Ma-t'ang was a rascal, a thoroughly dishonest and disreputable

creature. When Leupusie, their conductor, presented himself
at the customs office to pay the duty on his six boat-loads of
silk, Ma-t'ang refused to accept the money and denied him
passage in order to force him to offer more. Leupusie did so,
was refused again, increased the bribe further, still without success. Ma-t'ang, working through his clerks, simply told him to
wait. Days went by and Leupusie, who had contracted to reach
Peking by a certain date, was in despair. At last, unable to wait
longer and unwilling to pay more, he told one of the clerks
that Ricci had on board presents for the Emperor of a very
novel kind: it would be improper to delay him. When Ma-
t'ang received this intelligence he became interested. There was
both money and reputation to be made if he could get Ricci
into his clutches. He knew the Jesuit personally could not pay
much: his design was to take charge of the presents and himself
introduce him at Court, when, if the Emperor were pleased,
he, Ma-t'ang, would be promoted. So he entered his lacquered
barge and was rowed down to where the boats lay.

Ricci was not on board, for he had gone ashore. When he
had learnt that Ma-t'ang knew about the presents he became
uneasy and decided to ask the advice of the local Governor, an
official whom he had known some years back at Shiuhing.
This man was a person of integrity. Indeed, on his transfer later
the people of the town built a temple to house a statue of him.
But he told Ricci that the power of the eunuchs was increasing
so rapidly that even the most senior members of the Civil
Service could not hope to interfere with their malversations.
Now that Ma-t'ang knew about the presents, there was nothing to be done but to comply as graciously as possible with
whatever proposals he might make. To oppose him, said the
Mandarin, would be highly dangerous. He was both a cunning
and a cruel fellow.

While this conversation was in progress, one of Ma-t'ang's
peons arrived at the house to say that his master was waiting on
the Canal and wished to see the Jesuit at once. Ricci hurried
down to the bank. There was the lacquered barge moored be-

side his boat. He went on board and was shown into the main cabin. The eunuch received him with effusiveness. The presents were brought in and when he saw the pictures of the Saints he kotowed to them with unconvincing reverence, swore that His Majesty would hang them in his private rooms and protested he would immediately send forward the petition and see that it got into the right hands.

Ricci tried to disengage himself, saying that he had introductions to important officials at Court and that, though much obliged to Ma⁄t'ang, he would not dare to trouble him. At the mention of the Court officials, Ma⁄t'ang laughed heartily: his Reverence was clearly misinformed, for such Mandarins as he had mentioned could be of no service to him. He would be kept waiting indefinitely for an answer to his petition.

Finding that he could not shake off Ma⁄t'ang, Ricci thanked him with the best grace he could muster. The eunuch then suggested that the presents should be sent on shore to his house for greater security, but Ricci managed to elude this by pointing out that the clocks required constant attention, and that if he were parted from the pictures and other sacred objects, they might lose some of their virtue and so be less potent for good when presented to the Emperor.

Ma⁄t'ang, who was quite uneducated, seems to have been alarmed by these hints and did not press the matter. However, he moved the Jesuits and the presents on to a ship of his own, explaining that he personally would conduct them. Leupusie was sent off with his boats, on which no levy was made, legal or otherwise. But Ma⁄t'ang could not start at once. Apparently it was his duty to credit every six months the customs dues at the Treasury in Tien⁄tsin, and there was still a month to go. Ricci had to wait. His friend, the Governor, paid several visits and took the opportunity of impressing on Ma⁄t'ang the high esteem in which the Jesuits were held at Nanking. Ma⁄t'ang was cordial. The more important Ricci was, the more he should be able to get for introducing him. He even gave a party for him in his splendid residence, amusing the company after dinner with a troupe of acrobats, better than any Ricci had seen in Europe. The learned Jesuit mathematician was much taken with one item, the dance of a boy with an automaton.

Ma✕t'ang now modified his plan. He decided to send the Jesuits to Tien✕tsin in his ship under guard, he himself follow✕ing as soon as he could get away. But so as not to waste time, he addressed a letter to the Emperor, stating shortly that a cer✕tain stranger had arrived at Lintsing with presents and a petition for His Majesty, and that as he appeared to be a man of respectable character, he had thought it his duty to take charge of him, so that he should be spared all inconvenience. It was requested that he might be summoned to Court. This letter, wrapped in yellow silk, was put on board the ship with the usual ceremonies accorded to Imperial Correspondence, the firing of cannon and the proper number of kotows, and was entrusted to a messenger whose orders were to deliver it at Peking, and bring back an answer to Tien✕tsin, where Ricci should wait until it was received.

On July 18, having been delayed fifteen days, the Jesuits set off down the river. Ma✕t'ang bade them farewell in state, being carried by eight men to the wharf in his palanquin, accom✕panied by a band of gongmen and musicians. The voyage was comfortable, for at every stop the local officials came on board with supplies of meat, fish, fruit and wine. By the sixth day they had reached Tien✕tsin. The messenger went on at once to Peking.

On the 8th of August Ma✕t'ang arrived with about £30,000 of customs dues. No answer had yet been received from the Emperor. Accordingly he sent a second messenger. The first had delivered Ricci's petition and Ma✕t'ang's covering letter, not to the Board of Rites, which would have been the proper procedure, but to some eunuchs, friends of Ma✕t'ang's, who were asked to go direct to the Emperor, so that Ma✕t'ang could claim the whole credit. Why these eunuchs had been unable to procure an order for Ricci to come up was not known.

When two months passed without an answer, Ma✕t'ang's

manner became chilly. After all the trouble he had taken, it did not seem that he would make any profit. He ceased to invite the Jesuits to his house and posted six men on their boat to watch them. At the end of three months the second messenger returned with an answer, but when the Imperial Mandate had been read, everyone kneeling, it was found to contain no per-mission for Ricci to proceed, but only a demand for more in-formation. A detailed list of the presents was to be sent. This was submitted at once and another long delay occurred, appar-ently because the Board of Rites had seen the petition and was trying to take the matter out of the hands of the eunuchs. In November Ma-t'ang, now much put out, told the Jesuits that they must leave his ship, because it was wanted for other pur-poses. He transferred them to a house in one of the parks. They found the change not disagreeable, though the house was a poor one. But Ma-t'ang now became suspicious; someone had sug-gested to him that Ricci might be hiding valuables. So, a couple of days before he was due to return to his duties at Lint-sing, he came to the house with about two hundred persons whom he had instructed to shout and threaten. Frowning heavily he announced that he had received news from Peking that Ricci had a quantity of jewels in his possession, which he had not declared and did not intend to give the Emperor. Ricci replied quietly to this nonsense, inviting him to search the party's luggage. In the roughest manner Ma-t'ang ordered the boxes to be opened in the courtyard. Then shouting and raging he examined each bit of their private property as it was taken out. What did they call this? What was that for? Why did they bring that other? Why hadn't they shown him this? Ricci mildly answered each question. Finding nothing of any value, Ma-t'ang became more and more annoyed, making furious gestures or ridiculous lamentations. And whenever he saw anything he liked, he put it aside, as if he intended to keep it for himself.

This futile scene had been going on for some time and the Fathers thought they would escape with the loss of a few personal belongings, when the affair took a more serious turn. In a little box belonging to Father de Pantoja, Ricci's companion, Ma⁄t'ang's servants found a wooden crucifix, the Five Wounds depicted with red paint.

'What is that?' asked Ma⁄t'ang, making a strange face. And then: 'I know what it is. It is a spell! You have made it to kill the Emperor by magic! People who deal in such devilments are nothing but criminals. What have you to say?'

This was very awkward. The fact was that Ricci had always been careful to keep his crucifixes out of sight. They were shown as a rule only to converts. The idea of a crucified God, he knew well, would shock the generality of the Chinese. It was a conception totally foreign not only to Confucianism, but also to the popular cults of Buddhism and Taoism, a mystery which could only be explained after much preparation. The Nestorians who had brought Christianity to China during the T'ang dynasty (618–907) had been even more careful: they had never mentioned the Crucifixion at all. So, to be asked by an enraged and illiterate eunuch to explain forthwith its mean⁄ing was alarming. Ricci knew only too well that the repre⁄sentation of Christ on the cross might suggest sorcery. Not only in China, but all over the world witches modelled figures of those they designed to kill, piercing their limbs or bodies with pins or nails. The very excellence of the workmanship of de Pantoja's crucifix, the realistic manner in which the blood was painted, made it seem all the more potent a charm. Exag⁄gerated though Ma⁄t'ang's manner had been over the other contents of their trunks, there was no doubt he was now con⁄vinced that he had discovered a dangerous conspiracy.

Ricci decided that it would be impossible to say what the crucifix meant. To explain that it represented the crucified Son of the Christian God would have sounded like an attempt to conceal its real use by a clumsy invention. He therefore said that it was the representation of a great Western saint who had allowed himself to be put to death on the cross by a tyrant in order to save the people. As a perpetual memorial of his sacri⁄

fice it was the custom to carry about such crucifixes. Ma∕t'ang remained angry and suspicious. The sergeant of the guard was clearly shocked, observing that if what Ricci said were true, even so it was improper that sculptures of the saint should show him in such a predicament. The unpacking of the trunks con∕tinued and several more crucifixes were found, along with cer∕tain pictures of the crucifixion. The number of them had a calming effect on Ma∕t'ang. It did not seem possible that they were all designed for the Emperor's hurt. Tension relaxed somewhat and they all sat down.

There were three objects which Ma∕t'ang particularly fancied, a reliquary in the form of a cross, another in the form of a book, and the silver∕gilt chalice which the Jesuits used in the Mass. He said he would buy these and produced a sum of money. When told they were not for sale, he insisted. Ricci begged at least to be allowed to keep the chalice. It was a sacred vessel, he said, with which they sacrificed to their God, a vessel which a person not ordained might not touch. Superstitious though he was, Ma∕t'ang took the chalice in his hands and turned it with bravado this way and that. 'What do you mean—can't touch!' he exclaimed. 'I am touching it. Nothing happens.' Ricci offered to buy it back from him at double its weight in silver. Ma∕t'ang refused, but the sergeant of the guard became fright∕ened. 'I think it would be just as well', he said to Ma∕t'ang, 'to give them back the cup. If they offer double its weight, it must be a holy thing.' The eunuch hesitated. He certainly did not want to run the risk of provoking a holy thing to some occult vengeance. 'Take it,' he said at last, and handed it back.

But he kept the reliquaries and also other things he had put aside. Nevertheless, he was unappeased and, his suspicions returning, swore before he left that he would denounce them all to the Emperor. They would either be punished or expelled from China.

Two days later he returned to Lintsing. Ricci and his com∕panions were left virtually prisoners in their house, which was a wretched one for the cold of winter. The guard remained;

even their servants were not free to go out unescorted. There seemed no hope. Ma⁄t'ang, backed as he was by the eunuch clique at Court, was a most dangerous enemy. The Board of Rites might not believe the crucifixes to be connected with sorcery, but was it strong enough to put Ma⁄t'ang in his place? Deeply agitated, Ricci decided to write to his friend, the high Mandarin at Lintsing, explaining what had happened and asking for advice. The guard having become slack in its duties, a messenger was able to slip out with the letter.

The town of Lintsing was full of rumours about what Ma⁄t'ang proposed to do. It was said he intended to memorialize the Emperor accusing the Jesuits of attempted sorcery. Ricci's friend was afraid to receive the messenger openly, and he was shown in by a back door. In answer to the letter he wrote that he considered the Fathers' situation desperate, that he strongly advised them to escape from Tien⁄tsin and make their way back as best they could to Macao, even if that meant abandoning all their luggage and the presents. As for their crucifixes, the only safe course was to destroy them immediately, so that no trace of them remained. They might consider memorializing the Em⁄peror for leave to go, but he personally advised them to go while they could.

Ricci could not bring himself to accept this advice. For eigh⁄teen years he had planned to get to Peking. He had dreamed of being entrusted with the reform of the Calendar, of winning the Emperor's confidence, of converting the Court. Now with⁄in a few days' journey of the capital was he to take to flight? But the letter said they were in grave danger. Well, if that were so, he would stay and meet it. Even the threat of death would not frighten him away. Should they kill him, he would be a martyr. He had come out to the East prepared for that.

Then it occurred to him that the Mandarins in Peking, to whom he had introductions, might be able to help him. He sent one of the two Brothers secretly to them. This man, Mar⁄tinez, returned to report that they were afraid to compromise themselves, that to memorialize the Emperor was useless, they said, for he never acted without the advice of his eunuchs. The only thing for Ricci to do was to buy his life by giving Ma-t'ang the clocks and the clavichord.

Ricci relates in his *Opere Storiche* how suddenly their desperate situation was changed. 'In the month of December, 1600, things were as bad as they could well be. The weather at Tien-tsin was very cold and our house wretchedly uncomfortable. Then all of a sudden on the 8th of January the Emperor issued a Mandate that we should immediately bring up the presents to Peking. . . . It has never been clear why he delayed six months to issue this order nor how it was that after six months it occurred to him to do so. Our friends, however, told us afterwards that one day when he was alone he remembered reading some report or other about a clock and, calling his eunuchs, exclaimed: "What about that striking clock? Why haven't I seen it yet?" '

This story may be at least partly true. The various letters and the list of presents had not been sent through the proper channels, though, apparently, the Secretariat of the Board of Rites had got wind of them. The rival office which the eunuchs had established, no doubt inefficient as well as corrupt, may have kept them pending. Or perhaps, when put up to Wan Li, they were accompanied by a draft which he neglected to sign. But there are a dozen possible explanations. The Government of China had a great deal of business to handle.

On receipt of the Mandate, Ricci prepared immediately to comply. A Mandarin had been deputed from Peking to bring up the party. The clocks and the other presents were repacked. A few things had been stolen by Ma-t'ang and the sergeant, but on the whole they had lost very little. Ricci's mathematical books, however, had been confiscated. These Ma-t'ang had lodged in the Tien-tsin Treasury on the ground that the possession of books on mathematics without the Emperor's express permission was contrary to law. Such a law was, in fact, on the Ming Statute Book, though it was not enforced in the provinces. It seems that at the time when the early Ming Emperors made the Civil Service examination wholly literary in char-acter, this law was passed, partly to discourage the study of mathematics and partly to prevent would-be rebels from calcu-lating a Calendar of their own or otherwise using mathematics to further astrologically their rebellions. As it was essential to get possession of the books again if he were to make his way at Court as a mathematician, Ricci went to the Treasury to de-mand the box in which they were packed. He told the clerk in charge that the Emperor had summoned him to Peking with the presents, and let it appear that the box in question con-tained some of them. Though it was labelled 'mathematical books', fortunately the clerk could not read the characters, and flurried by the mention of the Emperor's name handed it over without further question.

On January 20, 1601, the Jesuits set out for Peking by road, the waterway being, perhaps, frozen. Eight horses and thirty porters had been supplied. The journey occupied four days, the nights being spent in the guest house of the local Magis-trates. On arrival at Peking, they were lodged with a eunuch who lived outside the walls. Ricci was still in the hands of the eunuchs. It must be supposed that Ma-t'ang, to whom a copy of the Mandate was sent, had now abandoned his idea of charging him with sorcery and had reverted to his original design of getting what reputation or reward he could for intro-ducing him with his novel presents. But as we shall see, the Board of Rites was not ready to allow this entrenchment upon its province without a struggle.

The morning after the Jesuits' arrival the eunuchs took the presents into the Forbidden City. It seems that they were im-mediately shown to Wan Li and that the larger of the two clocks, which struck the quarters, interested him. In the ordi-nary way Ricci would have been received in audience in due course, but when the clock ran down it was necessary to send for him at once, as no instructions had been given how it might be wound up. He was not, however, taken into the Forbidden City. The clock was brought to one of the gates and there he was asked by a eunuch of the Presence, who was in charge of the clock, to explain how to set it going. He did so, and it was further arranged that he should give all the necessary instructions to four eunuchs who were members of the Palace Board of Mathematics. During the next three days Ricci met these people and gave them a detailed explanation of the works. They took careful notes of what he said, improvising characters to express the various parts of the mechanism.

When the clock, which during the three days had been kept in the office of the Mathematical Bureau, was returned to the Palace striking properly, Wan Li was genuinely pleased with its novelty, and the four eunuchs who had been deputed to take charge of it were promoted, it is said. The clock was placed for the moment in the private apartments. There was talk of building a special tower for it—it seems to have been very large—and orders were issued that a copy be made on a yet larger scale. In short, Ricci had been quite right in thinking that a clock would amuse the Court. He was still, however, a long way from the realization of the first step in his plans, which was to obtain permission to reside in Peking. The Emperor had not yet seen him, though he sent to make enquiries about one thing or another and ordered a Court painter to make portraits of both the Fathers. They were asked, moreover, to teach four eunuchs of the College of Music how to play the clavichord. Their lodging had been moved to a house inside the walls not far from the Palace enceinte. The eunuchs kept a close eye on them, and hinted that if they could continue to interest the Emperor, they might hope to be made Mandarins.

This flattering talk was, of course, all nonsense. The eunuchs —and it seems that Ma-t'ang had arrived on a visit—intended him to stay only until Wan Li, according to custom, had made him return presents, when they would take their percentage, a high percentage, and send him away. Ricci had some suspicion of this, and desired to get into touch with those Mandarins to whom he had introductions. But he was forbidden to go into the streets, for the eunuchs did not want the news of his arrival to reach the Board of Rites. Yet he managed on several occasions to slip out. At that period it was usual for pedes-trians of the upper class to wear a veil, partly to keep the dust out of their eyes and mouths—it was very bad on dry days—and partly so as to avoid the elaborate civilities which etiquette demanded on meeting an acquaintance. Making use of a veil Ricci called on several persons of rank. In result, news reached the Board of Rites that the Jesuits had arrived in the city. Enquiries were instituted, and it was soon learnt that they had given their presents and were being held by the eunuchs pend-ing the Emperor's orders.

This intelligence angered the Board. For some years the official hierarchy had watched with dismay the growing power of the eunuchs. Their prerogatives were being encroached upon and an ever-increasing barrier erected between them and the Emperor. The Board decided to make the case of the Jesuits a trial of strength. It is not clear what papers had come before it, but I think it may be assumed that the members were not much more than aware that Ricci was expected. To learn now that he had arrived and that the eunuchs were managing his recep-tion was extremely aggravating. It was resolved to take drastic action.

On March 2 a posse of police entered the house where the Jesuits were lodged. Pantoja was at the Palace, but Ricci and the two Brothers were at home. The Sergeant stated that he had come to arrest them on the charge that they had memorialized the Throne through an improper channel and had concealed themselves when they should have reported their arrival to the Board of Rites. Aware that he could easily explain how he had been forced, Ricci made no objection. Pantoja coming in was also arrested. The Jesuits were then taken, though without the customary violence, to the police-station, where they were locked up.

The news of the arrest was not long in reaching the eunuchs, and Ma-t'ang's agent, he himself having left the city, immedi-ately went to the police-station, where he made so violent a scene, threatening the constables with torture and death for interfering with the Emperor's *protégés* and, he alleged, robbing them as well, that they lost their nerve and all of them, including the Sergeant, fled. The eunuch then reconducted the Jesuits to their house.

This rescue was not at all to Ricci's liking. He believed that his prospects would be better with the Board than with the eunuchs. During his long stay in China he had always managed to win the esteem of the scholar class because he himself was a scholar. He was out of his element with the uneducated eunuchs. So during the night he argued with Ma-t'ang's agent that it would be prudent to present himself before the Board on the following day; otherwise an uproar might ensue which would turn the Emperor against him. The eunuch agreed, and next morning they rode to the Board office.

The Members were sitting to consider the memorials of a number of other visiting strangers. The eunuch thought that a high line would probably succeed as well with them as with the police, and entering the Council Chamber complained that the police had wrongfully interfered by arresting the Fathers and repeated the accusation that they had been robbed. The President, however, was not alarmed, and firmly told him that everything had been done in accordance with law. He rebuked him for his intrusion and ordered him out. Ricci would presently be called in and examined.

When his turn came Ricci entered and knelt before the President. He had come voluntarily, he said, to submit to the Board. He then recounted frankly what had happened at Lint-sing, how he had been practically Ma-t'ang's prisoner and had been obliged to do what the eunuchs directed. He further pointed out that strictly speaking his position was not that of a foreigner, as he had resided already so many years in China. His object in visiting Peking was to obtain permission to settle there. At the end of an examination which lasted three hours the President withdrew the charges against him, but directed that he and his party should lodge until further orders in a building called the Strangers' Guesthouse. This meant that his case had been classified as that of a visiting foreigner, and that there was little chance of the Board supporting his request to stay on at Peking.

The Strangers' Guesthouse was more properly a strangers' quarter, for it consisted of a block of buildings sufficiently numerous to house ten thousand people. This number sounds very large, but it includes servants and a bazaar. Some of the accommodation consisted of sheds, but the Fathers were allotted apartments reserved for the superior class of visitor, which were luxuriously furnished with beds, armchairs and silk hangings. The meals were free and very liberal. On the third day they were taken with a crowd of other visitors to one of the inner courtyards of the Forbidden City to kotow the Imperial Throne. The details of the ceremony are recounted by Ricci, and they hardly differ from those observed by the Dutch fifty-five years later, except that on the latter occasion the Emperor appeared in person. It seems that during the reign of Wan Li an audience for visitors of minor importance meant no more than the kotow before the empty throne. The Fathers duly went through the elaborate prostrations, which in no way bridged the gulf between them and the monarch they dared to dream of converting. They were dressed in the red robes prescribed for the occasion and—a curious detail—were obliged to cover their mouths with an ivory tablet, two palms long and four fingers wide. I have not seen an explanation of this.

The Board of Rites, having forcibly asserted its authority and made Ricci comply with the ordinary procedure for gift-bearing foreigners, had now to advise the Emperor about his disposal. Although it had been considerate and polite, for some of its members knew very well the high esteem in which Ricci was held in learned circles at Nanking, that, in fact, he was a scholar and a gentleman, qualifications that had tremendous weight in China, the circumstances were such that they were bound to memorialize against him. He had been taken up by the Court eunuchs: the Board had lost face, had been obliged to seize him. It was a test case; he could not be recommended for special consideration. As for his wish to stay, that was out of the question. There was no precedent for any such course. The memorial should be read in the light of these factors.

'The man Ricci', it began, 'would appear to be a mendicant.' This word may have meant religious mendicant, like a wandering Taoist sage. But it was far from complimentary, as religious mendicants were considered frauds by such bodies as the Board of Rites. 'Where he comes from it is impossible to say, the alleged name of his country being untraceable in our records. Wherever it may be, it has certainly had no relations with this Government and must be entirely ignorant of our institutions.' The memorial then points out that Ricci after a residence of twenty years in China wished to present gifts to the Throne and did so through the eunuch, Ma-t'ang, in contravention of the rule that foreigners should apply to the office of the Viceroy of the Province by which they enter and that they should not proceed until authorized by the Board of Rites. As Ricci had fully explained the pressure put on him by Ma-t'ang and his explanation had been accepted, this allegation is so disingenuous that one must suppose the Board to have been more concerned to give the eunuchs a slap in the face than to state Ricci's case correctly.

The memorial then speaks of the presents: 'As a rule the gifts of tribute-envoys or others are rare and valuable, but Ricci's presents are merely curios—for instance the portraits of the Master of Heaven and his mother!' Referring to the reliquaries, which it seems were presented, the memorialists observe: 'He also brought the bones of Immortals, as if Immortals did not take their bones with them to Heaven!' (Immortals were Taoist saints or sages who had ascended into Heaven in the manner of Elijah.) Without any mention of the clocks or the clavichord, they warn the Emperor not to take such presents into his palace. Bones might be haunted by evil spirits.

They quote the definite precedent of a bone of the Buddha having been rejected for that reason.[1]

The memorialists then come to the point: 'There are no grounds for permitting Ricci to remain in the capital. He should be sent back to Macao, where it can be left to the Viceroy's discretion whether or not to embark him for his country. Before he leaves, His Majesty may present him with a hat, a girdle, a ceremonial robe and some rolls of silk. His companion, Pantoja, may also be given rolls of silk. Further, a sum of money should be paid equal to the estimated value of the presents.'

When Wan Li received this paper, he found himself in an awkward position. While it was a matter of indifference to him what was done about Ricci, a dispute between the Board of Rites and his eunuchs was not at all to his taste. If he accepted the Board's recommendation and disposed of Ricci like any visiting foreigner, he might find himself obliged to

---

[1] The reference here is to Han Yü's (A.D. 768–824) famous memorial. Han Yü or, to give him his posthumous title, Han Wên Kung, was a noted writer of the T'ang Dynasty, whose tablet is in the Temple of Confucius. It has been customary for punctilious scholars to wash their hands in rose-water before opening his works. His memorial to the Emperor against bringing a bone of the Buddha into the Palace is considered one of the masterpieces of Chinese literature. Buddhism at the time was fashionable at Court and the Emperor had sent for the relic, which was to be borne to the Palace in procession. 'Buddha was a barbarian,' submitted this stout Confucian. 'His clothes were ill-cut, he had not read the classics, he had no pretensions whatever to be a gentleman. Supposing this Buddha had come to the capital as an envoy from his state, what course would the then Emperor have taken with him? At most he would have received him in audience and after admonition have entertained him to dinner, bestowing upon him a suit of clothes and sending him back to the frontier under escort. But Your Majesty proposes to admit a bone of his into the Palace!' He goes on to point out that bones may be haunted, but that in the case of the present 'disgusting object' no precautions of any kind have been ordered. He advises the destruction of the bone and expresses himself quite ready to take on his shoulders any misfortune arising therefrom.

The felicity of his style was such that it caused the Emperor to abandon his intention.

proceed against Ma-t'ang and other eunuchs for their interference. To reject the memorial was also distasteful. Its recommendations were strictly in conformity with precedent. There
was no ground on which he could reject it. Yet to accept it
would be to admit that his eunuchs had been in the wrong.
His reign had now lasted twenty-two years. Eunuch favourites
had obtained gradually a great hold on him. He still governed,
indeed, under the constitution of the Empire. Public business
was strictly conducted according to law. Nor had he any intention of ruling otherwise. It was easy enough to reward his
minions without openly flouting constitutional usage. Now
this unfortunate case of Ricci brought into the light of day
what was better kept in darkness. The more he considered it,
the less possible did it seem to refuse to act on the memorial,
yet the more disinclined did he feel to do so, particularly as his
favourites had told him that the whole affair was in reality an
attempt by the Civil Service to curb the influence of the Court.

Confronted with this dilemma he decided to do nothing.
He would pass no orders whatsoever, either in favour of the
Board or the eunuchs.

A month passed. Ricci was detained in the Foreigners'
Guesthouse, though allowed, with an escort, to visit his
friends. The Board grew agitated when no reply came. Perhaps it had gone too far in directly accusing the eunuchs of
illegal interference. A fresh memorial was submitted, leaving
out that part. It was calculated that this would enable the Emperor to pass a mere routine order about a foreigner without
raising any other issues. But by this time there had been so
much gossip that the issue was directly between the Board or
the eunuchs. Not that the eunuchs wanted Ricci to stay indefinitely. What they desired was to get him back into their
hands, for only so could they recover the loss of face they had
suffered in having him taken from them.

The second memorial displayed an amusing solicitude for
Ricci. A longer stay in Peking could only injure his health,
argued the Board. Like all true Sages the proper place for him

was a mountain retreat. Such a retreat might be found in Kiangsi, which was a thousand miles away on the road to Canton. The mountains there were much frequented by Taoist philosophers, and it was reported that they lived to an extreme old age.

But Wan Li still refused to answer. The Board accordingly submitted a third, then a fourth, and finally a fifth memorial in which they omitted their sarcastic references to Ricci's character and presents, each successive memorial detailing more flatteringly than the last the Board's admiration for his profound knowledge. But it could not bring itself to recommend his staying on, nor was there any hint of an apology to Ma-t'ang. Tactful though these memorials were, they did not alter the situation either for Ricci or the Emperor. The deadlock continued, for still no answer was returned.

Ricci now made a move. It was May, and he had been detained in the Guesthouse three months. Its Superintendent had been appointed to this post through the good offices of a Mandarin who happened to be one of Ricci's friends. This Mandarin now approached the Superintendent to allow Ricci to live in a house of his own. The Superintendent pointed out that it was not in his power to give such permission. He was accountable to the Board of Rites. The Mandarin threatened that if he did not do so, it might be no harder to deprive him of his job than it had been to provide him with it. The Superintendent considered these two alternatives, and then suggested that if Ricci submitted a petition to him stating that his health was affected by his residence in the Guesthouse, there would be an excuse to allow him to go, more especially as their Lordships of the Board of Rites had already expressed such concern for his health. Two conditions must be imposed, however. When he had taken up his residence outside he must continue to draw his rations from the Guesthouse and take into his employ, free of charge, of course, as were the rations, one of the servants attached to it. In that way it could be represented to their Lordships, concluded the Superintendent, that Ricci was still, to all intents and purposes, in his keeping. The Mandarin agreed that these conditions were no obstacle and on May 28 Ricci moved out.

The result of this arrangement was that Ricci began to live in Peking as he had petitioned that he might be permitted to live, with the added advantage that by drawing free rations and service from the state he was as it were under official protection. The news of what he had done reached the ears of both the Board and the Emperor. But neither took any action or showed that they were aware of it. Maybe for both it was a happy solution. Theoretically Ricci was still at the Guesthouse awaiting the orders of the Board, which therefore had lost no face. Actually he had passed beyond its authority, and the eunuchs could feel that its seizure of him had come to nothing.

He took a house in a fashionable quarter and immediately a number of officials who had heard of him called to make his acquaintance. For nine years he lived in Peking, dying there on May 11, 1610. He never met the Emperor, he was not asked to reform the Calendar and he made very few converts, but for all that his stay had consequences of great historical importance.

## IV

# The Wide Consequences of Ricci's Attempt

What Ricci did at Peking was to collect round him, as he had done at Nanking and the other provincial cities, those members of the scholar class who had a taste for mathematics and science. The astronomer he had written for in 1598 did not arrive, but he was able to teach his pupils—for these Mandarins regarded him as their master—a good deal. He himself was aware of his limitations. In a letter dated February 15, 1609, he says: 'Although up to the present I have taught them nothing but a little mathematics and cosmography, they are so grateful to me that, often with my own ears, I have heard it said by distinguished persons that we have given sight to Chinese eyes.' In a letter of the previous March he had again asked for an astronomer, 'who can continue what I have begun with my small energies, my few books and my little knowledge'.

He was very busy. The eclipses of the moon on June 15 and December 9, 1601, and of the sun on July 4, 1602, on May 11, 1603, and February 26, 1607, gave him opportunities of demonstrating that his calculations were more correct than those of the Board of Mathematics. He made a translation into Chinese of Euclid which was published in 1607, and several translations from the works of Father Clavius, his old tutor at the Collegio Romano. Gradually a centre of scientific culture, a college where it was possible to learn, not all the latest scientific theories of Europe, but as much of them as Ricci knew, was established in the Chinese capital. His real aim, the conversion of his

MATTEO RICCI IN HIS CHAPEL AT PEKING
*From Nievhoff's 'Embassy'*

pupils to Catholicism, was not concealed, though he had to proceed with the greatest caution. He succeeded in avoiding offence, for he was allowed shortly before his death to build a small chapel wherein he celebrated the Mass. The Emperor, though he had never received him, granted on his death a piece of land for his tomb, an honour equivalent to public recognition of his services. An inscription was set up, composed by Wang Ing-lin, Prefect of part of the city, in which were mentioned the names of the eminent persons who had given him countenance, Viceroys, Board Presidents, Censors, Historiographers, Treasurers, an Imperial Tutor, Hanlin Academicians, and Grand Secretaries.

The death of Ricci did not mark the end of the Jesuit mission to Peking. It was, on the contrary, the beginning of it. A demand had been created for certain kinds of Western knowledge, and only the Jesuits were able to satisfy it. What followed is tolerably well known. A series of Jesuits of great talent went to China and, thanks to Ricci's pioneer work, had no difficulty in establishing themselves in Peking, where they found an audience ready and eager to attend their scientific lectures. Each of them had something new to propound. The discoveries connected with the names of Copernicus, Tycho Brahe and Galileo were an exciting sequel to the old Ptolemaic system which, explained by Ricci, had seemed so wonderful. Before the end of the seventeenth century they were able to reveal the new methods in astronomy, mechanics and physics which had changed the intellectual outlook of Europe and provided it with the information which the eighteenth and nineteenth centuries were to turn to such practical account. Many of Ricci's dreams came true. The Jesuits won an extraordinary position at Court. Adam Schall stood high with the last Ming Emperor, and we have seen how he impressed the Dutch when they met him at the Court of the first of the Ch'ing. He became a Mandarin and the reform of the Calendar was entrusted to him. The second Ch'ing Emperor, K'ang Hsi, happened to be a natural mathematician and was delighted to learn all the

Jesuits could tell him. During the early part of his reign Verbiest had the position held by Schall in the last reign. But
Ricci's theory that if the Jesuits could become the tutors of the
Emperor in science and mathematics they would be able by a
synthesis to bring together Confucianism and Christianity did
not work out in practice. Year after year the Fathers brought to
China a wealth of modern scientific knowledge; they toiled to
explain it and to make it useful. But the more they laboured at
such tasks, the more clocks, watches, telescopes, cannon and
astronomical instruments they introduced, the further they
seemed to be from achieving their real object. It was an insuperable difficulty that the Emperor was the Confucian
Pontiff. There existed no more likelihood of the Son of Heaven
putting off his pontificate and submitting to the Pope than of
the Pope dissolving the Catholic Church and calling the Son
of Heaven the Holy Father.

The Jesuits had built up their reputation by the tactful, diligent and, apparently, single-minded way they offered their
scientific knowledge to the Chinese. They seemed like true
sages in the best tradition of classical China. But towards the
end of the seventeenth century K'ang Hsi began to suspect that
they were not sages, but the emissaries of a scheming foreigner.
It was a strange *malentendu*. At first it had not struck him that
they had any designs against Confucianism. When they had
talked warmly of the Pope and Catholicism he believed them
to be merely commending their chief on the ground that his
tenets were Confucian in character. He honestly thought the
Pope would become a Confucian like every other barbarian of
sense. That is why he wrote and offered to take one of his
nieces as a concubine. In that famous letter he speaks of himself as 'the most powerful of all powers on earth, who sits on
the Dragon Seat to expound the word of God'. It was a ridiculous *malentendu* and could never have arisen if the Jesuits had
been a little less tactful. When the Pope did not send his niece
to the Concubinate, did not even answer the letter, but instead
proceeded to contradict K'ang Hsi, who had recently concurred

with the finding of an erudite Commission that the Christians, whether they knew it or not, worshipped the God posited in the Confucian books, the Emperor considered that he had been wasting his time with an impertinent ignoramus, who had never read the classics and was totally uncultivated. He saw at last what the Jesuits really meant when they spoke of their God and their Pope, at the same time praising Confucianism and hinting that the two systems were not incompatible. It was not, as he had thought, that they were referring to a compatibility where Catholicism would merge in a Confucian world system under himself, an obvious arrangement and one which other barbarians had invariably adopted: they had the effrontery to propose exactly the opposite. He was astonished and painfully undeceived. How could the Son of Heaven, on whose right actions depended the proper balance of heaven and earth, merge in some outer cult? The idea seemed to him so topsy-turvy that he suspected a political motive. With remarkable acumen he perceived that the Jesuits were the vanguard of a civilization which was potentially dangerous. In a confidential paper written to guide his successors he noted: 'The kings of France and Portugal have taken pains to send me good subjects, clever, well versed in science and the arts, who have served my dynasty well. But if our government became feeble, if we had civil war or were invaded by the Mongols, what would become of our Empire? The Europeans could do with China as they pleased.'[1]

After these disclosures or apparent disclosures K'ang Hsi's respect for the Jesuits waned. He and his successors in the eighteenth century continued to tolerate and employ them as cartographers, artists, architects and mechanics, but they were regarded more as handymen than as sages. Yet in a paradoxical way they were sages in the Chinese classical sense. They had offered China two things—Catholicism and that knowledge by means of which the Western world was later able to make

[1] J. Brucker, *La Mission en Chine. Revue des Questions historiques.* Paris, 1881.

itself so powerful. They believed that if the Chinese accepted the first they would be saved from the damnation which other-wise awaited them according to Catholic dogma. But it was actually the second, if the Chinese had taken and developed it, as it was about to be developed in the West, which would have saved them from the torments they suffered in the nineteenth century and are suffering today, torments which were due to their weakness when faced by inventions, the product of the very knowledge they had been offered, an offer which proved incidentally that the Jesuits were innocent of any political *arrière pensée*. Had China turned to as dynamic account what the Jesuits revealed to her as did Europe what she learnt from the rediscovered Greek books, she would have taken the path of modernization along with Europe in the seventeenth century instead of postponing her inevitable entry upon it for three cen-turies, instead of waiting until 1912, when she had already suffered terribly for her idleness and, her awakening being so tardy, was fated to suffer incomparably more.

But, it may be objected, surely she did receive with enthusiasm the new learning which the Jesuits brought? In a sense she did receive it; a small minority of intellectuals studied it eagerly. But it did not sink in, it was not applied; the Government did not take it up; the examination system remained unaltered; generations of Mandarins continued to be educated in the old way; the official outlook was unmodified.

The Chinese missed the point of the knowledge which was brought to them over the ocean. It was dynamic knowledge and its dynamism should have been obvious as the years passed and as Europe became stronger for all to see. But, as the pure scientist, discovering an explosive stronger than any known, will have his own satisfaction in the chemical fact, it had for most of them only an academic interest. Others, less intellectual, were mere dabblers and amateurs or childish enthusiasts for amusing novelties; others again, the extreme conservatives—and the Government seems to have been composed of such men—were concerned only to employ the new knowledge to buttress their old system as when, first, Ptolemy and, then, Copernicus were used to correct the Calendar so that the astro/ logical side of Confucianism might be made more exact.

Full of ironies as is the story of the Jesuits in China it had a sequel no less ironical in Europe. If the effect of their teaching in the first was to strengthen Confucianism—even those they converted were allowed to observe the Confucian rites—the effect of the books and letters about China which they pub/ lished in Europe aroused so much interest among thinkers and writers that, in the words of Reichwein, 'Confucius became the patron Saint of eighteenth century Enlightenment'. This is surely one of the strangest paradoxes in history. If the Chinese took little or no interest in Europe and its culture, Europe found China's culture so attractive that for the greater part of a hundred years she regarded her with veneration, held up her institutions as a model, copied her arts and made wide use of her most important exports. Not that the Pontiff/Emperors of The Great Within nor their *literati* would have thought there was anything surprising in this. For them it was so natural as to have been inevitable. The Outer Barbarians, as soon as they came into contact with the superior civilization of the Celestial Empire—properly so called because it was the only Empire governed on cosmographical principles—had always copied its laws, its administration and its manners. Why not then also that tribe of barbarians, so/called the Red, which lived in Europe, a race more disreputable, and so more in need of enlightenment, than any in Asia? For of the disreputability of Europeans in general the Chinese continued to be convinced as if Ricci, Schall and Verbiest had never been. Even as late as 1724 the third Ch'ing Emperor, Yung Chêng, could write in an Edict, which was directed against his brothers and their acquaintances: 'There is not a depraved priest, physician, soothsayer, rowdy, actor or European, who is not of their gang.'

This attitude of absolute superiority, which had been bred out of their experiences in the past, was a symptom now of a fossilized intelligence, of a civilization without sap. But that

Europe was anxious to learn, could become enthusiastic over China, proved her civilization to be living and progressive.

This *volte-face* of a Europe which had naively set out to bring China into the Catholic fold is so curious that it requires illus-tration, even though the facts are fairly well known. Their repetition will at least serve to refresh our memory and enable us to draw certain conclusions.

To begin with, here is the Jesuits' opinion of the Emperor K'ang Hsi (1660-1722), written immediately after his death. 'This great Prince, whose demise we rightly lament, was not only admired by all the nations of Asia: his extraordinary merit and the glory of his reign have become known beyond the wide oceans which separate us from him and have attracted the attention of the whole of Europe. One may say, indeed, that he possessed to an altogether remarkable degree the art of ruling and that he united in himself all the qualities which go to make a great man and a Grand Monarch. His manner, his build, the set of his features, an air of majesty tempered with mildness and good nature, inspired in all who saw him affection and respect, and marked him at once as the master of one of the greatest empires in the world. He had a lofty intellect, an acumen which no subterfuge could delude, a happy memory for the smallest details, a firmness of spirit which no crisis could shake, a sense of justice and a solidity of judgment which guided him surely to sage decisions. Always calm and master of himself, he gave no clue to his secret thoughts, knowing supremely well how to hide his plans. Able to conceive of the grandest enterprises, he was no less capable of carrying them out. Far from depending for his information upon favourites or Ministers, he made himself directly acquainted with all the problems of his vast territories. Autocrat though he was, he never forgot justice and equity, his edicts being strictly in conformity with law and the honours he distributed almost always the reward of probity and merit. A calamity at once aroused his compassion; he would remit the revenues of whole provinces, open the reserves of grain and give liberally, even in his sympathy cancelling court festivities. He always considered himself the father of his people. On visiting the provinces he permitted even the poorest to approach and petition him. Though very wealthy he was frugal in his tastes, yet ready to spend lavishly in the public interest. Disliking luxury and the soft life, he used to pass some of the year in the mountains of Tartary, hunting big game and continually on horseback, though without neglecting the affairs of state. Multiple as were his activities he found time to cultivate the sciences and the arts.'[1]

This eulogy, a picture of the perfect Confucian ruler, is typical of the narratives which the Jesuits sent home from about the year 1670 onwards. The critical reader may want to know why they lauded in this way a mere pagan prince, whom they planned to lead captive to the steps of St. Peter's, after they had proved to him that his entire philosophy of life was erroneous. It seems that they were really dazzled by the Court of China, infinitely flattered at being accepted there, and that their conception of its conversion was not vulgar but intellectual, involving the union of the East and West under a common syncretic philosophy.

In addition to accounts of the greatness of the Ch'ing, the Jesuits began publishing in Europe translations of Chinese texts. In 1687 a rendering in Latin of the principal Confucian classics appeared in Paris, under the title *Confucius Sinarum Philosophus*, in which the sage was thus apostrophized: 'Sapientissimus et moralis philosophiae pariter ac politicae magister et oraculum.' This was only one of a great many such translations.

The learned world of Europe was astonished by the wisdom of the old Chinese master; and it found him eminently to its taste. Men had freed themselves from the limitations imposed by mediaeval theology and its scholastic metaphysics; they were tiring of the half-mythological speculations of the Renaissance; they had set their feet in a new rational world. The condition of human society and the structure of the state, these were the practical problems which they were trying to pose and solve.

[1] P. xxxii. *Lettres edifiantes et curieuses*. Vol. 16 of edition of 1781.

What was therefore their surprise at perceiving that two thousand years previously in China a philosopher had devoted his
whole attention almost precisely to what occupied them now.
The parallel was quite extraordinary. Like him, they aimed at
reconciling culture and religion, autocracy and justice, and
hoped to do so by positing virtue, in the sense of right behaviour, humanitarianism and so the happiness of all, as the
ethical basis of their system. They found this ethic in Christianity shorn of its dogmas, a Christianity hardly distinguish-
able from Deism. Confucianism seemed to them precisely such
a Deism. Their approach to Chinese thought differed from
that of the Jesuits in that it was the Society's ambition to blend
the revelation of Christ with its attendant dogmas into the
framework of Confucian behaviour. Christ's revelation would
provide an authoritative basis for that behaviour and give precise information about the shadowy God who lay behind it. It
would thus be possible for a Chinese to be both Christian and
Confucian, for the first was merely an amplification of the
second. The learned world of Europe, however, did not wish
revelation to be the reason why a man did a good act. He must
act well, not because the mystical tradition which the Church
had fostered enjoined this course, but because virtue was based
on right knowledge and right knowledge could be acquired by
the reasoning mind. This movement was wholly modern in
character; it was clearly connected with the great advance then
taking place in mathematics and the natural sciences. But it was
fundamentally irreconcilable with Catholic theology. How
strange, then, that it should have been the missionaries of the
Catholic Church who directed attention to Confucius, thereby
providing their opponents with an ally and a precedent!

Leibniz (1646–1716) made great use of Jesuit publications.
In a letter dated 1687 to the Landgrave Ernst of Hessen-Rhein-
fels he mentions 'the work of Confucius, the king of Chinese
philosophers, which has been published this year in Paris', and
makes it clear that he has read the book carefully. Two years
later he met Father Grimaldi, who had just returned from

China. As a result of a long correspondence with him, he published in 1697 his *Novissima Sinica*, in which he argued that though China had much to learn from Europe about mathematics and science, she had as much to tell Europe about government and morality. Just as Europe had sent missionaries who had given instruction in the first, so China should send hers to teach the second.

Holding such views it is not surprising to find that his metaphysics are tinged with Confucian ideas, his doctrine of Monads and of 'pre-established harmony' being more obviously related to Eastern than to Western philosophy.

If Leibniz was the first of a number of notable European men of letters to urge that the study and application of Confucian principles of conduct and government would be the saving of Europe, Voltaire (1694–1778) was the last. The most fervent Confucian might have composed the following from his *Essai sur les Mœurs* (1756), where he sums up the Master's place in history: 'Le temps le plus heureux et le plus respectable qui fut jamais sur la terre, fut celui où l'on suivait ses lois.' And in his play, *L'Orphelin de la Chine* (1755), the plot turns on the thesis, of which the Chinese were so fond, that as soon as Outer Barbarians come under the influence of Confucian culture they mend their evil ways and lead the moral life. That Voltaire should have been moved to demonstrate this would have seemed to the Chinese, had they bothered to acquaint themselves with barbarian literature, ample proof of his reputed attainments.

One cannot leave this matter of the indirect influence of the Jesuits of China on European thought without mentioning the name of Quesnay (1694–1774), for he was known as the European Confucius. It will be remembered that it was he who, after a study of the Chinese classics, formulated a political philosophy derived from them with the practical object of inducing the Monarchy in France to model itself upon the Imperial Government of China. He saw that the French government was heading for bankruptcy and revolution and believed that it could be reformed and saved if Louis XV should become an enlightened despot in the Chinese classic sense. His book, *Le Despotisme de la Chine* (1767), marks the zenith of Chinese influence in Europe.

It is a melancholy reflection that while at that date there was Western knowledge of moment to which China should have given her attention but did not, little in Confucianism was then of real value to Europe, though her thinkers gave up a great deal of their time to it. Quesnay's theories, though they had an influential backing at Court, even Louis XV himself dabbling in them, were largely nonsense. The French monarchy was doomed; Europe was advancing towards a new theory of government, democracy; she could derive no more than academic benefit from the study of Confucius.

Moreover, Europe was making two capital mistakes about China. In the first place, the Confucian theory as understood by the learned world of the West did not correspond with the actual state of China. The reader will know that for half a century before 1644 she was abominably governed by a clique of eunuchs. The ethics of Confucius might not have existed under the late Ming. The Ch'ing cleansed the stable, but they were foreigners, speaking a different language and maintaining them-selves on the throne by means of a large standing army quar-tered throughout the provinces. The second Ch'ing Emperor, K'ang Hsi, was, no doubt, a great man; as the description of him already quoted shows, he modelled himself on Confucian standards and aspired to be a real Son of Heaven, the link be-tween God and his people, the just man, the Philosopher King, who ruled by goodness. But in actual fact he was a conqueror, and his power and reputation depended on his armed might. The position of the Ch'ing was, indeed, precarious for the very reason that it was not a true Confucian government. The Chinese people were not satisfied; they were not happy; they were not obedient by conviction. Universal harmony did not prevail. This discordance between the theory and the facts was unperceived by European men of letters, though as the eighteenth century went on it gradually became clear to Europeans who had to do directly with China. More will be said of this in the next chapter.

The second mistake that Europe was making about China is less easy to explain, but it was equally important. Confucian-ism was only one of three native modes of thought. The other two were Mahayana Buddhism and Taoism. At the period we have been considering neither of these religious philosophies attracted any attention in the West. European scholars thought that they were mere pagan superstitions, confined to the lower orders. It is true that in seventeenth-century China they were not fashionable. Their rituals were popular and mixed with magic. This, however, was not of their essence. They had had a remarkable history. Many great thinkers had been Taoists and Mahayanists. A knowledge of them was essential for a full understanding of the Chinese scene. Chinese art was unintel-ligible without a study of them. And in the seventeenth and eighteenth centuries the true Chinese art was not understood in Europe.

One must always bear in mind that learned society in Europe built up its picture of China largely from missionary writings. It was a tremendous achievement for the Jesuits to have learned Chinese, translated the classics and presented that side of Chinese thought in such detail and with such scholarship. They had not the time to push their studies further. Nor did they conceive this to be necessary, for with their grasp of Con-fucianism they were equipped to deal with the ruling classes, and that was their policy. Moreover, even had they been able to discover the Mahayanist metaphysic and, say, the *Tao Tê Ching*, neither would have interested them. The age was scien-tific, and its thoughts were directed towards the plain sense of things. It felt no desire for a new vision of the absolute. If the Jesuits had written of Taoism and the Mahayana and trans-lated some of their texts, these would have met no demand. There was, moreover, a further point. It was at least arguable that a Chinese might be able to reconcile Confucianism with

Catholicism, and without abandoning the first adopt the second as its amplification. But neither a Mahayanist nor a Taoist could merge his beliefs in Catholic theology. If they were of a popular character, he had his own theology, his revelation, his saints and his way of salvation. If he were an esoterist, he had his vision of truth, to which Christian revelation, Catholic theology and its dogmas were wholly irrelevant. For Mahayanists and Taoists to become Catholics meant the complete abandonment of their own faiths. There was no bridge, no possible compromise. The Jesuits were well aware that the conversion of the Chinese multitude was an undertaking without end. That was a major reason why learned Europe was told nothing of the Mahayana or Taoism, and it was this lack of knowledge which accounted for the superficiality of their conception of Chinese art.

The rococo period in Europe which covered roughly the first half of the eighteenth century coincided with a passion among the upper class for certain kinds of Chinese objects of art. These were not works of major importance such as antique bronzes, specimens of the work of the great calligraphists, sculpture of the Wei and T'ang dynasties, nor paintings of the T'ang and Sung and their porcelains. The Chinese themselves always treasured such things, but what eighteenth century Europe admired were porcelains of the Ch'ing, Canton lacquer, cabinets, wall-papers, cloisonné and embroideries. The Jesuits had written home about these kind of objects, particularly about porcelain. During the seventeenth and eighteenth centuries great quantities of them were imported along with tea and silk. It was found that by a curious chance they fitted into the rococo and enhanced the effect of that style, making it more amusing, ingenious, delicate and luxurious. They even harmonized with the music of Mozart.

The consequence was that polite society became interested in China at the same time as did the men of letters, but for different reasons. Ladies of quality, who might not have read a line of Confucius, were enthusiastic in filling their drawing-rooms with porcelain. As the demand for Chinese decorative objects exceeded the supply, the whole of Europe proceeded to copy them. German and Dutch glazed wares were made to resemble Ch'ing porcelains. In France the famous Martin made lac-quered cabinets as good as any you could buy in Canton. Masters like Watteau did not think it beneath them to adapt Chinese designs in their drawings and prints. Sedan chairs became the rage. In 1707 the Duchess of Namur was carried in her sedan by relays of French 'coolies' from Paris to her château at Neufchâtel, a distance of one hundred and thirty miles.

All this and a great deal more—shadow plays, gold-fish, masques in Chinese costume, gardens, pavilions, tea in K'ang Hsi cups—had the effect of depicting China as a delicate, flowery, coloured land, where the upper classes were exqui-sitely refined, where the lower classes knew their place, and where there was music and parasols and birds and chrysan-themums—and Confucius in the background.

This misunderstanding, supported by the more learned mistake that the Celestial government was the best in the world, was sufficient to give Europe an erroneous idea of China.

One should beware of thinking, however, that eighteenth-century Europe wrongly admired Confucianism and certain Chinese decorative objects. On the contrary, she exhibited in-telligence and taste. Confucianism was one of the great philo-sophies of the world; Ch'ing porcelain, cloisonné and lacquer still delight us and, though we know now that the best Chinese art is not delicate, charming and refined but visionary and austere, we still pay very large sums for what our ancestors of the Rococo admired. The mistake was only in taking the part for the whole and in turning China into a masquerade and believing that to be the reality.

But fashion changes, dreams dissolve. Before the end of the eighteenth century Europe began to see China in a less favour-able light. Europeans became irritated at what had once amused and impressed them. Picturesque China, Confucian China, became China the tiresome and, at last, China the impossible. On her side, China had never seen Europe in a favourable light. She had consistently held her inhabitants to be un-civilized. So when Europe attacked her, it was no surprise. The Red Barbarians had always been suspect.

PART III

# The Ruin of the Great Ch'ing

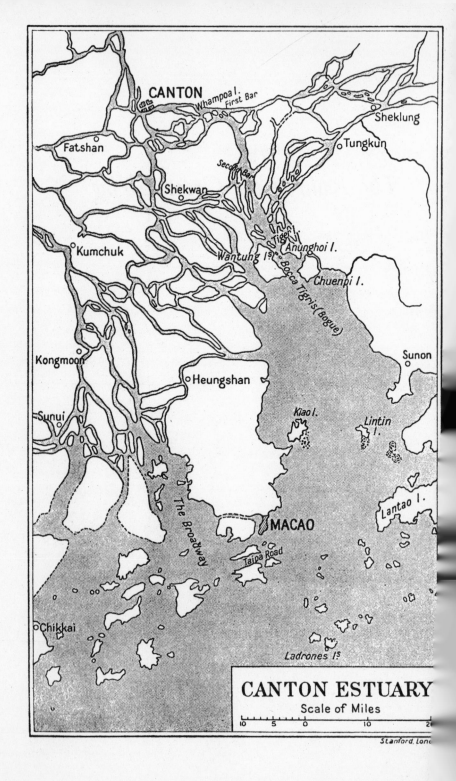

CANTON

Whampoa I.
First Bar

Sheklung

Fatshan

Tungkun

Second Bar

Shekwan

Tiger I.

Anunghoi I.

Wantung Is.

Kumchuk

Bocca Tigris (Bogue)

Chuenpi I.

Sunon

Kongmoon

Heungshan

Kiao I.

Lintin I.

Sunui

The Broadway

MACAO

Lantao I.

Taipa Road

Chikkai

Ladrones Is.

## CANTON ESTUARY
### Scale of Miles

10    5    0         10        20

Stanford, Lond

# I

# Captain Weddell jostles them at Canton

We must now take a new stance and examine the picture from a further angle. In Part I we were inside the Chinese system; in Part II we observed a certain interaction between it and the outside; here in Part III we shall see this interaction producing a clash.

The Chinese conceived their country as a world state at the head of which was the Son of Heaven. The nations outside had not to be conquered; as soon as they heard of China they became dazzled, sent envoys and presents and acknowledged her overlordship.

Neither the Portuguese nor the Dutch succeeded in modify-ing this view. The Jesuits, who sought to reverse it by its opposite, failed. It was the English who reduced it to an absurdity.

The English appeared in China seven years before the fall of the Ming dynasty. This, their first visit, was short but revealing. All the elements of what was to happen later were demon-strated in the course of it.

In 1635 Charles I found himself in need of money, as did a favourite of his, Endymion Porter. Porter suggested a gamble in the East India trade. The Crown had already granted a mono-poly of that trade to the East India Company, but the royal shares were paying no dividends. A certain Sir William Courteen was anxious to fit out a rival venture. Porter induced the King to sanction this, though to sanction a rival company was contrary to the terms of monopoly already granted to the East India Company.

Courteen got together four ships and two pinnaces and placed in command of them a Captain John Weddell, who had formerly been employed by the East India Company and knew the Eastern seas. Not only did Charles authorize the venture and take shares in it to the amount of ten thousand pounds, but he issued a Royal Commission to Weddell and several letters of Instructions by virtue of which the Captain was empowered to exercise martial law, to take prizes in certain circumstances, and to fly the Union Flag at his mast-head. He was to proceed first to Goa, the capital of Portuguese India. The Viceroy of that place had in January 1635 entered into an agreement called a 'Truce and Free Trade to China' with the East India Company. Weddell was to draw his attention to this and claim that it entitled the Courteen Association to Portuguese help at Macao in China. It was calculated that the East India Company would only raise technical objections as it had not extended its operations to Chinese waters.[1]

Captain Weddell left the Downs on April 14, 1636, and on October 7 arrived at Goa. No-one seemed very pleased to see him. Methwold, the President of the East India Company, whose headquarters was at Surat, a little way up the coast, wrote to say that the Association would be the ruin of the Company. Dom Antonio Telles de Menezes, the Viceroy, though he welcomed the English with 'the best peale of Ordnance that I ever yett heard', as Peter Mundy, the chronicler of the voyage, writes, was not inclined to implement the 'Truce and Free Trade in China'—it was his predecessor who had signed it—and, in consequence, Weddell left for Macao without having received any letter of recommendation from him to the Portuguese Viceroy of that place.

He arrived there on June 27, 1637, now with three ships, the *Dragon*, the *Catherine* and the *Sun*, and one pinnace, the *Anne*, the *Dragon* being flagship. The ships were armed merchant-

[1] One ship, the *London*, had been sent in 1635, but did no trade.

men, hardly inferior to the frigates of the period. Mundy, with the merchants, Nathaniel Mountney and a Mr. Robinson, who could talk Portuguese, was despatched ashore to deliver Charles's letter to the Viceroy, Dom Manoel da Camara de Noronha, a gentleman with a very grand name, but, it was alleged, a Eurasian by birth and the son of a tinker. This may be a libel, but illustrates the low opinion in which the Portuguese were held by the English. Charles addressed him as 'Captain of the Fortress of my Brother of Spain',[1] reminded him of the agreement made at Goa in January 1635, and asked him to assist his servants to open trade. Weddell also sent a covering letter wherein, after making out that the Viceroy of Goa had been more obliging than was actually the case, he declared: 'We shall await here your Excellency's answer to my Master's letter, and are at your Excellency's orders, whose reply I await, as also your Excellency's instructions how I am to act. I am in good health and hope that your Excellency enjoys the same.'

The Viceroy's reply discloses the true facts of a delicate situation. Writing to Weddell he says: 'Would that my power to serve your Worship were equal to my desire to do so.' He then points out that he has received no orders either from Spain or Goa to assist the English to share in the China trade, and adds that even had he such authorization he could do very little because the Chinese, on whose goodwill he entirely depended, were wholly opposed to additional foreign traders entering their ports.

All this was incontrovertible. The city of Macao existed on sufferance. The Canton authorities, within whose jurisdiction it lay, were extremely strict. But the English did not believe this. They took it to be merely jealousy on the part of the Portuguese. It seemed incredible that they could be afraid of the Chinese, for the English at that date were afraid of nobody. When the Port Officer came on board some days later with provisions, Weddell thought him a lying rogue when he spoke of his difficulties in the face of Chinese opposition. 'He began to unfold

[1] Portugal was under the Spanish Crown from 1580 to 1640.

a tedious lamentable discourse, as false as prolix, of their miser-able subjection to the Chineses,' who would penalize them heavily, he said, if they gave the English any facilities.

For a fortnight Weddell waited in Taipa road, a few miles from Macao, when being now certain that the Portuguese would do nothing to put him in touch with the Canton government, nor were able themselves to supply him with Chinese merchandise, he decided to go up the river to Canton and find out personally what could be done. As a first step he sent his pinnace to explore. Canton is about eighty miles inland from Macao. As the map on page 192 shows, the way is up the estuary past Lintin Island to the Bocca Tigris, often called the Bogue, the entrance to the Canton River. Ten miles further is the Second Bar, then, ten miles again, the First Bar, which is fifteen miles short of the city. The pinnace sur-veyed the river as far as the First Bar and returned on July 22 to report.

Robinson and Mountney, who were on her, stated that after trying in vain to induce certain boatmen whom they met to pilot them to the city, they were stopped by a fleet of twenty junks commanded by a high official. The Chinese had on board a few negroes, fugitives from the Portuguese, and these, acting as interpreters, asked them roughly what they meant by coming up the river without permission. Robinson replied that they only wanted to trade, and would like to get into com-munication with the port authorities to that end. The Chinese at this seemed more affable and invited Robinson and Mount-ney to board a junk and go with them to Canton. The pinnace must anchor where she lay, because they could not allow an armed ship to approach any closer. The two Englishmen agreed, but when the junks reached the First Bar, orders were received from Canton that they were to return to their pinnace. If they wanted to trade, they should put in a petition through the local authorities at Macao. The Chinese were polite, but it was clear they regarded the strangers as doubtful characters, probably pirates.

On receiving this report, Captain Weddell made further efforts to persuade the Viceroy of Macao to help, but on July 27 he was told by some merchants sent by him that it was hopeless to expect the Chinese to permit any nation except the Portu-guese to trade in their ports. In the circumstances the Viceroy trusted that he would go away. 'Butt I conceave', writes Mundy, 'that they kept the Maine cause of all to themselves, which was thatt our Comming in Would quickly eatt them out of all trade.'

Convinced that nothing but Portuguese jealousy lay between him and a lucrative trade, and that if he could explain his King's motives for sending him out to the head authorities in Canton all would be well, Weddell resolved to take his ship into the river. So on July 29 they weighed from Taipa road and stood up towards the Bogue, which was said to be fortified.

On the 30th, whilst they were riding to the eastward of Macao, ten sail of China junks came and hovered about them. They had been warned that the Chinese might attempt to send down fire-ships and took certain precautions. 'Other hurt from them wee feared nott, were they 10 tymes as many,' says Mundy truculently.

On August 1, near the Nine Isles, a Chinese officer went aboard the *Dragon* and desired Weddell to anchor until advices were received from Canton. He refused and continued towards the Bogue, reaching Chuen-pi Point at its entrance the following day. But the wind and currents were adverse and he could not make the river. On the 4th forty sail appeared and surrounded him, and he was again told to anchor. This time he did so, and 'kept especiall good watch thatt Nightt, not knowing as yett how to trust them'.

Our Captain, of course, knew nothing of China, its laws and customs. But he believed that as his objects were reasonable, the representatives of her government would meet him fairly when they understood what he wanted. If the real situation was not plain to him, it is clear enough to us. Under standing orders no foreign ship might enter the Canton river without special authorization from the Council. The officials concerned had reported Weddell's numbers, his cannon and alleged wants, and had been directed to hold him up, for he looked like a pirate. They should get rid of him by address, if possible, but if not, by force.

On August 6 a number of them came aboard and he explained his intentions. For answer he was desired to anchor at the mouth of the river near the Anung-hoi forts on the eastern bank, pending orders from Canton which were alleged to be on the way. On the opposite side of the river were the Wantong forts situated on two islands. While he lay where he had been ordered, he noticed great activity in the Anung-hoi forts, batteries being installed and manned and flags run up. 'They fell to work about the Castle,' he writes in a letter, 'and planted by night 44 peeces of Ordinance upon it. . . . The Ordinance they tooke out of the Junkes and they being all mounted in the Castle, the Junkes went farther up into the river supposinge the Castle sufficient to keep us from goeinge further.'

Apparently the authorities had allowed the forts guarding the entry to the river to fall into disuse. Under threat of a possible pirate fleet they hurriedly armed them. When we remember the condition of the metropolitan fortifications and armies in this year of 1637, when Li was making his preparations to fall upon Peking, we need not be surprised that in the far south the military administration was even more lax.

For three days Weddell waited in the Bogue for the instructions which were represented as coming from Canton. He knew that he was giving the Chinese an opportunity to prepare measures against him, but as his orders from the King, his master, were to open trade by agreement, he was loath to use force. Not till he were attacked or until his ships were gravely endangered would he be justified in departing from those orders. But he was not naturally a patient man. To Methwold, who at Goa had written to him complaining, civilly enough, of his coming in at the head of a rival venture, he had sent a scorching reply in the tumbling manner of the seventeenth century: 'Wee are

MING MEN-OF-WAR JUNKS
*From a drawing by Mundy*

—

not taken with a few flashes and peremptory jeering menaces. ... Be assured that if ever you attempt the least underhand injury ... (which indeed wee feare not) ... eyther you or yours shall answer it to no mercenary man.' And he had done some fighting, for when employed by the East India Company he had been in command in 1622 at the taking of Ormuz, the Portuguese fortress guarding the entrance to the Persian Gulf. That had been a strong fort, and he now eyed with disdain the belated efforts of the Chinese to fortify the Bogue. He was fifty-four years of age, 'a gentleman of valour and resolution', as his late employers, the East India Company, had reported in 1634. His address was Ratcliffe in the County of Middlesex. As for his crew, their fathers had sailed with Drake and Hawkins.

On August 9 he sent ashore a party to enquire whether orders to let him trade had not arrived, and receiving an unsatisfactory reply decided to clear for action. 'Wee Fitted our selves as well for offence as Defence, Displaying our bloudy ensignes on our poopes.' This ensign was the Flag of Defiance used from the thirteenth to the nineteenth centuries as a signal to engage and to give no quarter. The Union Flag also was flown at the main top and boarding nets (or what corresponded to them at that date) were stretched over the waist.

The Chinese read these signs as menacing, and immediately sent a messenger to beg Weddell to wait six days more and to promise him provisions, of which he stood in great need. Choking down his irritation he agreed, but during the next few days got very little food from shore.

On the 12th he sent his barge to take soundings under the fort of Anung-hoi in case he should require to bring his ships close in. While so engaged, the Chinese fired on her three times with cannon, the balls flying over or short. 'Hereupon', wrote Weddell, 'I Called all the Commanders and merchants together and demaunded their opinions what was beste to be done; in reguard wee found nothinge but delayes and, that there was noe hopes of anie trade by faire meanes, we were all of opinion to laye all our shippes as neere the walls of the Castle as wee Could well Come and to batter it about their eares. Soe wee waied presentlie with the flood and with our shipps an/cored within musquett shott of the Castle.' The 'bloudy Ensign' was again hoisted and the engagement began. Weddell had his three ships and the pinnace. Before he could bring his cannon to bear, the Chinese fired thirteen shots, 'yett not one that touched soe much as hull or rope, until one which cutt the maine halliards of the *Dragon*, a little abuove Man height, The Admiral then walking on the halff Decke'.

The Chinese gunnery was extremely bad, ridiculously so, considering the range. Their powder was indifferent, for some of the balls 'Dropte downe outt off the Mouth of the peece close under the walls'. There seemed to be no gun/laying, the cannon being touched off as they lay in the embrasures. When the English ships had swung on the flood into position, they opened fire with their broadsides, 'with sound of Drummes and trumpetts,' to such effect that the Chinese could not serve their guns. The cannonade lasted half an hour, when it was noticed that one company of Chinese soldiers began to desert the fort. This was the right moment for an assault. A strong landing/party pulled ashore. The remainder of the Chinese garrison then turned and fled. 'Our people beeing landed and finding the gates open', says Mundy, 'entred the Fort, tooke Downe the China Flagge, hung it over the wall and thereon advanced our Kings coullours.' Later they transported thirty/five of the Chinese cannon on board, defaced the battlements and burnt the houses within. Mundy, who had never been in a battle before on land or sea, was astonished at the ease with which the place was taken. There was neither difficulty nor danger, the exploit 'rather shewing the Manner than Deserving the Name of the taking of a Fort'.

Such was the action fought by Charles I against the Ming. But Weddell's troubles were far from over. As Mundy wrote, summing up the engagement: 'In Conclusion, the peace is broken and Now more than ever it behooves us to stand uppon our guard.'

'The Allarum', says Weddell, 'flew up to Canton which is as farre distant as London bridge is to Eriff.' He was in an awkward situation for a man who wanted to secure dividends for his Sovereign. What was to be done next? He decided to write to the authorities and reiterate that his sole desire was free trade. Happening to capture two junks on the following day, he sent some of their people with a letter.

Meanwhile provisions were running short. Many men had scurvy and badly needed fresh food. Robinson was ordered ashore with seven musketeers to see what he could buy. About a mile inland he took up his position in the porch of a pagoda. Apparently the inhabitants were not afraid to do business, or perhaps they were so frightened that they dared not refuse. Whatever was the fact, fowls and pigs were offered, but while Robinson was paying for these, he suddenly saw a force of about 350 Chinese, armed with swords, lances and shields, advancing upon him. 'And beinge approached very neare, they began to rayse a confused shoute after the manner of the Irish hubbub.' The recent fighting in Ireland had given the English much experience of the curious war-cry of her inhabitants.

Robinson felt himself to be in a tight corner. Seven men, armed with breech-loading fire-locks, and a mile from their boats, can only save themselves from the assault of 350 swords-men by a disciplined retreat. The Chinese tried to cut them off, but the musketeers, divided into two companies of three and four, discharged their weapons alternately, each falling back under cover of the other's fire, until they reached the waterside. Weddell, who had perceived their danger, sent reinforcements and they were able to drive off the Chinese, return to the pagoda, collect the provisions they had bought and get them on board. They lost no-one, but some of the Chinese were killed or wounded. Yet for peaceful traders this second engage-ment was a further misfortune. It was one more act of violence to be explained.

There is no reason to suppose that the local officials were puzzled by Weddell's behaviour. They had had to do over years with all sorts of pirates, for the seas were full of them. Pirates from the far West, so their experience went, generally put about some story of trade in order to effect an entry. They might even pay the country people for provisions, the more rapidly to secure them. They were not always, of course, pirates *de carrière*; in the present case Weddell might be some sort of a rough adventurer who for his own barbarian purposes wanted a cargo of this or that and, when told that China did not trade with such persons as he, had turned nasty and shown fight. The usual course was to get rid of such intruders as quietly as possible. Accordingly they sent down a junior official who knew Portuguese with instructions to use diplo-macy. The man they selected for this job was at one time employed in Macao, where he had been converted by the Jesuits and baptized as Pablo Noretti, which name, instead of his Chinese name, he gave when with a flag of truce he boarded the *Dragon*.

Weddell entertained him and explained that he had been forced into a violent course by the unwarranted opposition of the authorities. All he wanted was fair trade. Noretti did not tell him that the officials responsible had acted under standing orders, and that there was no possibility of his being granted leave to trade. On the contrary, he pretended that if he returned the guns taken from the fort, the Mandarins would be sure to grant all his requests, though, of course, he would have to pay the usual duties. Weddell was deceived by this apparently reasonable proposition, and so was induced to return the cannon.

Noretti seems to have held the rank of Assistant Sub-Prefect and to have been attached to the military department of the Prefecture. Certain officers of higher rank awaited him on shore close by, and he was seen to rejoin them. The party then left to make their report. That same night he returned in a junk and stated that he had authority 'to carry upp such as should be appointed to Canton, there to tender a petition and to con-clude farther upon the manner of our future proceedings'. He also alleged that it would give him great pleasure to forward their case with what influence he possessed, for he would like to see them cut out the Portuguese, who had treated him badly during his employ at Macao. What he said was so convincing and reassuring that Weddell gladly sent Mountney and Robinson along with him. But he was playing a double game, as will appear.

On August 18 the two merchants had audience in Canton with the military commander, to whom they submitted a petition to be allowed to trade. Noretti acted as interpreter, and they understood from him that the Tsungping, as the officer was called, would accede to their request. A letter was later handed to them which on their return to the ships Noretti translated as the required permission. The letter also empowered him, he said, to assist them in every way. Not until some considerable time later did they discover its real meaning, which was exactly the opposite to what had been told them.

It had been issued jointly by the military and marine departments of the government of Canton, and began by a recital of the facts: four ships manned by Red Barbarians had approached the Bogue forts and demanded passage; this was refused by the authorities concerned, and the Barbarians were told to return from whence they came; but they had adopted a threatening attitude and attempted to force trade. The letter then admonished and warned them in these terms: 'You have shown great effrontery by daring to force trade upon us. On receipt of this letter you will immediately weigh anchor and put out to sea. If you have the boldness to damage so much as a blade of grass or a chip of wood, the military and naval forces of this Government will make an end of you.'

Why did Noretti conceal the real purport of this letter? The answer throws additional light on the corruption of the Ming bureaucracy. He considered there was an opportunity of making money out of the English. He and his confederates—who they were and whether senior officials were also involved is not clear—would secretly arrange for them to get some trade. A large squeeze ought to be possible. To be broker in a case where the buyer does not know and cannot find out the correct market price is the happiest of chances.

Weddell was entirely ignorant of this conspiracy. On August 21, when Noretti gave him the fanciful translation, he believed that he was authorized by the Government of Canton to direct his merchants to explore the market. Accordingly on the 24th he sent back to Canton Mountney, Robinson and John Mountney, the former's younger brother, with 22,000 reals. They were smuggled into the city by Noretti disguised as Chinese, for Noretti, of course, had to keep their arrival secret. Officially the fleet was supposed to have sailed. It had dropped down from the Bogue by agreement with Noretti and was anchored at the mouth of the estuary, eighty miles from Canton.

Noretti first directed the merchants, who were not allowed to leave their lodgings, to pay 10,000 reals in advance for customs dues, a sum which presumably went into the pockets of himself and his friends, as it could not have appeared in the official books. He then procured them eighty tons of sugar, some ginger and silk, so as to encourage them to lay out more money. Meanwhile the fleet, threatened by a typhoon in the lower waters of the estuary, moved up again to the Bogue, though forbidden to do so, and passing through it anchored at Tiger Island, which is three miles inside the river. This movement of the fleet was too public for Noretti's liking, and he seems to have asked the merchants to urge Weddell to go down again. But he refused.

By September 5 some of the goods bought began to arrive by junk and were loaded on the ships. Noretti sent word they would have their full cargoes within a month. It was about this time that the Portuguese of Macao heard of what was going on. They became seriously alarmed, feeling sure that if the Canton Government should discover the truth and that its orders had been disobeyed, it would suspect them of complicity and penalize their trade. They therefore addressed Weddell, begging him to go. 'We hope that your Worships will accede to our friendly request, and with all justice we ask you to put to sea with your ships, as your presence is a great prejudice to this city. . . . We beg you earnestly to deliver us from the trouble you have brought upon us.'

The Captain ascribed this attitude wholly to jealousy and wrote a violent reply in Portuguese. It began: 'Having received your offensive letter, accompanied by a formal but worthless protest, we have concluded with astonishment that you consider us so despicable, that you appear to think your letter, full of groundless threats, will induce us to abandon an undertaking both profitable and certain. . . . This land, as you yourself acknowledge, is not yours, but the King of China's. Why then should we wait for license from the King of Castile or his petty Viceroys in these parts?' The Captain then threatened to bombard Macao, and concludes: 'We are too occupied at present to answer your vulgar letter more at length.'

Weddell, of course, was able to take this high line, because he believed he had secured the ear of the Canton Government and was well on the road to fame and fortune. That very day he entrusted Noretti with a further ten thousand pieces of eight. In fact, as we are aware, his situation was extremely delicate. He was in league, though without his knowledge, with a disreputable Mandarin to obtain goods contrary to the orders of the Government. It was only necessary for the Portuguese to lodge information against him in the proper quarter for all his plans to go awry. The Canton Government would have power to bring the strongest pressure, for his chief merchants were on shore and a large sum of his money was out. Had he been aware of his danger, no doubt his letter to the Viceroy of Macao would have been phrased more discreetly.

As it was, the truth did get out and the probability is that the Portuguese made sure that it did. The departments concerned instituted enquiries, and confirmed that the English merchants were hidden in Canton and that the ships were anchored at Tiger Island. They were furious and decided on drastic action.

What happened very nearly was the end of Weddell and his venture. On Sunday, September 10, the ebb was due to set down at 2 a.m. at Tiger Island. There was no moon that night. The four ships rode in line one behind the other, the pinnace, *Anne,* being at the north end, and behind her the *Catherine,* the *Sun* and the *Dragon,* in that order. When the flood ceased, they lay a moment in the slack water and then began slowly to swing athwart the river. At this moment the watch on the *Anne* saw several large junks under sail, close to their bows. They hailed them, got no answer, but though suspicious did not fire, thinking they might be bringing them cargo. The junks then seemed to steer down on the *Catherine,* which opened on them. At that instant three of the junks burst into flames and began to drift with the ebb upon the three English vessels. Their crews were observed to have jumped overboard. The greatest of all dangers that can threaten wooden ships at anchor are fire-boats, and these were fire-boats. As Mundy says, it was 'Not now tyme to looke on', and the *Dragon* and her consorts cut or slipped their cables. The ebb, having only just begun, was running gently, and the fire-boats, therefore, approached at a slow pace. Weddell and his Captains had time to set some sail. A light breeze was blowing off shore and they steered into it. So close were the fire-boats, however, that they would have fouled some of his ships, had not the seamen quickly launched the lifeboats and towed them a little off their course. There was also the help of a slight tidal set outwards, owing to the configuration of the land at that place. 'They all Drave withoutt us,' says Mundy. 'The Fire was vehementt. Balles of wylde fire, Rocketts and Fire-arrows Flew thicke as they passed us, Butt God bee praised, not one of us all was toutched. . . . Great and sodaine was the amasement and affrightt att such a tyme of the Nightt to see such a Fearffull Daunger redy to Destroy us. The Fire was very high and violentt and the brightness therof soe great in that Darcke nightt thatt the hills reflected lightt. The Confused Noise was Noe lesse, as well of the Marriners on the one side crying and calling to their Fellowes about the shippes, worcking with their heedlesse hasty runinge on the Deckes, as allsoe of the Crackling of the burnt Bamboes, whizzing of the rocketts, Fireworckes etts: Frome the Fiered Flaming Junckes. . . . I Doe somwhatt enlarge, bee´ cause it is the first fire Daunger that ever yett have seene my selff in.'

Next morning, when they had somewhat recovered them´ selves, they began to wonder what was the explanation. They had felt particularly happy and secure. Could it be that the Chinese had tried to take revenge for the bombardment of the Bogue fort? But if so, why had the merchants been allowed to go to Canton and begin to trade? Or had the Portuguese engineered the attack? But the fire´boats were manned by Chinese and came from the direction of Canton. One thing seemed fairly certain. Noretti must be in it. There must be some double dealing. They had captured one Chinese, having speared him with a pike when he was swimming away from a fire´boat. While the surgeons were dressing his wound, he said something, but no´one could interpret it. But later, when they put him in irons, he seems to have been able to explain that it was the Chinese authorities who had engaged him to do the work. If the Chinese had turned against them, Weddell saw his position was very weak. They must already have seized his merchants and the large sums of money he had sent with them. Could he rescue them from Canton itself? It was impossible. But he must do something. He had had no news from them for eight days.

Feeling that the anchorage at Tiger Island exposed him to a second attempt by fire´boats, he fell down the nine miles to the Bogue and anchored beside the empty Anung´hoi fort. There a runaway Portuguese slave, a half´caste, came to him. He told a long story, which they did not know whether to believe, that the attack on them had no doubt been made under orders of the Government of Canton, but that the Chinese had been insti´ gated thereto by a deputation from Macao, the Portuguese brib´ ing right and left and making promises to pay higher customs duties if the English were driven off. He added that the Govern-ment was preparing fresh fire-boats and had called up a num-ber of Fuhkienese seamen, reputed the most resolute on the coast, who would attack them in a fleet of junks well armed with cannon.

This information was no doubt generally true, but it prob-ably exaggerated the influence of the Portuguese. As we know (though Weddell did not as yet), the Government had from the first threatened to destroy the English ships unless they departed at once. The Portuguese by the use of their money were at most able to hasten the Chinese to put that threat into execution.

When Weddell and his captains had weighed all the facts available to them, they came to the conclusion that it would be useless to warn the Portuguese that if they did not help to rescue the merchants Macao would be bombarded. The right course was to frighten the Chinese. The ease with which the Bogue fort had been taken showed how unready they were. There was no proper defence of the Canton river, not a defence which could meet English armed merchantmen. Their men-of-war junks were so unhandy, their gun-laying so bad, that even a fleet of them was no match for Weddell's four ships. No doubt his position was precarious. His provisions were short, he could not force his way into Canton, he might be worsted by guile. The only course, it was decided, was to make a demonstration, burn villages, sink boats, make captures, and, when the Chinese were thoroughly tired of them, say they would go away quietly provided the merchants and their money were restored.

This reading of the Chinese character was sound, or rather a true estimation of the Chinese bureaucracy in its decay. It was then, and in later years it remained, possible to intimidate Man-darins by threatening to cause such an uproar that their seniors in the official hierarchy would hear of it and make enquiry. There was nothing which a corrupt Mandarin feared more than an enquiry by his superiors, because he had much to conceal, had enemies who would take such an opportunity to petition against him and because his superior, also being corrupt, would welcome every opportunity to harm him in order to extort money. These observations are, of course, true of all corrupt bureaucracies. Though Weddell was a sea-captain, he seems to have been aware of this, for Mundy, under the date of September 18, noting on the decision taken by the Captain, says: 'Our best course was held to Doe all the spoile wee could unto the Chinois, thatt complaint Mightt come to the higher powers.'

Accordingly that very night some of the boats, well manned and provided, were sent away. Before dawn they had burned five junks and a small town, captured one man and seized thirty pigs. During the following days they burnt a large junk, killed eight persons on land and blew up the walls of Anung-hoi Fort, which had remained empty since the first attack upon it. During these operations they lost one man only, the quartermaster of the *Sun*, Christopher Barker.

A short letter now arrived from the two Mountneys in Canton to the effect that they were confined in their lodging, feared that they might be imprisoned any day, and had lost sight of their money. Robinson was not with them. They asked Weddell to sail up to Canton and threaten the city. But this course he considered too dangerous. Canton was three times as large as London.

The full story of what had happened to the merchants was known later. It will be recalled that August 28 was the day they entered Canton in disguise. On August 30 the fleet moved to Tiger Island. A week or so later the Government became cognisant of both these facts. On September 10 it sent the fire-boats against the fleet, and at the same time arrested Robinson and kept him on a junk. The other two were not arrested, but a guard was put on their lodging, no-one was allowed in or out, and provisions were cut off. The owner of the lodging and his son were taken to prison in chains and Noretti was arrested, and they 'so bebosted that poore dogge, that they have scarce left him worth his skin'. For the following three days the

Mountneys sustained themselves with biscuit and spirits. They were in great anxiety, having no idea what had angered the Government. As far as they were aware, it had sanctioned their visit and had appointed Noretti to act as their broker and inter-preter. They were unable to ascertain the reason for its change of attitude. On September 14 they became desperate and decided to cut their way down to the shore, seize a boat and try to reach the ships. They had swords and pistols, and they planned to set fire to the house and to make a rush from it as the flames spread and threw the quarter into confusion. They had begun to kindle the fire with a burning glass when a guard saw them. He be-came agitated and begged them to do nothing rash until he had summoned the Mandarin in charge. They agreed to desist for the moment and soon that official hurried to the house. To him they complained violently of injustice and swore that if there were no redress they would fire the town and sell their lives dearly.

The Mandarin was aware that the fire-boats four days pre-viously had failed in their purpose and that Weddell was furiously ravaging the river. In the circumstances he deemed it prudent to use diplomacy. In any case he desired to avoid a disturbance, for which, if it occurred, he would certainly be blamed. He therefore assumed a mild air, assured them they had nothing whatever to fear, and directed that the gates of the courtyard be unlocked. On his departure, however, the merchants perceived that the guard was there as before and that no food was allowed to pass in. So hungry did they become that the younger Mountney went to the gate and with a drawn sword in one hand and money in the other obliged those on their way from market to sell him provisions.

The result of Weddell's depredations in the river was as he had hoped. The Canton authorities decided to compromise. Their object in this was to get rid of him and his ships as quickly as possible, so that the news of his ravages and of his destruction of the Bogue forts—or rather the only Bogue fort which was armed and had resisted his passage—should not be

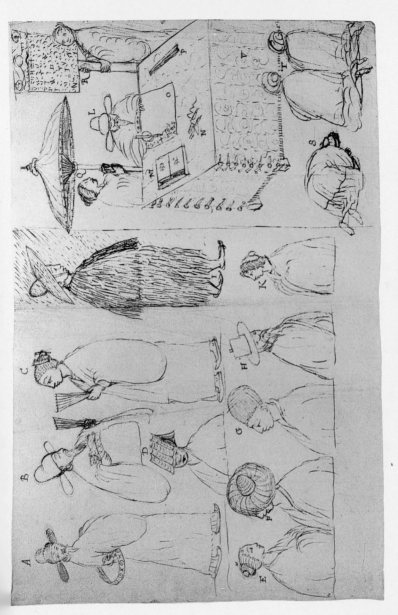

MING TYPES AT CANTON:
A MAGISTRATE AT WORK

*From a drawing by Mundy*

carried to the capital, when the neglect of their duty which would thus be apparent might have sufficed to lose them their appointments. They accordingly wrote him a letter stating that if he undertook to depart and never to return, his merchants would be sent down, his moneys, which had been impounded, would be released and arrangements made to provide him with cargoes.

At the moment he was at Lintin, the island anchorage in the estuary fifteen miles from Macao, where he had gone in ignor-ance that the Chinese were giving in and with the intention of bringing pressure on the Portuguese to help him, a course which he had first dismissed as unlikely to be profitable. From there he wrote a letter dated September 27 to the Viceroy, Dom Domingos da Camara, accusing him and his people of treachery, to which he received an immediate and civil reply that a Jesuit called Father Bartholomeo de Reboredo would wait on him forthwith and explain everything. Needless to say the sea-captain was no match for the Jesuit Father, who convinced him without difficulty that the Portuguese had had nothing what-ever to do with the detention of the merchants. That they were not primarily responsible was, of course, true, but there can be no doubt they saw to it that Noretti and his confederates were exposed.

On September 30 there occurred an episode, which throws so much light on the outlook of Weddell and his crews that it cannot be omitted. A great Spanish galleon sailed into the estuary and anchored in the road beside them. This galleon was the treasure ship which crossed the Pacific once a year from Acapulco in New Spain or Mexico to Manila in the Philippines. It had come to Macao to load a cargo of silk pre-paratory to returning to Acapulco and had a quantity of money on board. Spain and Portugal were at the time, as has been stated, both subject to the same Crown, and England was at war with neither, but the presence of the galleon so whetted the appetite of these sons of Drake's men that they debated whether to seize her or not. After some discussion it was decided to spare her because Weddell feared that her seizure would embarrass him too much in his negotiations for the return of his merchants, both with the Chinese and the Portuguese. This decision, notes Mundy, 'bredd great Murmuring in our whole Fleete amongst the Commonalty'. The galleon had come in before dawn, and it is amusing to note that when it was light enough for her Captain to see the English ships, he weighed immediately and sought a safer road. Small wonder that the old settled Government of China regarded Weddell as little better than a pirate.

A few days after this episode representatives of the Government got in touch with him and delivered their offer. On October 9 he agreed to the compromise, writing that if the authorities handed over his merchants and the money, which amounted altogether to sixty thousand reals (or in lieu of the money its equivalent in goods) he would depart peacefully and never return.

The Government kept scrupulously to their side of the bargain. On November 28 the merchants returned safely, having been able to spend the whole of the sixty thousand reals on a cargo of sugar and ginger, with a little silk and porcelain. It is true that Weddell had a further eighty thousand reals of the Courteen trading capital, which he could not use; moreover, he would have to report to Charles I a failure to open a trade with China. But on the whole he had not done so badly. If the defences of Canton had been kept in sufficient repair to implement the Imperial policy of excluding foreign merchants, he would have been turned back, either by the forts or the river police. Further, had he understood the true purport of the first letter from the Military and Marine Departments, he would hardly have dared to send his merchants into Canton. Indeed, he could not have done so, unless Noretti had planned to line his own pocket. The thing was an imbroglio, into which he had blundered and from which he now escaped, thanks to his resolute front, in far better guise than he had grounds to expect.

Before he sailed for home, he received a letter from Noretti, who seems to have recovered from his beating and disgrace, in which that irrepressible rascal declared that the Viceroy of Canton was now ready to grant them free trade and land for a factory on an annual lease. The news only caused merriment; they knew better now than to believe it. But the letter was highly characteristic of the Chinese provincial official view that you could cheat the Red Barbarians again and again. This Noretti continued in the Civil Service, and was the very man whom the Dutch envoys of eighteen years later employed as their inter-preter. It will be recalled that it was his murder in Canton in 1656 which, along with other disagreeable signs of official dis-pleasure, alarmed them so much that they left the place in a hurry.

The fleet weighed from Macao road on December 29, 1637, exactly six months after it had anchored there. A few days before there had occurred a last and highly coloured passage with Dom Domingos da Camara de Noronha, the Viceroy. Disappointed as he had been when he learned that the Chinese were letting Weddell have cargoes, he felt obliged also to allow him to make a few purchases in Macao. But it was a grudging concession and little trade was done. Now, there was a stand-ing rule that any Portuguese desiring to leave for Goa or else-where should travel by a Portuguese ship. No less than a hundred and forty residents, however, prevailed on Weddell to carry them, because by doing so they escaped export duty on their goods, and also for the reason that they would be safer on his ships than on board their own, for the Dutch used to waylay Portuguese merchantmen in the Straits. Dom Domingos considered Weddell's action in taking them a poor return for all his civilities, allowing him trade and once giving him dinner, so that when on December 26, just before they were due to sail, Mundy went ashore to settle a trifling matter of business with him, a scene took place at Government House. It appears that His Excellency had only just heard that his com-patriots were on board the English ships and he was in the first transports of a Latin rage. He did not wait for Mundy to be

shown in, but went out and met him on the steps. The Englishman prepared to salute him, but was assailed immediately by
a flood of abuse. Did not the English know where they were?
Well, he could tell them: they were in the King of Spain's
dominions. They thought they could behave as if they were in
London: let him assure them that they could not. He was Viceroy and he knew how to deal with rogues, aye, and with
drunkards, and with traitors, too. If he found one of them on shore
next day he would hang him, yes, hang him—and confiscate
his property! With that he rushed back into the palace, Mundy
having been unable to get in a word.

It was this exhibition which convinced the English that
Dom Domingos' father was, in fact, a tinker.

The ships sailed away. Weddell kept his word that never
again would he trouble them at Canton, for he perished somewhere in the Indian Ocean, the *Dragon* being lost with all
hands. The *Catherine* also was never heard of again. The *Anne*
had been sold at Macao, so that only the *Sun* made her home
landfall. On December 15, 1638, 'Wee came to Dover roade,'
writes Mundy, who travelled by her. 'Thatt evening wee tooke
post horses and rode all nightt. Early in the Morning, beeing
Sonday, wee came to London, the end and period off this
voyage. . . . Gods Name bee praised For our preservation and
saffe conduct to this our Native land and wished Port, Amen.'

It had been a great voyage, lasting two years and eight
months, the ships having covered 36,204 miles, 'which is
14,604 Miles More then the compasse off the whole world is
accompted to bee'. Looking back on it, after he had recorded
meticulously its daily incident, Mundy suddenly lifts it into the
region of romance—to which indeed it properly belonged—by
his description of two old sailors of the *Sun*. Of one of them he
says shortly—yet how much is concentrated there—that his
name was 'Antonio Gonsalez, a Portugall, who was taken by
Sir Francis Drake, was with him in the West Indies when hee
died, married an English woman, and now homeward bound
grew blind, a good honest poore old Man'. So when they

stormed the Anung-hoi Fort, and when they murmured because Weddell would not seize the Spanish galleon, among them was actually one of Drake's men, who had been with him at Porto Bello, where he died forty years before.

The other old man belongs to Conrad's world. His name was Avery, they called him Father Avery, and he was their cook. His peculiarity was this, that during the entire voyage he never set foot on land. For the whole two years and eight months he remained aboard, a fabulous, splendid, ancient sea-dog. They were months at Goa, months at Macao, lying near the shore, boats going to and fro, but he had no interest in India or China, he loved the ship, would not leave her for an instant. When at last they sighted their native land, turned into the Thames estuary and anchored at Erith, he was carried ashore there to be buried, having died as the ship came up the river.

Let us now stand back and attempt to see Weddell's exploits in a wider perspective. What was their significance from the Chinese point of view? Sometimes by reversing the elements in a situation one is enabled to understand it better. Suppose, then, that in 1637 four Chinese armed merchantmen had entered the estuary of the Thames and, after being ordered by the marine authorities to come no further, had silenced and taken a fort guarding the approach to London. To say that such an event would have caused the greatest interest throughout the country would be to use a stupid understatement. It would have been regarded as one of the most astonishing events in English history. Every bit of information which could have been obtained about China, her aims and resources, would have been eagerly collected. The endurance of her ships, the quality of her guns, the extraordinary skill of her mariners and their incredible daring and presumption would have been debated by high and low with the utmost excitement in every household. Had it appeared that the Chinese Commodore, in spite of his rude action, had a reasonable proposition to put forward about a mutual trade, his proposals would have been considered and if an arrangement profitable to both sides could have been made, it certainly would have been—the English thereby exhibiting an attitude of mind both intelligent and reasonable.

But if intelligence and reason are characteristics of advanced states, one might have expected to find them more developed in Ming China than in Caroline England, for the first was vastly richer, more ordered and sophisticated than the second, and for two thousand years had made reason and intelligence the pivot of her national cult. Indeed, China had been a civilized state for so much longer than Britain that to suppose four of her ships going to London was more inherently probable than that four English ships should come to Canton.

But Chinese civilization did not develop in that way; the Chinese had become less and less interested in the world be-yond their borders; and Weddell's entry aroused none of that intellectual curiosity which one associates with intelligence, nor induced the accommodation to new facts and the desire to profit by them which is suggested by reason.

The Chinese should have taken cognizance of the following relevant facts: that the English were a more manly and resolute race than the Portuguese with whom they were acquainted: that they had defeated the Spaniards, whose king was overlord of Portugal, in a whole series of naval battles: that inasmuch as they were doubtless acquainted with that scientific knowledge to which Father Ricci had drawn the attention of the *literati* until his death in 1610 and which Father Schall was at that time laying before the Court, they were formidable because they had begun to apply it to the adjuncts of war, to cannon, ships, navigation and trade: that it was therefore common prudence to learn as much about them as possible, bring the resources of China to a level with theirs and come to an arrangement which would ensure China's sovereignty while it enabled her to repair what was weak in her dispositions. This was the attitude which was eventually to be taken up by the Japanese—certainly very late but just in time—and which enabled them so to increase their power that they have overrun China and even threaten the West, to such an extent that were their warships to appear now in these waters, say, in conjunction with German U-boats, it would cause little surprise.

Why was it that the Chinese, intelligent and reasonable, the heirs of a great tradition, of a civilization resting on the stored wisdom of ages, why was it that they saw nothing in Weddell's visit which demanded their close attention?

We are informed already of the main reason. The Confucian principles which guided policy had become with age so august and absolute that a nimble and pragmatic policy towards current events was impossible. A Red Barbarian or foreign devil (devils were always red) came to learn, not to teach, to admire and worship, never to claim that he knew what China did not.

In Weddell's case there were also certain particular reasons which in fairness should be mentioned. The Ming dynasty was close to its destruction by rebels within and by enemies without; the bureaucracy was corrupt, and timid because it was corrupt; and the central government had been usurped by a clique of eunuchs who were the last people to assess at its proper value the mere incursion by a Red Barbarian into a provincial port fifteen hundred miles away.

Indeed, no Chinese government, however clear-sighted, could have assessed altogether at its full significance this visit. It could not have foreseen that Weddell was the first of a great host of Englishmen who would come in, grow more vociferous as they became more powerful, and more irritated as their demands continued to be ignored, until all patience exhausted they made the old Captain's destruction of the Bogue fort seem a small thing beside their burning of the Summer Palace and their sack of The Great Within. For his part, Mundy, in spite of the way his King's overtures had been received, in spite of the poor showing of the Chinese gunners and the weakness and corruption of the officials he met, was impressed by the greatness of China and had an inkling of vast possibilities. Expressing, no doubt, the view of Weddell and of the merchants, he writes under the heading 'Chinas excellencies': 'This Countrie may bee said to excell in these particulars: Antiquity, large-nesse, Ritchenesse, healthynesse, Plentiffullnesse. For Arts and manner of governmentt I thinck noe Kingdome in the world Comparable to it, Considered alltogether.'

# II

# Captain Anson explodes the China Legend

Incurious though the Chinese might be about Weddell and what he represented, it will have struck the reader as strange that they should have neglected the defences of Canton, their largest southern port, to such an extent that its principal fort could be silenced by a few discharges of ordnance. If this was characteristic of Chinese military science, how had that Empire retained the respect and admiration of Asia from the remotest antiquity? But the condition of the Bogue forts was by no means characteristic, for the military dispositions of the Government of China were directed to meet danger from a different direction.

For millenniums there had been only one military problem in China. This had to do with the nomad riders of the Steppe. All along the northern frontier were Mongolian tribes which raided when they could, and which on several occasions had raided to such purpose that they overthrew the dynasty of the day. How to keep them out was the problem which each dynasty set itself to solve. To that end the Great Wall had been built, and was maintained, century after century, by garrisons throughout its length. Behind it were fortresses, one of which was Peking, the capital from the thirteenth century. That the capital should be fixed in the northern march showed that the Government considered the restraint of the nomads their greatest preoccupation.

In this way all eyes had been turned to the north. The countries lying to the west, such as Burma and Annam, were harm-less. The sea bounded the east and south, and during the immensity of Chinese history no danger had threatened from the sea. Pirates there had been, particularly Japanese pirates, and in 1592, when Ricci was trying to get to Peking, the Shogunate of Japan had attempted to conquer Korea, a tributary state on the Chinese northern flank. But the attempt was not on China herself, and was an exceptional event explainable by the ambition of the restless Shogun Hideyoshi.

It was therefore natural that the fortifications of Canton should be designed to stop no enemy more formidable than an occasional sea-rover.

But Weddell was symptomatic of a greater danger than any pirate, because he represented the first thrust of a maritime power which was destined not only to abase the power of China, but also to put an end to her ancient civilization. Neither Canton nor the Imperial Government had the smallest conception that the country was fated thenceforward to be assailed on the frontier which was undefended. While she continued from a habit of centuries to look north, there was creeping in from the south a mortal peril.

With a lofty superiority which eventually became idiotic the Government continued to ignore what was happening under their eyes. They took no steps to strengthen their sea frontier or to size up the power and ambitions of the Western world. On the contrary, K'ang Hsi and Ch'ien Lung, the second and the fourth Ch'ing Emperors, exerted themselves in the opposite direction, and in a series of campaigns extended their frontiers far into the Steppe. They added to the Empire nomad territories which had been independent of it since the seventh century, at a time when they would have been better employed in building a navy and fortifying their ports after a study of Western models.

Weddell's bombardment of the Bogue was therefore profoundly ominous, more especially because it was the English (rather than those who had been ahead of them in Eastern adventure, the Portuguese and the Dutch, and in a lesser degree the French) who were to fix their teeth into China, until in Shanghai and Hongkong they possessed the two richest and most powerful cities which any sovereign state has ever been able to plant inside the territories of another. The Chinese had no need to trade with England in order to maintain their tradi/tional way of life. But it was of vital importance to England, if she were to keep that influence on the continent of Europe which was the corner/stone of her national security, that a world/wide trade should provide her with adequate resources.

So it fell to the English to demonstrate to the Chinese the practical operation of that knowledge to which the Jesuits had introduced them. English traders became the protagonists in China of the modern world. It was their insistence that she must abandon her ancient cult of self/sufficiency and admit the Son of Heaven to be what in fact he was, a Sovereign among many and not the Sovereign of all, which eventually tumbled down the whole theory of The Great Within.

The story of Captain Weddell has served as a prologue to this drama of East and West; the story of Captain Anson will carry the plot a step further.

Anson came to Canton in 1742, one hundred and five years after Weddell had left it. During that interval, as we already know, the Ming gave place to the Ch'ing dynasty. The Ch'ing invasion was an example of danger from the north, though in this case the invaders were sinified nomads. In 1655 we noted the Dutch Embassy, which failed to open Chinese ports to European traders. During the reign of K'ang Hsi (1662–1722) the Jesuits continued their great efforts to bring China into the world of Catholic states and, in spite of their success at Court, their learning which was admired and their great services to the Throne, were unable to effect any change whatever in her outlook. On the contrary, as has been shown, the result of their labours was if anything to strengthen the Confucian system and make the Chinese more extremely conservative.

In 1685, however, K'ang Hsi issued a Mandate which on

the face of it was a departure from precedent. He gave orders that foreign ships might enter his ports and take cargoes, pro- vided that they obeyed certain strict regulations. But this depar- ture was not an opening of the country to trade in the modern sense; K'ang Hsi was not primarily concerned to promote the prosperity of Canton or other ports, nor to build up a great mercantile community with business connections in the outside world. His object was much narrower and more personal. The Court itself wanted to make money. A most ingenious method was evolved by which a large revenue would flow to the Palace. The Emperor appointed as his direct representative an Admini- strator of the Canton Customs (the permission to trade became restricted to Canton). In Chinese this person was called the Hai-Kwan Pu, corrupted to Hoppo by the English. He paid a handsome sum for his appointment and he had to remit what was calculated to be the utmost, after allowing for his commission, which could be squeezed out of foreign traders without dis- couraging them altogether. To effect this he did not depend altogether on the imposition of customs dues; he also sold the right of trading to a small guild of merchants known as the Hong. These monopolists, in consideration of being able to buy at current prices and sell to the foreigners, who were, of course, forbidden to buy from anyone else, paid the Hoppo a gigantic squeeze. How big that squeeze was may be estimated from the amount of money they had left after paying it. How- qua, a Hong merchant in the heyday of the system, himself admitted to an estate worth over five million sterling, probably the largest mercantile fortune in the world of that time.

The trade at first was small: there was no rush of ships from Europe. In England, 1685 was the year of the Monmouth rebellion; in 1688 the Stuart dynasty fell; and from the begin- ning of the eighteenth century the campaigns of Marlborough occupied all our attention. The first ship sent by the East India Company was in 1689. By 1715 a settled policy had been adopted. The Chinese allowed an English warehouse, or factory as it was called, to be built at the western end of the suburb which lay between the city wall and the river. Every year two or three Company ships arrived on the S./W. Mon/soon about October, anchored at Wampoa some six miles short of the city, and unloaded their cargo, shipped another, departing on the N.E. Monsoon in January or February. The dues, exactions and tips were confusing and often heavy, and the prices demanded considerably above the real prices current in China, but as the East India Company was itself a mono/poly it had not to face competition in England and so was able to make its profit. It was not a pleasant trade, however; the merchants knew they were being exploited, and they had no direct appeal to the Viceroy or the senior mandarins.

Moreover, they had to put up with almost penal regulations. Confined to the factory during the trading season, they were obliged to depart with the ships at the end of it, either to Macao, where they had a house, or back to Europe. No European women were allowed on shore. Credit could not be carried over to the next season. Chinese servants might not be em/ployed. They must not use sedan chairs. Even rowing for pleasure on the river was forbidden.

Nevertheless the trade was well worth while. The prices they could obtain in Europe left a large margin for profit. Bribery, cheating, insult and a very dull time outside business hours—these were supportable for so good a return. Moreover, they had one trump card. If they were pressed too far, they could always threaten to refuse to trade. And the Hoppo knew he must keep trade going or the Court would dismiss him.

As an indication of the state of the trade at the time of Cap/tain Anson's arrival in 1742, here are the Canton figures for 1741. Five English ships called that season, with a total ton/nage of 2,600 tons, their crews amounting to 500 men. They took cargoes of tea, silk and porcelain. There were also two French and two Dutch ships. (It may be noted here that by the end of the century the number of English ships had mounted to an average of twenty/five, while that of the French and Dutch remained very small.)

What brought Anson to Canton—it had nothing to do with trade—was this. England had gone to war with Spain over Jenkins' ear (and for some stronger reasons) and the Government decided to send a squadron into the Pacific via Cape Horn to do what damage it could to the Spanish possessions in South America and their trade to the Philippines, with special reference to the Acapulco treasure galleon, which still sailed annually between Mexico and Manila. George Anson, who held the rank of Captain in the Navy, was appointed Commodore of the squadron. He was a man of about forty-three years of age, a kinsman of the Earl of Macclesfield, and has been described as polite, handsome, humane and well-bred. These adjectives sum up the qualities which were valued in the eighteenth century, a period when good sense, good family, good manners and good looks had greater importance than they have today, for it was our classical period and reason, balance, clarity and virtue were more esteemed than enthusiasm, intuition, push and business acumen—all of which goes to explain why Confucius then had so much vogue in Europe.

Captain Anson's flag-ship was the *Centurion*, sixty guns, four hundred men, and he had under his command two men-of-war of fifty guns, one of forty, a fourth of twenty-eight, a sloop of eight guns, and two pinks. Among his Commanders were the Honourable John Murray and the Honourable Edward Legge—descendants of the latter are in the Navy today. The expedition was, in fact, a thoroughly eighteenth-century affair, the officers being all members of the aristocracy or of the landed gentry, the men mostly bumpkins collected by the press-gang. In addition to the sailors were five hundred marines. These were to have been drawn from a regiment of Foot, but at the last moment that could not be arranged. Accordingly the Commandant of Chelsea Hospital was instructed to supply five hundred of his out-pensioners. Such persons at that time consisted of soldiers who on account of age, wounds or other infirmities were incapable of service in marching regiments. When Captain Anson learned that his marines were to be aged invalids, he was 'greatly chagrined,' as Mr. Richard Walter, M.A., Chaplain of the *Centurion* and chroni-cler of the voyage, expresses it,[1] for he knew that they would mostly die of scurvy and hardship before they reached the scene of action. He was further chagrined when only two hundred and fifty-nine came aboard, 'for all those who had limbs and strength to walk out of Portsmouth deserted, leaving behind them only such as were literally invalids, most of them being sixty years of age, and some of them upwards of seventy. Indeed it is difficult to conceive a more moving scene than the imbarka-tion of these unhappy veterans.' They knew well what was in store for them, and were both depressed and indignant 'to be thus harried from their repose into a fatiguing employ, to which neither the strength of their bodies, nor the vigour of their minds, were any ways proportioned and where . . . probably they would all uselessly perish by lingering and painful diseases; and this, too, after they had spent the activity and strength of their youth in their Country's service.'

Such a fate could never have overtaken aged men in China. No Chinese, old or young, was ever sent by the Son of Heaven to die on the other side of the globe. How mad Europe seems in comparison! How much saner, more humane, the Chinese vow to stay at home! Yet that was the essence of the impending clash. European interests were already world-wide and Eng-land, for all the urbanity of her classical age, was obliged to send Chelsea pensioners to fight in the antipodes.

At the last moment Anson succeeded in obtaining 210 marines detached from different regiments in place of the 240 invalids who had deserted. These were raw undisciplined youths who had never fired a shot and 'had scarcely anything more of the soldier than their regimentals'. However, he was lucky to get them, and on September 18, 1740, the squadron weighed from St. Helens with a contrary wind.

The voyage was highly unfortunate. The most dreadful

[1] *A Voyage Round the World by George Anson, Esq.,* compiled by Richard Walter, M.A. London, 1748.

storms were encountered at the Horn and in the southern Pacific. Ship after ship was lost; the men died of scurvy at a crippling rate. However, Paita, a town on the Equator in Peru, was sacked at the end of 1741 and a treasure taken worth £30,000. Exciting though the episode was, it cannot be related here. It was a happy interlude in their hard life, though the treasure was small compared to what they hoped for, should they encounter the galleon, which was reputed the richest ship in the world. But they failed to sight her, when in March 1742 they cruised off Acapulco, for the Spaniards heard they were there and cancelled the sailing for that year.

So on May 6 they set sail for home across the Pacific, steering for Canton, where they hoped to replenish their stores and refit. By this date the *Centurion* had lost all her consorts except one, and that one she now lost, so that when she arrived in Macao road on November 12 she was alone and her complement was reduced to two hundred and fifty men. Adding her proportion of the marines to her original crew of four hundred, three hundred of her people must have perished in all. She herself was very foul and urgently needed to be careened. But weakened, dirty and battered though she might be, she was a British man-of-war, the most formidable engine of destruction which had been seen in those seas, for no ship of the Royal Navy had ever come to China before.

Macao had gone downhill somewhat during the century since Weddell was there. The Viceroy had as splendid a name, but the hidalgos, sauntering with their swords in the square before the cathedral or by the steps of São Paulo, were poorer, if as proud as ever: Captain Hamilton, I think, remarks—he visited the place at the turn of the century—that they tended to stop strangers and ask for a loan—repayable next month on the word of a gentleman.

Anson was aware of the rule that no ship of war might enter the Bogue. The trading season had begun and four English ships were lying at Whampoa in the river of Canton, properly called the Pearl River. He would have preferred to sail in and join

226

them, for he wished to secure from the Government as speedily as possible leave to avail himself of the facilities of the port. But to do so, he knew, would be an embarrassment for his com-patriots, on whom the Chinese would no doubt visit their dis-pleasure. He resolved therefore to wait at Macao until he had received the necessary permission to come up. It was not that he was afraid to sail through the Bogue and anchor by the city. 'For it is certain', wrote his Chaplain with some truculence and a great deal of truth, 'that he might have entered the port of Canton, and might have continued there as long as he pleased, and afterwards have left it again, although the whole power of the Chinese Empire had been brought together to oppose him.'

By 1742, although the fame of China, the reputation of her arts and her laws, were at their height in Europe, it seems that the English had already taken her measure as a naval power.

So, as a preliminary, a civil letter was addressed to the Vice-roy of Macao in which Anson requested him to advise on the proper manner of approaching the Government of Canton. It should be recalled that Portugal was now governed again by its own Royal Family and that war between England and Spain concerned her not at all except in so far that as a neutral she might not wish to favour either belligerent. But evidently it was thought that at so great a distance from Europe the Portuguese would not trouble about a technical neutrality; the world was then a very large place. As to China, since she stood outside the comity of Western nations and still spoke of them as Outer Barbarians, it was impossible that she would raise the question of her neutral status, a conception which had no place in her law or her practice.

In point of fact the only difficulty Anson foresaw was that the Chinese might classify the *Centurion* as a merchantman and insist on her paying the port dues. This he was resolved to refuse, for men-of-war were exempted in every European har-bour from such charges, and he held that to pay them in China would be derogatory to his country's honour. No doubt also, as a Captain in the British Navy, he had no fancy to be confused with a merchant Captain, even by such people as the Chinese.

The Viceroy of Macao, in his reply to the Commodore's letter, stated categorically that should the *Centurion* proceed up the river, dues would be demanded, and he advised, if the ship must be careened, that this be done in Taipa road adjacent to Macao, at which the Chinese officials would probably wink, were it to come to their knowledge.

Anson, assuming he could get what he required from Macao, took this advice and moved to Taipa, which was some nine miles to the southward, where he anchored in about five fathom water.

Next day going over to Macao in his barge, he asked the Viceroy whether he could supply him with provisions and such things as might be necessary for refitting his ship. His Excellency, though declaring his eagerness to be of any service, explained that he could do nothing without the previous sanction of Canton. This answer was annoying, and the Captain replied that in that case he would go to Canton himself in a local boat and see what arrangements could be made. The Viceroy looked doubtful, but made no remark.

Next day, having hired a rigged sampan, Anson was embarking on it for the eighty mile journey, when the Chinese official in charge of the customs of Macao forbade him to start. Efforts were made to induce him to withdraw this prohibition, but they were of no avail. On the following morning Anson told him that unless a permit were issued he would 'man and arm his boats to carry him thither; and asking at the same time who he imagined would dare to oppose him. This threat immediately brought about what his entreaties had laboured for in vain: The permit was granted, and Mr. Anson went to Canton.'

Then began a long comedy. On reaching the city he consulted with the officers of the four English ships and the merchants in charge of their trade. How was he to get at the Canton Viceroy? They told him it was impossible to address that high official directly. All relations between the English and the Government of Canton had to be carried on through the Hong merchants who handled the trade. When Anson objected that what he wanted had no connection with trade, he was informed that the Chinese would regard it as falling under that head. Seeing no other way to effect his purpose he agreed to let his countrymen put the matter to the Hong merchants. These, as soon as it was explained, were all smiles and promises. Let the Captain leave it to them; they would arrange an audience for him.

Anson then took up his residence in the English factory. Downstairs were the warehouse and offices, and upstairs the bedrooms, dining and sitting rooms; a little garden stretched to the river-side. Behind, about a quarter of a mile away, rose the high wall of the city, with a gate, known as the Petition Gate, a short distance along it. Days passed and the English traders entertained their distinguished guest as far as the amenities of the place allowed, and took the opportunity of explaining to him the irritating disabilities under which the trade was carried on, how they never knew for certain what they might have to pay in duties and how they were unable to appeal against the assessments of the Customs' officials except through the Hong merchants, who were in league with them. The third Ch'ing Emperor's reign had come to an end seven years before —he who had taken the reign-title of Harmonious Rectitude (Yung Chêng) and had in an Edict already quoted classified Europeans with actors and soothsayers. His successor, whose reign-title was Enduring Glory (Ch'ien Lung), was a young man. From all reports he seemed to have inherited some of his grandfather, K'ang Hsi's, aptitude for public business and followed him also in his employment of Jesuits. But there was nothing to show that he would be prepared to protect the European traders. In any case, it was wholly impossible to approach him. If they had never been received by the Viceroy of Canton, were not even allowed to petition him, how could they aspire to an audience at the Court of Heaven? All this meant that there was no appeal against injustice and insult. They begged

Anson to put in a word for them, when the Viceroy received him, should he perhaps do so.

A fortnight passed. The Hong merchants had not reported any success, but almost daily they sent messages to assure the Captain that they were giving the matter of the audience their anxious attention. Sometimes they declared they expected to arrange it that very day, sometimes it was the next day they felt sure would see it settled. At the end of a month Anson sent word that unless they could fulfil their promises forthwith, he would have to take the necessary measures himself. This brought them running to the factory. Pressed to state what exactly they had done, they confessed they had done nothing at all. 'You have made no application of any kind!' exclaimed Anson. 'None,' they declared, smiling nervously. They had been asked to do something impossible. The Viceroy was far too great a man for humble people like themselves to address. 'In that case', said Anson, 'I will petition him direct.' Much alarmed, they begged him to do nothing of the kind, and, turn-ing earnestly to the English merchants, urged them to restrain him, for it would only mean unpleasantness; the Government would certainly be gravely displeased, and that would do the trade no good.

They had professed willingness at first, no doubt, because they looked to gain time in an awkward situation. It was, in truth, out of the question for them to inform the Viceroy that a British man-of-war was in the estuary, that her Captain wanted provisions and assistance to refit and that he was actually in Canton at the moment. Had they done so, they might very well have been accused of complicity in Anson's arrival, which was against the rules. Moreover, the news that a powerful warship was off Macao would have caused the Government to bring pressure on them to induce both Captain and ship to leave at once. There were, indeed, a hundred reasons for keeping clear of an incalculable affair. They knew from long experience that to startle the Viceroy, particularly in a matter which really did not concern them, would be the most stupid thing they could do. Mixing oneself in affairs of state was not the way to prosper in business. Whenever there was any unpleasantness they always had to bear the brunt of it. To blurt out something about a battleship and a Captain would be a quick road to bankruptcy and perhaps to prison. And if Anson himself petitioned the Viceroy, they would be blamed for not having prevented him.

The Chaplain, whose narrative we are following, was some-what at a loss to understand all this underground working. Nevertheless, he makes a very shrewd guess when, truculent as ever, he writes of the merchants in the starched language of his day: 'I impute their behaviour to the unparalleled pusillanimity of the Nation, and to the awe they are under of the Govern-ment: For such a ship as the *Centurion*, fitted for war only, had never been seen in those parts before, she was the horror of these dastards, and the Merchants were in some degree terrified even at the idea of her, and could not think of applying to the Vice-roy (who is doubtless fond of all opportunities of fleecing them) without representing to themselves the pretences, which a hungry and tyrannical Magistrate might possibly find for censuring their intermeddling with so unusual a transaction, in which he might pretend the interest of the State was immedi-ately concerned.'

Anson was no fool, and for a man so well-bred, humane and handsome he had more guile than you would expect. He ceased to press the merchants, professed to have abandoned the idea of petitioning the Viceroy direct, and said that in the cir-cumstances he would take his ship to Batavia in Java, where he would be able to procure all the assistance he might require, but that to go there he must have certain provisions.

The merchants heard him say this with evident relief. They promised him provisions, though even in this, they pointed out, it would be necessary to use every discretion. The best course would be to load the meat and flour by night on to the English merchantmen in the river. These were sailing shortly and the goods could be transferred to the *Centurion* as they passed Taipa road.

When this was settled, Anson returned to the *Centurion*, 'seemingly resolved to proceed to Batavia'. In fact, his ship was in no condition to go to sea. Her main mast was sprung in two places, and she had a leak which her carpenters could not stop until she was beached. His intention was to careen her in Taipa road. He had secured his most urgent requirement, fresh food for his crew. But he also wanted skilled assistance and certain appliances. These he proposed to acquire in his own way, by taking the line he had originally proposed and from which he had been dissuaded against his judgment. He would write to the Viceroy himself from Taipa. In this way he would not involve his countrymen.

So on December 17, which was the day after his return, he had a letter composed in Chinese, wherein he declared who he was and the situation in which he found himself with a sprung mast and a serious leak. He desired nothing better than to be gone as soon as possible, but he could not go until he had re-fitted. He had come up to Canton in the hope of an audience, but as a stranger could not ascertain how to procure one. He had therefore been obliged to write and now hoped His Excel-lency would send him carpenters with the necessary materials.

The point in this letter which was likely to commend itself particularly was the declaration that he desired to take himself off. When satisfied that he could not go till refitted, the Viceroy might well decide to grant facilities, rather than have a row with a man capable of making himself unpleasant.

These anticipations proved to be perfectly sound. The letter, which was delivered under protest by the Chinese Customs of Macao, brought in a few days a Mandarin of the first rank and two inferior Mandarins with a retinue of servants, in eighteen sampans, decorated with streamers and furnished with a band, which struck up as they anchored near the *Centurion*. A message was sent on board to say that the Viceroy had ordered them to examine the condition of the ship, and asking that a boat be sent across for them.

While the boat was on its way, Anson made hasty preparations to receive the distinguished visitors. His crew, now hardly numbering more than two hundred men, was mostly far from well. However, 'a hundred of the most sightly of them were uniformly drest in the regimentals of the marines, and were drawn up under arms on the main deck.' When the Chief Mandarin came up the side, 'he was saluted by the drums and what other military music there was on board; and passing by the new-formed guards, he was met by the Commodore on the quarter-deck, who conducted him to the great cabbin.'

The Mandarin immediately made a very good impression. He was brisk and affable and, they found, extremely intelligent. The carpenters he had with him were soon inspecting the leak and the sprung mast, while he sat at a table with an official form in front of him, in column I of which was a list of ques-tions and in column II a space for their answers. When he had filled in column II and had received a report from his car-penters that the leak was as bad and the mast as unsafe as they were alleged to be, he expressed himself fully satisfied and, on Anson inviting him to dinner, accepted with an agreeable show of manners.

As they sat down, Anson warned him not to expect a good dinner because his provisions were very low and he had not so far been able to replenish them. Whereupon the Mandarin wrote out an order on the spot addressed to the Chinese Customs at Macao, directing that supplies be sent on board every morn-ing, an order which from that time forwards was punctually obeyed. At dinner he and his two junior colleagues had diffi-culty with the knives and forks, utensils which in China are only used by servants to cut up meat to be eaten with chop-sticks, a vastly more elegant method of eating in the opinion of those who are able to manipulate them. Nor need this view be assigned only to such persons, for it is an arguable point that the table-knife differs too little from the butcher's knife and that the fork is too like a kitchen utensil for either of them to be held superior to two ivory or jade wands wielded to lift morsels delicately to the mouth.

Such was certainly the view of Anson's guests, and before dinner had advanced very far they required their attendants to cut up their meat for them. However, they did very well for, Mr. Walter remarks, 'the three Mandarins compleatly finished the white part of four large fowls.' Nor were they at all backward in drinking. Anson was a teetotaller in an age when abstention from wine was very rare. 'But there being another Gentleman present, of a florid and jovial complexion, the chief Mandarine clapped him on the shoulder . . . and insisted on his bearing him company.' Between them the Chinese finished five bottles, but rose from table perfectly cool.

The dinner had been a great success, and before leaving the senior Mandarin assured Anson it would be his pleasant task to convince the Viceroy's Council that the request for carpenters and materials was reasonable and should be met.

Within a comparatively short time the carpenters arrived and contracted after some bargaining to do the work for £600. The *Centurion* was hove down at a convenient place. By March 3 the work on the hull was completed, but not until the beginning of April had they new-rigged her, stowed their provisions and water, and fitted her for her long voyage home. 'Before this time', remarks Mr. Walter, 'the Chinese grew very uneasy and extremely desirous that she should be gone,' so much so that, as a strong hint, they cut off the supplies of fresh food three days before her departure. At last on April 19, 1743: 'she, at three in the afternoon of that day, weighed and made sail, and stood to sea.'

But, as we have seen, Captain Anson possessed a pleasing guile. He had no intention of sailing home at the moment. His officers, his crew, the Portuguese at Macao, the Viceroy of Canton, the English merchants, who had given him letters for London—all these he had convinced he was returning to England, though the S.-W. Monsoon was on the point of breaking and the wind would be against him all the way to the Cape. But the *Centurion* seemed such a wonderful ship and her people so skilful that no-one doubted she could do the impossible.

However, Anson had a far more attractive plan than tacking backwards and forwards for months in the teeth of the monsoon. When land was out of sight, he called the whole ship's company on to the quarter-deck. It numbered now two hundred and twenty-seven, about thirty of whom were boys and twenty Lascars recruited at Macao. The crew's six months' stay at Taipa had restored them to health and they were all in fighting trim and spirits. So when he told them his real intention was to hunt the Spanish galleon, a loud cheer rang out.

It was just over a year since they had lain outside Acapulco waiting for the galleon to start for Manila. Her sailing being cancelled for that season, the time had come round again and Anson's plan was now to watch for her off the Cape of the Holy Ghost, which is on the eastern coast of the Philippines on the approach to Manila, about a thousand miles sailing from Macao. It was possible that there might be two galleons, a year having been missed. Were there to be but one, it would still be a great prize. The Spaniards, like other Europeans, mostly paid cash for their purchases of Chinese goods, because there were few articles they produced which were saleable in China. The cargo of the galleon on its outward journey was therefore chiefly pieces of eight, for the eight-real piece had for centuries the standing which the pound sterling has now. She might have a million pieces in her strong-room. That was the reason the crew of the *Centurion* had cheered so loud. For over two years they had been battling with the sea, suffering all the vicissitudes of tempest and disease, their booty a wretched £30,000. Now they might recoup themselves in one blow and 'all declared their determination to succeed or perish'.

There was a certain risk they might not succeed, for the Acapulco galleons were large ships, stoutly built, and hardly to be distinguished from men-of-war, for they were reputed to carry as many as fifty guns and to have a complement of five hundred men. No match for a *Centurion* of sixty guns, had the full crew of four hundred been aboard, there was a chance that if such a galleon laid herself alongside and her five hundred swarmed over upon Anson's two hundred and twenty-seven, the latter might be overwhelmed. And should there be two galleons that risk would be doubled. Moreover, it was said that the sides of the galleons were so thick that cannon-shot could not penetrate them. But Anson told his men not to believe such stories. In any case 'he would fight them so near, that they would find his bullets, instead of being stopped by one of their sides, should go through them both'. But the crew did not need such assurances. They were so certain of taking both vessels 'that they considered themselves as having them already in their possession'. This came out in an amusing way. The Commodore had provided himself with some Chinese sheep for his own table, and noticing that no mutton had been served for some days asked the butcher whether they had all been eaten. 'The Butcher very seriously replied, that there were indeed two sheep left, but that if his Honour would give him leave, he proposed to keep those for the entertainment of the General of the galeons.'

It was calculated that the galleon or galleons would pass the Cape of the Holy Ghost some time during June, for March was the month they left Acapulco and the passage across the Pacific took three months. Anson was able to reach the Cape on May 30. He felt sure he was in time, and proceeded to cruise at a distance of thirty or forty miles from shore. It seems that the Spanish coastguards caught sight of him one dawn when the tide had carried him within twenty miles of the Cape. The Manila merchants, when they knew of it, petitioned the Governor to send a squadron against him, but it was impracticable, as their principal ship was not ready for sea. They knew quite well who he was, his presence at Macao having been reported. It had even been proposed to attack him at Taipa while he was careening, but this was not carried out, no doubt because such an encounter would have annoyed the Chinese, with serious consequences to Spanish trade.

Anson continued to lie off the cape, keeping a sharp look-out and giving his men daily musketry practice. How many

Chelsea pensioners remained is not stated, but no doubt there were some of these much tried old soldiers. On June 19 he became anxious. That date New Style was June 30. The Spaniards had been using the New Style since Gregory's re/form in the sixteenth century, but the English did not adopt it till September 2, 1752, nine years later, their Old Style dates being eleven days short. As the galleon was due before the end of June N.S., Anson began to give up hope. However, the very next day at sunrise the masthead watch discovered a sail in the S.E. quarter. Anson immediately stood towards it, and at half/past seven one of the expected galleons was clearly identified. She was coming up on the wind. It was thought she would put about as soon as she was aware of what was on her path. But she held on and continued to bear down on him. Afterwards they heard she knew well it was the *Centurion*, but was resolved to fight her, having learned she was under/manned and trusting to her own superior numbers.

'About noon the Commodore was little more than a league distant from the galeon, and could fetch her wake.' As he was tacking towards her, this means that at the end of the next tack he would be just astern of her. He could then close on her with the wind, being the faster vessel. 'Soon after, the galeon haled up her fore/sail, and brought to under top/sails, with her head to the northward, hoisting Spanish colours, and having the standard of Spain flying at the top/gallant mast/head.' As the *Centurion* was coming up on a southerly tack, it followed from this manœuvre that she would fall alongside the galleon and not, as before, cut her wake.

While the distance was shortening, Anson made his dis/positions. He picked out thirty of his best marksmen and dis/tributed them among the tops. This not leaving him enough men for the usual gun/crews, he stationed two men only at each gun, whose duty was to load, and arranged for the guns to be fired by parties which ran from piece to piece. Salvoes or broadsides were thus impossible, but it meant a continuing fire, and as Spaniards were known to have the trick of taking cover when a broadside was due, it was thought discharges coming without interval might be an advantage.

With the men at their stations, the *Centurion* drew nearer the galleon, which was occasionally obscured by squalls but always reappeared as before, resolutely lying to. Her people were throwing cattle and lumber overboard to clear the decks, and the *Centurion*, which by one o'clock had come within gunshot, opened with her chase-guns to embarrass them in their work. The galleon returned the fire with her stern-chase. As Anson drew in, he rigged his sprit-sail yard fore and aft, so that if necessary he might be ready for boarding, and was amused to see the galleon do the same out of bravado.

Soon after he came abreast, keeping to the leeward. This put him on her larboard quarter, which, as she was lying north and south, was to the westward of her and so between her and Manila, a position he took in case she might wish to run for it, then or later. He was within pistol shot and now saw her name clearly, *Nostra Signora de Cabadonga*; her Commander he knew afterwards was Don Jeronimo de Montero, 'the most approved officer for skill and courage of any employed in that service'.

Anson did not lie, however, squarely on her larboard quarter, but turned into the wind till he stood nearly across her bow. From this position he was able to rake her with the greater number of his broadside, because his ports were unusually wide and allowed enough traverse, while few of her guns could be brought to bear on him. She was much the bigger ship, and her armament, it was observed, consisted of thirty-six guns of heavy calibre, and twenty-eight four-pounders on her gunwale, quarters and tops. Her men, afterwards known to number five hundred and fifty, were well supplied with small arms, and she was protected against boarding by a strong network of two-inch rope laced over her waist and defended by half pikes.

When Anson, firing gun after gun in the manner pre-arranged, began to rake her, mats which were stuffed into the netting immediately took fire and burnt violently, blazing up half as high as the mizen-top: his wads had dropped on to them.

This alarmed him nearly as much as it did the Spaniards. What if he were to burn his treasure or, worse still, that while burning she drove on to his quarter and burnt him! But the Spaniards were able to cut away the netting and throw the whole flaming mass into the sea.

The cannonade proceeded, the *Centurion* maintaining her advantageous position across the galleon's bow and firing with precision, while her marksmen 'having at their first volley driven the Spaniards from their tops, made prodigious havock with their small arms, killing or wounding every officer but one who ever appeared on the quarter-deck, and wounding in particular the General of the galeon himself'.

By the end of half an hour Anson could not prevent himself from drifting alongside the galleon. She now was able to bring her guns to bear 'and continued to fire briskly for near an hour longer, yet at last the Commodore's grape-shot swept the decks so effectually, and the number of their slain and wounded was so considerable, that they began to fall into great disorder'. Don Jeronimo, who at first had been the life of the action, was no longer capable of exerting himself nor were his officers able to prevent the crew from deserting their stations. There was nothing for it but surrender, 'and she struck the standard at her main-top-gallant mast-head'. Sixty-seven of her crew were lying dead and eighty-four were seriously wounded.

As her flag fluttered down, the transport of joy among the crew of the *Centurion* was indescribable, says Mr. Walter. After so many disappointments, such misery, such labour, they had their hands at last upon a great treasure. At that moment of triumph one of the Lieutenants whispered in Anson's ear that the *Centurion* was dangerously on fire in the after hatchway by the powder-room. Smoke was now seen to be billowing up. But Anson kept his head, the seat of the fire was discovered and it was smothered out.

The securing and manning of the prize was the next step. The first Lieutenant, Mr. Saumarez, was placed aboard her, and the greater part of her crew and all the treasure were trans-

ferred to the *Centurion*. The prisoners were double the number
of their captors. When they saw this and that many of the
English were boys, they looked dangerous, and it was necessary to place them all in the hold, except the wounded and the
officers. The latter had Mr. Saumarez's cabin, as it was vacant,
and Anson took Don Jeronimo into his own. Course was
then set for Canton, as more provisions would be required and
the prisoners had to be landed somewhere. It was now revealed
that the other galleon had arrived in Manila before the *Centurion* reached the Cape.

On the way back the treasure was counted, and was found
to be 1,313,843 pieces of eight, and 35,682 ounces of pure silver,
to the value of close on £400,000. For eighteenth-century England that was a gigantic sum: it had five times the purchasing
power of today. I do not know the ratio of the prize-money,
but we may be sure that each man on board was due to get
enough to set him up for life. It was the chance of such rewards
which sweetened the tyranny of the press-gang and the miseries
of the lower deck. And if only ten of the two hundred and
fifty-nine old pensioners drew prize-money—well, at least those
ten must have been glad they were forced to sail.

The *Centurion* with her prize reached the Canton estuary on
July 14 and anchored short of the Bogue forts. Anson had not
called at Macao and one can well understand his reason. To
have reappeared, and with a Spanish prize in tow, would
have embarrassed the Portuguese past words. He can hardly
have expected, however, that the Chinese would be any more
pleased to see him. They had helped him to refit at Taipa on
the understanding that he was returning home: after an absence
of three months, here he was again, having captured in the
interval a merchantman which was in the habit yearly of ex-
pending large sums of money on Chinese products, either at
Macao or by purchase from Chinese middlemen at Manila. He
alleged a state of war between his country and Spain, but the
Canton Government had no official information on this point.
For all practical purposes he was a disturber of the China seas,

a reprehensible person, no better than Weddell, and to say that was to say he was no better than a pirate.

If Anson knew this—and he must have had a shrewd idea of it—it did not deter him from anchoring at the Bogue and preparing to pass through into the river. Now that he had all this money on board it was essential to find a safe anchorage until the N. E. Monsoon set in about December. He could not start for Europe till then, and he must renew his provisions for that long voyage. Tiger Island would suit him well enough, the very place at which Weddell had anchored and where the fireboats had been loosed against him, though it is hardly probable that Anson was aware of this.

No sooner was he swinging opposite the Anunghoi fort at the Bogue, than the military officer in charge put off to interrogate him. The *Centurion*, having been kept at Taipa on the previous visit, was not known by sight to the officials higher up the waterway. The officer had no idea what ship she was, and had to be told the story from the beginning. Anson said bluntly the whole truth and that he wanted to pass the Bogue and anchor at Tiger Island, whence he would depart with the shift of the Monsoon.

'What arms and ammunition have you on board?' asked the official.

'Four hundred firelocks and between three and four hundred barrels of powder,' said Anson, who believed in a policy of the bolder the better.

On hearing this the Mandarin 'shrugged up his shoulders and seemed to be terrified with the bare recital, saying that no ships ever came into Canton River armed in that manner; adding that he durst not set down the whole of this force lest it should too much alarm the Regency'.

To this Anson made no reply, leaving it to the Mandarin to write down what he liked, but making it clear that the *Centurion* must enter the Bogue and anchor at Tiger Island, for she was exposed where she lay to the full force of any typhoon. The Mandarin warned him not to move until an answer was received to his application. And a Chinese pilot, who was on board, received strict orders to take him no further.

The forts of the Bogue were no stronger than they had been in Weddell's day: indeed, they do not seem to have been as well equipped. At the Anung-hoi fort on the starboard side there were eighteen embrasures, but not more than twelve cannon, and these no larger than six-pounders. To larboard was the Wantung fort with about ten cannon of the same calibre. The passage is hardly a mile broad, but clearly such fortifications could have been no obstruction to a sixty-gun man-of-war of the British Navy, even had they been well supplied with gunners and ammunition, which there was every reason to doubt.

On the day after the Mandarin's visit, the weather being threatening, Anson weighed and directed the pilot to carry him by the forts. The man protested that he could not until orders were received from shore. To this Anson replied that he must, and that if the ship ran aground he would hang him to the yard-arm. 'The pilot, awed by these threats, carried him through safely, the forts not attempting to dispute the passage.' Shortly afterwards, the *Centurion* let go her anchor in Tiger road. The pilot was paid and dismissed. It transpired later that hardly was he on shore than the police arrested him. He was punished by a severe beating. Subsequently he returned to the ship and demanded compensation. 'Mr. Anson, in com-miseration of his suffering, gave him such a sum of money as would at any time have enticed a Chinese to have undergone a dozen bastinadings.' The Mandarin in charge of the forts was also arrested and dismissed the service.

From his safe anchorage at Tiger Island Anson now ad-dressed a letter to the Viceroy, informing him of the facts and of his wants, and stating that he proposed to pay him a visit. The Viceroy was responsible for law and order, the Hoppo for the trade. But he had his share in the profits and, so, a strong per-sonal interest in supporting the Hoppo. Moreover, that officer had the ear of the Court and if it were whispered there that the

Viceroy had allowed a foreign warship to enter the river, thereby setting at naught all the regulations, he might, should the
Court take fright or believe their profits were threatened, be
relieved of his exceedingly lucrative post. Get rid of Anson he
must and as quickly as possible. The Englishman might pro-
fess innocent motives, he might not, in fact, be a direct danger,
but he had burst through the Bogue without permission, and
there was no telling what he might do next or what the English
merchant captains might do at his instigation. Face had been
lost, also, and just as the subordinate responsible for that loss
had been punished by him, so might he also be punished by
the Emperor, unless he handled the matter with the greatest
tact. Accordingly, when Anson's Lieutenant, the bearer of the
letter, arrived at Canton and presented it to the officials at the
Petition Gate, instructions were sent to inform him that an
answer would shortly be returned.

Meanwhile Anson had allowed some of the Spanish officers
to go to Canton on parole. These gentlemen bore him no
malice, for it had been a fair fight, they themselves having proposed to take the *Centurion*. Furthermore, he had treated them
very well on board his ship. They considered him to be a
gentleman, and when the Mandarins of Canton interrogated
them, which was done as soon as they landed, they said so, an
admission which, coming as it did from persons who might
have been expected to abuse him, created an excellent impression among officials brought up on the ideals of behaviour
taught in the classics. The Viceroy was relieved. Anson might
turn out more amenable than he had expected. It should be
possible to handle him without further loss of face. It might
even be possible to regain some face. Not that the situation was
changed in essentials—he must be got rid of. But this might be
effected, he now hoped, without that hullabaloo which was so
distasteful to the Chinese bureaucracy.

His first step was to send three Mandarins to Tiger Island.
They arrived on July 20 with a vast retinue. Coming on board
the *Centurion* they informed Anson that the Viceroy had

arranged for provisions to be supplied daily, and was also prepared to allow him to move another eight miles up the river to the second bar, which is a matter of twenty miles from the city. As for an audience with His Excellency, they regretted it would be impossible to arrange that at the moment. The weather was very close; an audience of such importance would entail the presence of all the provincial officials and troops; the Captain would understand how exhausting that would be on a hot day; His Excellency must positively forbid him to fatigue himself unnecessarily. Later, when the days were cooler, in September, it would be time enough.

This refusal to see Anson was no doubt dictated by several considerations. In the first place the Viceroy did not wish to commit himself. Then, he could not tell how Peking would take such a step: if things did not go well later he might be held to have exposed the government to a further loss of face. It would be safer to reserve the audience for the very end, when Anson was on the point of departure. Alternatively, to be free to refuse it then might come in handy as a way of regaining face.

Having thus reserved the question of the audience, the Viceroy's emissaries put forward two demands, both of which, if conceded, would have the effect of restoring the face lost by Anson's sailing through the Bogue. The first of these was that he should pay port dues. Merchantmen paid dues at the Bogue, and if the *Centurion* now paid it, she could be described as a merchantman, when it would be an easy matter to enter her payment of dues against the date she passed the Bogue, thereby legalizing that act.

Anson, however, refused this demand at once. He was not going to help the Viceroy to save his face by accepting a status which afterwards might involve him in all sorts of exactions. And it would be a dangerous precedent and also an insult.

The Mandarins then proceeded with the second demand—that he should release his Spanish prisoners. Anson himself was extremely anxious to get rid of them: they were a great encumbrance and his humanity revolted at the necessity of keeping them confined in his stuffy hold. 'However, to inhance the favour, he at first raised some difficulties; but permitting himself to be prevailed on, he at last told the Mandarines that to show his readiness to oblige the Viceroy, he would release the prisoners whenever they, the Chinese, would send boats to fetch them off.'

Having gained this point the Mandarins departed, glad to be able to report to the Viceroy what they knew he could represent, if necessary, to Peking as a concession by Anson which had been forced on him by fear. In the matter of the port dues, they held a reserve card. Anson was getting daily pro-visions, but what he also required was a stock of food for his six months' voyage home, particularly salt meat and biscuit. It should be possible to make the supply of this contingent on his paying the dues. The connection between the two need not be stated so plainly as to annoy him, but he could be left to find out that there was a connection and, by a process of calculated procrastination, could be steered into a frame of mind when rather than endure further delays he would pay the dues and have done with it. Such a course required much tact. He must not be so irritated that he resorted to violence. Nor must he be delayed beyond the shift of the Monsoon. It was now the end of July. He could not leave before December. In these five months they ought to be able to get the dues out of him. Then the whole affair would be regularized. All loss of face would be made good. The *Centurion* would have become a merchantman, a fact which they could use as an answer to any awkward ques-tions asked by Peking or, for that matter, by the Spaniards. Their papers would be in order, and in China, where bureau-cracy developed earlier and was carried farther than in any other state on record, to have your papers in order was to be unassailable.

Anson, of course, understood nothing of all this curious underground working. He was a sailor who had made one of the richest seizures of treasure ever made by any sailor, and wanted to get home as soon as possible. He ordered a quantity of salt meat and biscuits from the Canton merchants, who promised to have them ready for him in plenty of time before he sailed. It would be necessary, no doubt, to get permission to ship them, but he saw no reason to believe that the Viceroy would refuse this, particularly as he had hinted that an audience would be granted later.

The *Centurion* and the galleon moved up to the second bar. August passed. In September Anson sent to Canton to enquire whether the merchants were getting on with their contract. Answer was returned that the goods were ready and could be shipped any time. Not a biscuit or a cask of meat arriving, further enquiry disclosed that the contractors had done nothing. They had not even procured the necessary authorization from the Viceroy to undertake the deliveries. This was alarming news. Did it mean that the Viceroy had forbidden the contractors to proceed? But why should he do such a thing? It did not occur to Anson that there was some connection here with the port dues. He and his officers could make nothing of it. Mr. Walter observes: 'After all, it may be impossible for a European, ignorant of the customs and manners of that nation, to be fully apprized of the real incitements to this behaviour. Indeed, this much may undoubtedly be asserted, that in artifice, falsehood, and an attachment to all kinds of lucre, many of the Chinese are difficult to be paralleled by any other people.' This view, he feels, is very 'contradictory to the character given of them in the legendary accounts of the Roman Missionaries', but, he concludes, it is their true character. And he proceeds to give examples of the extreme ingenuity the tradespeople showed in increasing the weight of the daily provisions they sold on board, making the ducks and fowl eat stones and injecting water into the carcases of pigs.

It will be recalled that here and there Peter Mundy, a century earlier, spoke slightingly of the Chinese. Between his date and Anson's all the numerous books published in Europe about that nation, its country and government, had been eulogistic. Here in Mr. Walter's book is the first sign of a reaction, a realistic view founded upon direct experiences met with in Canton. It is interesting to note that there is no sign of irritation with the Chinese in Nievhoff's book on the Dutch Embassy of 1655. But that was written just before the wave of enthusiasm. And the Dutch Envoys did not expect much. Moreover, they were the guests of the Government, not traders or in-truders, and had to do as a rule with a better class. Their experiences at the end with the Viceroy and the Tartar General were insufficient to outweigh the many other kindnesses they had received.

At the end of September, after Anson heard that the con-tractors had taken no steps to bake his biscuit and salt his meat, he decided to make another effort to see the Viceroy. On the 27th he sent a message to a Mandarin who attended on the *Cen-urion* 'to inform him that he, the Commodore, intended on the first of October to proceed in his boat to Canton; adding that the day after he got there, he should notify his arrival to the Viceroy, and should desire him to fix a time for his audience'. In pursuance of this plan he selected a boat's crew of eighteen and dressed them up like Thames watermen 'in scarlet jackets and blue silk waistcoats, the whole trimmed with silver buttons, and with silver badges on their jackets and caps'. It occurred to him that possibly the Chinese might seize him in Canton and then attempt to take possession of the *Centurion* and her great treasure. Providing for such eventualities, he appointed his Lieutenant, Mr. Brett, to command during his absence, with instructions to fall down below the Bogue in the event of any treachery. With the *Centurion* at large in the estuary, he thought it unlikely that the Viceroy would resort to violence, for it was common knowledge that his ship could destroy the whole commerce of the port.

On October 1, when he was preparing to step into his barge, the eighteen rowers being on the thwarts and his flag hoisted at the stern, the Chinese who was his interpreter came on board to report that the Mandarin in attendance had received a message from the Viceroy requesting him to postpone his visit two or three days. Anson therefore did not start, but in the afternoon another interpreter arrived and, apparently in much agitation, declared that the Viceroy had been expecting him all day, had drawn up a guard of honour and assembled his Council, and now at his failure to appear was much offended, indeed was so uncommonly incensed that he had directed the arrest of the other interpreter, to whose negligence he ascribed all the confusion.

To Anson this story made nonsense. He could not suppose that the Government of Canton was carried on in so slovenly a manner that its officials were incapable of conducting a simple matter without making a fool of their superiors. Could it be that the whole episode was a fiction, both the first message and the second? If so was it a strategem to cause him to lose face, the Viceroy first putting him off and then telling him he had been guilty of rudeness by not coming? Or were there subordinates who for private reasons did not wish him to see the Viceroy? Or was it that his message to the Viceroy had not been delivered by the Mandarin in attendance, so that on October 1 this official had to put him off, and having told him one thing by the first interpreter's message, told him its opposite by the second, hoping that thereafter he might be afraid to approach the Viceroy again for an audience.

Anson had not the smallest notion which of these explanations was the right one or if any of them was correct. Nor were the English captains and merchants who had just arrived at Canton for the season's trade able to enlighten him, though they were somewhat alarmed and argued that the Viceroy was clearly annoyed for some reason and might visit his annoyance on them. But Anson had heard that story before, and being quite convinced in his own mind that the way to deal with the Chinese bureaucracy was to show a bold front, he entered his barge on October 13, and attended by his own boats and those of the trading ships, which had come down to escort him, he rowed up to Canton.

It is well to remember that not only was Anson the Commander of the first English man-of-war to put into a Chinese port, but he was also the most distinguished Englishman who had been to China, the only distinguished Englishman the Chinese had ever seen. One may record here that on his return to England he was made a Rear-Admiral and appointed to the Board of Admiralty. Two years later he entered Parliament. By 1748 he had been raised to the Peerage and was Commander-in-Chief. In 1751 he became First Lord of the Admiralty. The English merchant captains held him in great respect and had directed their ships to fire salutes as he passed Whampoa road, an order that was carried out so that he landed on the Canton foreshore in such a way that the official world must have been fully aware of his arrival. No-one was deputed to meet him, however, nor was any move made to get into touch with him.

We have already explored the Viceroy's point of view. China, moreover, had no imperial navy, nor did she recognize the existence of other navies. There was no precedent for receiving a senior naval officer of a foreign power. Indeed, officially there was no such thing as a foreign power: there were only Barbarians who had or who had not submitted to the Son of Heaven.

But the Hong merchants, who called on Anson at the English factory as soon as he arrived, assured him that when the Viceroy learnt he was in Canton—and they would have much pleasure in reporting the fact—a time for an audience would be appointed. Next day, however, they declared that he was so busy over his despatches for Peking that he could not be approached for the present, 'but that they had engaged one of the officers of his Court to give them information, as soon as he should be at leisure, when they proposed to notify Mr. Anson's arrival, and to endeavour to fix the day of audience'.

Anson, who had now begun to understand the Chinese much better, could only smile at this patent evasion. But he again yielded to the persuasions of the English merchants not to try to approach the Viceroy directly and proceeded to make a bargain with the Hong merchants, settling with them to pay in advance for his stores and to take no steps to see the Viceroy, provided that the merchants on their part showed their goodwill by beginning at once and in an open manner to cook his biscuit and salt his meat. When these were ready—forty days was the term agreed—the merchants would then ask the Viceroy for permission to ship them. If they did not, Anson would be free to take what action he thought proper.

On November 24 the forty days expired. The merchants, who within certain business limits were perfectly honest, had got all the stores ready, but though they continually protested they were on the point of obtaining the Viceroy's permission to ship them, it seemed either that they had not dared to petition him or that some official pressure, the precise nature of which was not clear to Anson, prevented them from making any move. The truth was, of course, that they were in the official conspiracy to keep him waiting for the stores until the right moment came to confront him again with a demand for dues.

The N. E. Monsoon had now set in and Anson decided to act. He drew up a letter addressed to the Viceroy, asking for permission to ship his stores, and sent it by the hand of one of his lieutenants to the Petition Gate. A Mr. Flint, who was the only Englishman in the Canton factory who knew Chinese, accompanied the lieutenant. The official in charge of the gate accepted the letter and promised that an answer would be sent.

What sort of an answer it would have been will never be known, because now an event occurred which caused the bureaucracy to abandon its manœuvres.

On November 26 a fire took place in the riverine suburb where the English and other factories were situated. This had become, since Canton was opened to foreign trade, a mercantile quarter, full of warehouses and shops, hardly recognizable as the open space where the Dutch envoys had been entertained by the Viceroy and the Tartar General. The fire began in some boatman's hut and spread with great rapidity. Anson was staying, as before, in the English factory, and when he saw the smoke driving in his direction on the easterly wind, he went to give assistance, accompanied by his officers and the barge's crew. By the time he got to the fire, it was out of hand, and there was no sign of the fire brigade, whose headquarters were inside the walls. The houses were so closely packed together that the only way to control the flames was to demolish all buildings in their path, but this the local people had hesitated to do because they had not the requisite authority for so drastic a step. Anson thought the circumstances justified him in assuming that authority and, accustomed as he was to command and his men to obey in the hundred desperate occasions of a voyage round the world, he gave orders that certain sheds should be pulled down. The sailors were setting to work with a will, when some people came up to him and insinuated that as there were no officials present he would be answerable for any damage his men might cause. Somewhat huffed by this he left the place and returned to the factory to assist in securing the East India Company's treasure and effects, as there was clearly danger of the whole quarter being gutted.

At this point of the affair the fire-brigade arrived from the city, but the blaze was now so tremendous that the firemen were daunted, and it looked as if not only the riverine quarter but the whole city would be consumed. Certain stocks of camphor had got alight, sending up a great white leaping flame, which was visible on board the *Centurion* away at the second bar. Things looked so grave that the Viceroy himself appeared upon the scene. Someone then sent a message to Anson, begging him to help. With forty of his people he hurried a second time to the fire. The sailors, who were as handy and high-spirited as English sailors always seem to be when they get on shore, threw themselves into the fire-fight with enormous animation, 'so that it was not uncommon to see the most forward of them tumble to the ground on the roofs and amidst the ruins of houses which their own efforts brought down with them. By their boldness and activity the fire was soon extinguished,' but not before a hundred shops and eleven streets full of warehouses had been destroyed.

Not only did the sailors distinguish themselves as fire-fighters, but also as special constables, for at the height of the conflagration criminals seized the opportunity to begin looting, and some of the leading merchants, after obtaining Anson's leave, engaged sailors to mount guard over their houses.

Stiff though the Chinese bureaucracy was as a body, it was composed of human beings who were not proof against the emotions of admiration and gratitude. Everyone conceded that Anson and his men had rendered Canton a great service, and even the most meticulous officials now felt that to present him with a bill for port dues would be an ungentlemanly action. Moreover, it was no longer necessary for the Government to save its face. If Anson had flouted it when he sailed through the Bogue without permission, his services during the fire could be termed a handsome reparation for his former fault, and there were many precedents for accepting it as such. Such a repara-tion had the same effect of restoring lost face as if he had been manœuvred into paying the dues. This argument appeared so satisfactory to the Viceroy's Council that it was decided forth-with to answer the Captain's letter and give him an audience.

When Anson received the letter fixing a day for his appear-ance, he realized that the shipment of his stores would now be sanctioned unconditionally. He knew this because he was advised on all hands that for the Viceroy to agree to see him and then to raise difficulties would be contrary to Chinese notions of finesse. Their method was always indirect. His audience was, therefore, tantamount to his benevolent dis-missal. Such was the practice of the Court of Peking, and its practice governed procedure in the provinces.

At ten o'clock in the morning of November 30 a Mandarin came to inform him that the Viceroy was ready; on which, he set out at once with his retinue and accompanied by Mr. Flint, the young Englishman who knew Chinese. The English mer-chants had reminded him before he left to be sure to speak on their behalf. This he felt confident he should be able to do, for he could rely on Mr. Flint to translate whatever he might say, whether it were agreeable or not, 'a part which no Chinese Linguist would ever have performed with any tolerable fidelity'.

At the gate of the city he was received by a guard of two hundred soldiers, who conducted him through the streets to the square in front of the viceregal residence. Here ten thousand troops were drawn up and 'made a very fine appearance, being all of them new cloathed for this cerimony'. The Viceroy was seated on a chair of state under a canopy in the Hall of Audience, all the provincial Mandarinate being in attendance. Anson was given a chair, the position of which, it was observed, gave him precedence over all the officials present except the Senior Magistrate and the Head of the Treasury.

When he was seated he addressed the Viceroy through Mr. Flint, explaining that he would not have sent a letter direct had he received an answer to his applications made through the Hong merchants, who had not, he opined, forwarded them as they had undertaken to do. The Viceroy hastened to assure him that the first intimation he had of his arrival in Canton was the letter in question.

As there must have been an understanding between the merchants and the officials, Anson's remark shows that he still did not guess what had been happening, and the Viceroy's that he did not want him to guess. Next Anson made a reference to the trade between China and England, and on behalf of his compatriots submitted that the English merchants would esteem it a great favour if they were allowed access to His Excellency or his Council when they had complaints to make against subordinate customs officials. 'Here Mr. Anson paused, and waited some time in expectation of an answer; but nothing being said he asked his interpreter if he was certain the Viceroy understood what he had urged; the interpreter told him he was certain it was understood, but he believed no reply would be made to it.'

Here, also, we must pause for a moment. Why did the Viceroy make no reply to a request which on the face of it was reasonable and not inconsistent with the principles of good administration? The answer must be that he knew the English had cause for complaint, but that the way they were treated was a deliberate policy which gave lucrative returns in which he shared. Anson's request was therefore embarrassing. He had condescended to receive him because by doing so it was possible to get rid of him blandly, without unpleasantness or a wrangle, in short in a dignified manner. His criticism of the port administration introduced just that disagreeable tension which it was desirable to avoid. To discuss with him the inner workings of the Canton government was impossible. How could he be told that it was the Hoppo, the Emperor's direct representative, who controlled foreign trade and that the Hoppo had created the Hong system because it enabled him to remit to the Court of Peking the large sums which he was expected to remit? To allow the English merchants the right of appeal they desired, might result in a reduction of those sums, and what would the Court have to say to that? Yet it was awkward to receive such a request pointblank in audience, if the fiction was to be maintained that no connection existed between the government and the Hong. To concede the request was impossible, to refuse it would look bad. That was the reason no answer was returned.

Anson swallowed the snub and passed on to his own business, stating that he wished to leave for England at once, and only waited for permission to ship his stores. This gave the Viceroy the opportunity he desired of dismissing his troublesome visitor with the benign cordiality which it was Chinese etiquette to assume. Licence to ship would be issued immediately, he said, and wound up the audience by complimenting Anson on the way he and his men had fought the fire. He then added drily 'that the *Centurion* had been a good while on their coast and closed his discourse by wishing the Commodore a good voyage to Europe', a strong hint that he hoped never to see him again.

When Anson was out of the hall of audience some Mandarins pressed him to enter a neighbouring pavilion where an
entertainment had been provided for his amusement. But finding on enquiry that the Viceroy himself was not to be present,
he declined the invitation, reflecting, no doubt, that he had no
more to gain and being suspicious of the slights or familiarities
to which he might be exposed at a function the nature of which
had not been defined. Moreover, if it were beneath the Viceroy's dignity to attend, it could not be proper for him to go
there, for it seems that he regarded himself in some measure as
the representative of the King of England, and had an intuition
that his meeting with the Viceroy stood for issues far transcend-
ing the mere provisioning of his ship.

Next day the meat and biscuit began to come aboard, and a
week later, on December 7, 1743, over a year since her first
arrival in those waters, the *Centurion* unmoored and stood down
the river, still accompanied by her prize, the *Nostra Signora de
Cabadonga*. On December 10 the two ships passed out through
the Bogue.

The Chinese insistence on the value of maintaining appearances runs through all their life and statecraft. Even when these
appearances are transparently absurd they consider them worth
keeping up. We have already had several examples of this
idiosyncrasy, but what Anson saw as he sailed between the
Bogue forts is an extreme instance of the length to which they
will go on occasion. 'The forts were now manned with as
many men as they could well contain,' relates Mr. Walter, 'the
greatest part of them armed with pikes and match-lock mus-
quets. These garrisons affected to show themselves as much as
possible to the ships.' One man in particular arrested their
attention, 'a soldier of unusual size, dressed in very sightly
armour', who 'stalkt about on the parapet with a battle-
ax in his hand'. When you looked at him through a telescope, however, you saw that his armour was made of silver
paper.

At Macao the galleon was sold to the Portuguese for six

thousand pieces of eight, a very poor price, but Anson could not wait to bargain. He weighed for home on December 16, 1743, and on June 15, 1744, 'in the evening to their infinite joy they came safe to an anchor at Spithead'.

In 1748 Mr. Walter published the narrative of the voyage from which we have been quoting. At the end of it he gives his opinion of China and the Chinese. This opinion was very critical, and coming, as it did, at a time when the Chinese, their way of life and their institutions, were subjects of extra-vagant adulation in Europe, it aroused much comment, for the book was an exciting one, full of detail and coolly written, and had a wide circulation. 'From the description given by some of these good fathers', he says, speaking of the Jesuit missionaries, 'one should be induced to believe that the whole Empire was a well-governed affectionate family, where the only contests were who should exert the most humanity and beneficence: But our preceding relation of the behaviour of the Magistrates, Mer-chants and Tradesmen at Canton sufficiently refutes these jesuitical fictions.' Referring more particularly to the admini-stration, which he complains has been 'the subject of boundless panegyric', he remarks: 'The favourable accounts often given of their prudent regulations . . . are sufficiently refuted by their transactions with Mr. Anson: For we have seen that their Magistrates are corrupt, their people thievish, and their tribunals crafty and venal.' Moreover, he goes on, this government, 'so pompously celebrated for its refined wisdom and policy', is not even able to defend its own territories. China 'was conquered about an age since by a handful of Tartars; and even now, by the cowardice of the inhabitants, and the want of proper military regulations, it continues exposed not only to the attempts of any potent State, but to the ravages of every petty Invader. I have already observed . . . that the *Centurion* alone was an overmatch for all the naval power of that Empire'.

Well, Mr. Walter puts his finger here on a very important point. If he exaggerates about China's military weakness, his perception that she was defenceless on her sea frontier against a naval power shows him to have grasped at a very early date the chief cause of her eventual ruin.

His realistic view of her government and the character of her people, though certainly prejudiced on account of Captain Anson's experiences and limited because of his own ignorance and lack of understanding of what was admirable in Chinese civilization, was an aspect of the truth, which gradually be-came accepted as the whole truth by the English. As the eigh-teenth century went on, their trade with China increased till they out-distanced all their rivals. They thus acquired a more practical knowledge of the Chinese than other Europeans, and the greater the dealings they had with them, the less they esteemed them, until in the nineteenth century their annoyance boiled over and, their power having greatly increased, they began to exert it.

Even at the time his book was published some distinguished people in Europe, dissociating themselves from the current view, thought Mr. Walter was right. Thus the celebrated French man of letters, Grimm, in a letter dated September 15, 1766, says: 'The Chinese Empire has become in our time the object of special attention and of special study. The missionaries first fascinated public opinion by rose-coloured reports from that distant land, so distant that no one could contradict their falsehoods. Then the philosophers took it up and used its alleged excellencies as a foil for the evils in their own country. Thus China soon became the home of wisdom, virtue and good faith, its government the best possible and its morality the loftiest. . . . The famous Captain Anson has, I think, been the first to correct our notions of this Mandarin govern-ment.'

But Voltaire, whose admiration for China was of long date, was not to be deflected from his opinion. He read Mr. Walter's book, but in his *Essai sur les Mœurs*, published eight years later, he says: 'European princes and merchants in their voyages to the East have been in search not of wisdom, but of wealth,' and then, naming Captain Anson, he attempts to explain away his perverse reception by the Canton Government by calling that city a distant provincial town where it was only to be supposed the commonalty would be rascals and the officials pettifogging.

The truth is—and we are now in a position to formulate it—that neither Grimm nor Voltaire nor Mr. Walter, whose views, of course, are those of Captain Anson and of the English mercantile community, succeeded in defining very precisely the curious phenomenon of the Chinese Empire. The China of their day was the mummy of a once vital and marvellous civilization, but those who admired her believed she was still alive, and those who condemned her did not understand that the evils they perceived were no reflection upon the excellencies of her past, but were only the marks of her desiccation in the present. It was not appreciated that the Chinese Government and people were conservative to a degree that far transcended the normal meaning of that word. The conception of the Son of Heaven ruling the wide world dominated their outlook on foreign affairs in the eighteenth century just as much as it had done in those distant centuries when it approximated to the facts. They had abated not a jot of their vast pretensions, though they had become increasingly less able to give effect to them. A clash was therefore inevitable between them and Europe. It was impossible to reconcile the modern view of world relations which by Anson's time had taken shape in the West with the dream of the past in which they lived.

The next chapter will show how fifty years after Anson's visit the English made a frank attempt to dissipate that dream by sending their first Ambassador to the Forbidden City itself to suggest to the Son of Heaven that times had changed, new measures were called for, that the ancient Chinese conception of the Celestial Empire required modification, that, in fine, the hour had arrived when China must face the facts of life as it was then being lived in other parts of the globe. Had there been any substance in Voltaire's opinion that the criticisms in *Anson's Voyage* only applied to provincial China, the English envoy

would have met at the centre statesmen of vision. His experiences, however, were no more satisfactory than Anson's. He
was astounded and irritated to find that The Great Within was
as it had always been, and that the Dragon thought and spoke
as if the world had stood still for three thousand years.

# III

# *Lord Macartney converses with the Everlasting Lord*

During the half century between the departure of Anson and the sending of the first British embassy to China, England made a great advance upon the road of her imperial destiny. She lost America, but in India she became the paramount power. In Europe she outdistanced all her rivals. When France, in many ways her superior till that time, was overwhelmed by revolution in 1789, she was left the most stable and civilized kingdom in the West.

Her stability and her fitness to take advantage of her political opportunities were partly due to the successful application to industry of the scientific theories of the previous hundred years. In 1765 Watt transformed the steam engine from a mere toy into the most wonderful instrument which humanity had ever possessed. About the same time it was discovered that coal could be used to smelt iron, which was to become the working material of the modern world. After the steam engine came the power-loom, which multiplied the production of cloth. At the same time distribution was enormously improved by the digging of three thousand miles of canals. The progress of the nation was many-sided. Population more than doubled during the eighteenth century, and the increase of wealth was even greater than that of population. The loss of America only added to the commerce with that country. Industry had begun its great expansion which was to make Britain the workshop of the world. Moreover, the theory of wealth had been revolutionized by the publication of Adam Smith's *Wealth of Nations* in 1776, the most important book ever written, if we are to judge the importance of a book by the material results which follow the adoption of its principles. Not that the principles of the *Wealth of Nations* were immediately adopted, but their publication showed the trend of ideas and their final adoption ushered in the nineteenth century.

China, if not wholly ignorant of this extraordinary rise to a novel kind of power by a remote western island, gave the phenomenon little thought; does not seem to have understood that it had to do with the application to industry of the scientific and mechanical knowledge with which the Jesuits had enabled her to make some acquaintance; and did not deduce therefrom that the world was changing rapidly, while she remained motionless in her ancient ways, still convinced that the Celestial Land was perfect, with no room for improvement in its minutely organized life. The inventions of the West were amusing, but they had no significance. That they might one day threaten China would have seemed a mere fantasy.

This second half of the eighteenth century, though it was the period when the great middle class, which smelted the iron and made the machines, began to fill its pockets, was predominantly aristocratic, and Lord Macartney, destined to be England's first ambassador to China, was one of its typical representatives. His father was an Irish country gentleman of old family, whose estate was Lissanoure in the County of Antrim. He himself, after passing through Trinity College, Dublin, was entered as a student in the Middle Temple. While in London he became a friend of Burke's and Reynolds', and during a tour of the continent made the acquaintance of Voltaire, who seems to have taken a great fancy to him. This was about six years after the sage had written his *Orphelin de la Chine*, into which he had poured all his admiration for classical China, which he believed to be the same as the China of his day. On his return to London Macartney became a member of Dr. Johnson's literary club and also an *habitué* of Holland House. He was considered one of the handsomest and most accomplished young men in town. His manners were easy, his conversation brilliant, he was well read, a good linguist, a good listener, indeed a charming fellow. In 1764, when he was only twenty-seven years of age, he was knighted and sent as Envoy Extraordinary to the Court of the great Catherine, where he made an easy conquest of that highly susceptible lady. His first address to her on presenting his credentials in audience was described by Charles James Fox in a letter to him as 'One of the neatest things of the kind I ever saw; and I can assure you Edmund Burke admires it prodigiously'. When he left Russia two years later Catherine gave him a snuff-box valued at £600.

From this success with an Empress he passed rapidly to other honours. After marrying Lord Bute's daughter, he became Chief Secretary of Ireland in 1768. In 1774 he was elected to Parliament and raised to the Irish peerage. 1780 saw him Governor of Madras, and in 1785 he was offered and refused the Governor-Generalship of Bengal. In all these important offices he was eminently successful, being noted for his tact, intelligence and dignity. In sum, he was one of that long line of Irish gentlemen who have adorned and brightened the British administration.

It was natural, therefore, that when in 1792 the Government was looking for a suitable person to send as Ambassador to the Court of China, they should pick on Macartney, for the mission was likely to require consummate tact, the most lively intelligence and a dignity capable of weathering very insidious stratagems. The Ministry did not know very much about China, but it knew that it was a closed country, that the Court was a Forbidden City, and that the inhabitants had a rooted prejudice against all foreigners.

A glance at Macartney's instructions will show what it was hoped he might accomplish, and also how delicate the negotiation was deemed likely to be. One can perceive in them the Cabinet feeling its way. For instance, it frankly could not say whether the discouraging conditions under which the English merchants conducted their business in Canton were due to the corruption of a local administration or to the settled policy of the Imperial Government. That after nearly a hundred years definite information should still have been lacking on this vital point shows clearly how cleverly the Hoppo, the Hong and the Viceroy managed to conceal that they were all in league. We have seen them at work with Anson. He was never sure of their relations to each other or to the Imperial Government, for he continued to think that, could he but get in contact with the authorities at the top, all would be arranged. The British Ministers in 1792 seem to have suffered under the same delusion. They were sending Macartney right to the top in the sanguine expectation that the Emperor, Ch'ien Lung, once told the true facts, would act with that breadth and justice which was supposed to characterize the great Confucian Court. They even conceived it possible that Macartney might contrive to get on friendly terms with him. 'It is not unlikely that the Emperor's curiosity may lead to a degree of familiarity with you in conversing upon the manners or circumstances of Europe, and as Despotic Princes are frequently more easy of access than their Ministers and Dependents, you will not fail to turn such contingency to proper advantage,' wrote Mr. Dundas. He was thinking, no doubt, of the Court of France or Russia, or even of the Mohammedan Courts of Asia. But the Dragon was unique; as Macartney was to learn, there was not the smallest chance of engaging him in familiar conversation.

The specific concessions which were to be sought need not be detailed here. Suffice it now to say that Macartney was to try to rescue the English merchants in Canton from their oppressions, get a right of appeal conceded and, if possible, induce the Emperor to allow a British Ambassador to reside permanently in Peking. In short, the object of his mission was to establish modern relations between England and China.

The Cabinet did its best to make the Embassy as brilliant as possible. No expense was spared, no detail likely to enhance in Chinese eyes the reputation of England was overlooked.

Macartney's salary was £15,000 a year. He was given a distinguished staff; Sir George Staunton, Bart., his friend and a wellknown public servant, was appointed his Deputy, and he was accompanied by a number of artists and men of science. The *Lion*, a 64gun manofwar, attended by two merchantmen, was to carry him. No less than £13,124 was spent on presents for the Emperor, articles of a kind believed to be most acceptable in China, such as telescopes, lenses, guns and swords, globes, clocks and lustres, a planetarium and an orrery.

The credentials of the Embassy took the form of a letter from King George III to the Emperor Ch'ien Lung. This, needless to say, was not written, as it should have been according to Chinese usage, in the form of a humble memorial by an Outer Barbarian to the Son of Heaven, yet it was very politely worded. Ch'ien Lung was addressed as Imperator Augustissime. A high Confucian tone—or what was held to be so—was adopted. The Emperor was hailed as one whom Providence had seated on a throne for the good of mankind, and his sole desire stated to be the diffusion of happiness, virtue and knowledge among his subjects. George, 'by the Grace of God King of Great Britain, France and Ireland, Sovereign of the Seas, Defender of the Faith and so forth,' was also described as entertaining this same desire, and in furtherance thereof now sent his 'right trusty and wellbeloved Cousin and Counsellor, the Right Honorable George Lord Viscount Macartney, Baron of Lissanoure . . . a Nobleman of high rank and quality, of great virtue, wisdom and ability', to contemplate the Imperial 'virtues and to obtain such information of Your celebrated institutions as will enable him to enlighten Our People on his return'. Mixed in with this flattery was the suggestion that Macartney, if the Emperor agreed, might stay on in China to represent England, and it was hinted that he would have certain requests to make touching the conditions under which English merchants traded in Canton. He was further required 'to give, as far as Your Majesty shall please to desire it, a full and free communication of any art, science or observation either of use or curiosity, which the industry, ingenuity and experience of Europeans may have enabled them to acquire'. For this task his staff of experts had been provided.

One may perceive that the general tone of the letter to some extent followed what was understood to be the etiquette of the Court of China, but the Chinese were unlikely to find it alto, gether pleasing, for besides lacking the proper form of a memorial it contained expressions like: 'As We are Brethren in Sovereignty, so may a Brotherly affection ever subsist be, tween Us.' And King George signed himself: 'Vester bonus frater et Amicus'—hardly a way to address the Dragon!

But it had been a difficult letter to write. The Cabinet wanted to fall in with Chinese custom as far as possible without seri, ously suggesting that Britain was a suppliant or King George III a subject monarch. This was, indeed, the crux of the whole affair. Was it possible to have discussions with the Court of China in the modern sense? Was its etiquette of such a nature as to preclude negotiations or would statesmen be found there whose sense of actuality would prompt them to lay aside ancient precedent and get to business? The British Cabinet did not know. They must leave it to their representative's discretion how far to conform to Court usages and when to stand on his dignity. 'You will procure an audience as early as possible after your arrival,' writes Dundas in his instructions, 'conforming to all ceremonials of that Court which may not commit the honour of your Sovereign or lessen your own dignity.... Whilst I make this reserve I am satisfied that you will be too prudent and considerate to let any trifling punctilio stand in the way....'

But what if the Chinese insisted that the visit was a piece of ceremonial and nothing more? What if they declared it a tribute,embassy in accordance with precedent and treated Macartney as they had treated the Dutch Ambassadors a hun, dred and forty years previously? But that could hardly happen: in a hundred and forty years China must have accommodated her policy to events.

The narrative from this point will follow Lord Macartney's

private diary, supplementing it where necessary from Sir George Staunton's account of the Embassy published in 1797. The diary was not published until 1908, when Helen B. Robbins included it in her book *Our First Ambassador to China*. She, however, makes no comment upon it, beyond collating certain passages with extracts from Staunton's work and from the books of two other members of the staff of the Embassy. Nor, as far as I know, has it been the subject of detailed examina tion by any subsequent writer. Yet, it is a remarkable docu ment, for it was not written for publication, was entered up day by day, so that the writer's hopes and fears are apparent, and, withal, is the work of a man of great intelligence who was called upon to undertake what turned out to be an impossible task. It introduces us in a very direct manner to a number of the most distinguished persons at the Court of Ch'ien Lung, and, though Macartney never wholly realized that he was being made a fool of, it gives a vivid impression of an aristocrat of eighteenth century Europe moving among the baffling courtesies of the Clouds of Heaven.

We will take up the narrative at the date July 25, 1793, when the *Lion* arrived at Taku, the fort at the entrance of the Pei ho River, which flows down from Peking. Macartney had not gone to Canton like the Dutch envoys and proceeded thence overland. Having anchored for a few days at the Grand Ladrone near Macao, he had there got in touch with the Chinese authorities and was spared the long journey by river and canal, being permitted to bring his ship—a very great con cession—to within a few days' journey of the capital.

In 1793 the Emperor Ch'ien Lung had been on the throne for fifty seven years and was himself eighty three years old. His reign was the apex of Manchu power in China. On the military side, as we have shown, he carried on the steppe policy of K'ang Hsi. The Dalai Lama looked to him as suzerain, nor did the kings of Burma and Annam dare to deny that relation ship. At home his chief aim had been to conserve the Goodly Heritage, to cultivate what was old and tried, to discourage change. Traditional art and literature had his enthusiastic backing. He brought out a new and complete edition of the classics and of the twenty-four dynastic histories. Perhaps his greatest achievement was a literary encyclopaedia which embodied every book of importance which had ever been written in China, whether previously printed or not, each having its critical and bibliographical introduction, a publication without parallel in any country. He himself was a connoisseur, a prolific poet and a tireless calligraphist. The imperial collections, always large, were enormously increased by him. In the Forbidden City, in the Summer Palace of Yuan-ming Yuan, the Bright Round Garden, and at Jehol, his Manchurian hunting lodge about a hundred miles north-east of Peking, he had an accumulation of works of art, jades of all colours, porcelains, bronzes, pictures, both antique and modern, carvings in every sort of hardstone, agate, lapis and cornelian, with a great treasure of gems and gold. If he was the richest sovereign in the world, he was not, as he believed, the centre of the world, like his predecessors of the T'ang dynasty, but the centre of *a* world, a world apart.

As soon as the arrival of the *Lion* at the bar of Taku was signalled, two Mandarins of the second and third rank, whose family names were Van and Chou, came on board. They had been placed on special duty by the Emperor to bring up the Embassy. A great quantity of provisions were presented by them, for, in accordance with usage every member of the embassy, including the sailors, was the guest of the Government. Macartney was quite overwhelmed by his welcome. 'In truth,' he notes, 'the hospitality, attention and respect which we experienced . . . are such as strangers only meet with in the Eastern parts of the World.' Van, who belonged to the military department, was a hearty, good-natured man, very obliging. Chou was a scholar, had been an Imperial Tutor, and was grave, solid and careful. Their manners were perfect.

The journey up the river to Peking began on August 5, after the presents and luggage had been loaded on to the junks and sampans provided for their transport. Next day the Viceroy of Pechili, which was the metropolitan province, asked Mac-artney to meet him at a temple on shore. The Ambassador landed at once, accompanied by Sir George Staunton and the latter's son. This boy was somewhat of a prodigy. He was only twelve years of age, but was already fluent in Latin, Greek, French and German. During the voyage out he took up Chinese, and his gift for languages was so remarkable that he now knew it sufficiently to carry on a conversation and, more extraordinary still, had mastered enough ideograms for Macartney to employ him in writing letters.

At the gate of the temple the Viceroy received them 'with distinguished politeness and an air of cordiality', says Mac-artney. Staunton adds that 'he was a man of the most pol-ished manners, tottering with age, but not less dignified than he was venerable. In his reception of the Ambassador he be-haved with refined and attentive politeness, but without the constraint of distant forms or particular ceremonies.' Used though they were to the best society of England and France, they were fascinated by his ease and dignity. He informed them that the Emperor was not at Peking but at Jehol, and that he would grant them audience there.

On August 9 they reached Tien-tsin, where they were met by the Emperor's Legate, a Manchu who belonged to the Manchu Court set, the people who drew profits from the Canton trade through the Hoppo, their man. He was a very different sort of person from the Viceroy, who was a Chinese in the regular Civil Service. Macartney noticed at once that his manner was cool. 'I could not help feeling great disquiet and apprehension from this untoward disposition so early mani-fested by the Legate,' he notes.

On the way up the river to Tung-chao, the landing-place twelve miles from Peking, the Legate introduced the subject of the ceremonial usual at an imperial audience. It was cleverly done. He began by talking largely about the clothes worn by the various nations of the world, and pretending to examine the

Englishmen's remarked that the Chinese costume was more convenient as being quite loose and so giving the limbs room for the customary prostrations before the Emperor. 'I am afraid', said he, 'you will find your knee-buckles and garters greatly in the way. Perhaps it would be better to take them off before you go to Court.'

Macartney knew well that this matter of the kotow was likely to be a delicate question. So had Dundas when he wrote about trifling punctilios, but to be careful to do nothing derogatory to dignity. Well, the Chinese had brought up the subject quick enough. Macartney had given it some thought, and now replied that the Legate need not be uneasy about their buckles because it was certain the Emperor would prefer 'my paying him the same obeisance which I did to my own Sovereign'. 'But I suppose', returned the Legate with bland innocence, 'that the ceremonies in both countries must be nearly alike.' 'They differ somewhat,' replied Macartney, drily. The Legate opined that it would be difficult, if not impossible, to modify Chinese Court usages, particularly when there was no precedent. Macartney closed the subject for the moment by saying that, if on reflection the Legate continued to hold the English manner of paying respect to be insufficient, he would submit a memorandum on the subject in a day or so. In all this Van and Chou had acted as a sort of chorus to the Legate, though their manner was much more affable. Not that the Manchu was rude, but his compliments and professions were too extravagant to be sincere; they did not conceal his dislike of the Embassy. The suggestion here is that the Manchu Court party had already determined there should be no modification of the Hoppo system.

As they went up the river Macartney noticed that the flag on his houseboat bore an inscription. On enquiry he learnt that it read 'Tribute-embassy from Red Barbarians'. This was rather a shock, but he thought it prudent to conceal his knowledge. That they were labelled as a tribute-embassy did not, however, mean they were treated with want of respect. On the contrary, the guard turned out and saluted at every military post. But such was the traditional way of receiving important tribute embassies. The greater the honours paid, the greater by implica-tion the compliment to the Emperor, for the more important the tributary state, the more its submission did him honour.

On landing at Tung-chao it was arranged that before going to Jehol they should call in at the Summer Palace at Yüan-ming Yüan, a few miles beyond Peking. The more bulky presents were to be left there.

On August 21 they started up the Peking road in palanquins, on horseback and in carriages. The day before, Van and Chou had introduced again the subject of the kotow. 'It is so easy,' they said, 'nothing at all,' and they did a demonstration on the floor. 'Try it,' they urged insinuatingly, 'just to see if you could do it.' But Macartney had refused to be drawn.

Covering the twelve miles to Peking by 1 p.m., they entered the Tartar city by the East Gate. It had been a very warm jour-ney, the thermometer registering 96° F. inside the carriages. The road was much improved since the days of the Dutch embassy, being now paved with granite blocks and lined for a good part with ancient willows. Great crowds of people watched them pass. In spite of the dust and heat they found the journey enjoy-able after their long confinement on shipboard, and kept eagerly watching for the first sight 'of the greatest city on the surface of the globe', as Mr. Barrow, who was in charge of the presents, phrases it in his account of the embassy. Its popula-tion was estimated at three millions.

At the gate refreshments were served. The cortège then pro-ceeded to cross the capital, for the Summer Palace lay beyond it some eight miles on the north-west. On reaching the wall of the Imperial City, they turned north and then west, till they were at the North Gate of that enclosure. Looking through, what they saw 'had somewhat the appearance of enchantment', says Staunton—lakes and hills, pavilions clustered about them, and in the centre the yellow roofs of The Great Within. Someone pointed out the Coal Hill; they looked at it with attention and

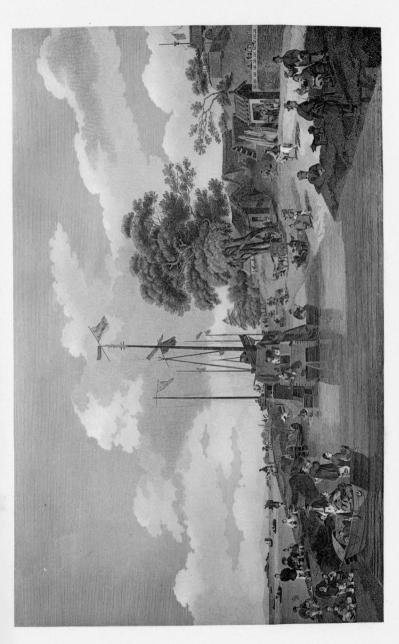

THE GRAND CANAL WITH THE EMBASSY'S BOATS

*From a painting by W. Alexander*

remembered reading how the last Ming Emperor had committed suicide there. It took two hours to reach the North-West
Gate, a space of time filled with many novel sights, one being
the Manchu ladies who rode astride, a patch of vermilion in the
middle of their lower lip. It was a hundred and fifty years since
the Manchus had come to China, but some of their women,
apparently, had not given up their out-of-door life. On the
whole the Embassy was rather disappointed. They had expected to see much grander buildings. But it was the residential
quarters of the Tartar City which they had been traversing. The
marvels of the Imperial and Forbidden Cities they had seen
only through a gap in the wall.

In the late afternoon they reached the Summer Palace in the
Round Bright Garden, a name which by classical allusion
means the garden where the mind becomes round and complete. And, indeed, Macartney was to need round clear thinking if he were to find a way out of the maze in which he soon
realized he was wandering.

But first we must get some picture of this famous garden. It
was computed by Barrow to have an area of sixty thousand
acres. K'ang Hsi laid it out, and it had been greatly embellished
by the reigning Emperor. The object of the designers was to
produce on a flat plain the illusion of a hilly landscape, and
particularly a series of view points or vistas, each of which
would be a picture in the style of the traditional masters of
painting. To accomplish this they undertook the enormous task
of making hills. The cavities thus left were turned into lakes
and canals, fed by the streams which flowed down from the
mountains on the horizon. The hills were then planted with
trees, flowering shrubs and, on terraces, with flowers, all of
these being carefully selected beforehand so that their size,
colour, grouping and significance fitted, from certain aspects,
into a composition which conformed like a painting to the
rules of balance, contrast and symbolism.

The bridge is a feature of Chinese paintings, and in Yüan-
ming Yüan there was a multitude of bridges over the winding

canals, bridges whose white marble balustrades were reflected in the water, so that where the bridge was hump-backed a circle was formed, half-real, half-reflection, a circle that seemed like a round gateway such as Chinese gardens often have, when the bars of the gate are made to resemble the ideogram that wishes you every blessing. Thus, on a day of calm, looking through such a bridge to the beautiful landscape beyond, this circle was enough to suggest to a mind sensitive to allusions that here was the gate to the Taoist paradise of the poets.

In this ideal setting were built the palaces. There seem to have been some two hundred principal structures, widely distributed over the grounds. Thirty may have been Imperial residences, the rest being for the Court, its eunuch servants and for officers of state, or pagodas and temples or lake-side pavilions. One row of these palaces was very strange. It appears that Ch'ien Lung asked Castiglione, the most talented of the Jesuit artists in his employ, to build for him some European palaces. The Italian, in collaboration with the French Jesuit, Benoist, created what was unique, a Chinese dream of the baroque. We have seen in an earlier chapter how, inspired by Chinese designs, the artists of that elaboration of the baroque, the rococo, produced a phantasy of the Celestial Empire. Here, in Yüan-ming Yüan, the opposite took shape, a vision of contemporary European architecture dreamt in China. The Jesuits had had many dreams. They had dreamed of converting the Son of Heaven and with him the countless subjects who worshipped him. That dream had dissipated, and now they built him the sort of palace in which he might fittingly have lived had he chosen to call the Pope his Holy Father. These baroque palaces were not curiosities; they were the authentic work of artists who, disappointed in their hopes as priests consoled themselves by a projection of them into architecture. For it may truly be said that if the Court of China had become Catholic it would inevitably have taken on a baroque appearance.

To this strange beautiful garden there came on Wednesday, August 21, 1793, Macartney and his well-bred companions,

WEST GATE OF THE TARTAR CITY OF PEKING AND THE ROAD
LEADING TO THE SUMMER PALACE AT YUAN-MING YUAN

*From a painting by W. Alexander*

having no thought, indeed, to turn Ch'ien Lung into a Christian, but possessed by a fancy no less extravagant of inducing
him to become a believer in Adam Smith. They were allotted
a group of pavilions among walks that wound down to a ser-
pentine canal, but found them too much like summer-houses,
unswept and draughty, though the dinner provided was very
delicious. 'The best soup I ever tasted,' says Barrow, 'their
vermicelli excellent, and their pastry unusually light and white
as snow.'

During the following days the heavier presents were set out
in the main Hall of Audience. On one side of the throne was
placed the terrestrial globe, on the other the celestial. The
lustres were hung from the ceiling, and the planetarium, orrery,
clocks, barometer and some Derbyshire porcelain arranged
down the east side. Macartney was very pleased with the result.
'An assemblage of such beauty', he notes, 'is not to be seen
collected together in any other apartment, I believe, in the
whole world besides.' He was to be disillusioned later.

On September 2 the Embassy started for Jehol, Macartney
with young Staunton travelling in his English post-chaise, 'the
first piece of Long Acre manufactory that ever rattled along the
road to Jehol'. The others, seventy in all including the guard,
rode, were carried in palanquins, or drove in carriages. There
were two hundred porters. Occasionally Van and Chou would
take a turn in the post-chaise. In their engaging way they would
open and shut the windows or pull the curtains, laughing
happily or paying compliments. During the days at the Summer Palace Macartney had submitted his memorandum about
the etiquette he proposed to follow at the audience. He would
kotow, he said, provided a Chinese official of equal rank
kotowed to a portrait of George III. The Legate shook his head
on learning of this proposal, but Van and Chou had seemed
delighted and offered to prostrate themselves there and then to
the portrait, when, as all his objections would have been removed, the Ambassador could begin at once to practise the
kotow. Macartney, of course, had meant that a Chinese official

should be authorized by the Emperor to perform the kotow publicly. With some difficulty he had restrained the eager Mandarins.

This matter of the kotow merits a few words. To kotow to the Emperor meant in the Chinese view that you acknowledged him to be Lord of the World. It was in the nature of things that a tribute-envoy should kotow, for his sole reason for coming with presents was to salute the Emperor as his suzerain lord. He would not, indeed, have been allowed to visit him in any other capacity. To come as an ambassador to discuss matters affecting the relationship of China with the country you represented was not a recognized procedure. Such an ambassador would not be received with honour; he would not be received at all. That Macartney had been welcomed, was a guest of the Empire, was being treated with every respect, signified that he had been accepted only as a tribute-envoy. For him to make difficulties about the kotow at this stage was therefore disconcerting. If he persisted the Emperor would lose face. Much had been made of him so that the significance of his kotow should appear the greater. His refusal to kotow would therefore be the greater slight. Yet from Macartney's point of view, it was impossible for him to kotow, for the object of his mission was precisely to terminate the fanciful idea that England was tributary to China and to induce the Emperor to enter into relations which corresponded with the realities of the modern world. So, as he bowled along the Jehol highway in his post-chaise, his mind was much occupied with the coming audience. Was a solution possible? It seemed the most difficult problem he had had to face in the whole course of his long career.

Taking the journey in easy stages of sixteen to twenty miles a day they arrived at Jehol on September 8 and went straight to the building reserved for their accommodation. The Legate now returned Macartney his memorandum about the ceremonial and asked him to present it to the first Minister. Strictly speaking there was no such post in China as a premier ministership. The person referred to was one of the Grand

Secretaries, who composed the inner Cabinet, Ho Shen by name, a Manchu who had become the Emperor's favourite minister. Under the late Ming such favourites had been eunuchs. The Ch'ing had so far succeeded in keeping eunuchs in their place. But like the Chief Eunuchs of the past Ho Shen had used his position to enrich himself. Now, when Mac-artney met him, he was the richest man in the world, for his estate was officially valued, when he fell six years later, at three hundred million pounds sterling.

So immense a sum as this must delay us a moment. If a Grand Secretary, after thirty years' service, was able to acquire such a fortune, what must have been the accumulated wealth of the Ch'ing after a hundred and fifty years of sovereignty? Again, if a Grand Secretary could misuse his authority to so blatant an extent, what must have been the corruption gener-ally among officials? Clive had been impeached for taking one-thousandth of what Ho Shen had taken, and that in a foreign land and after a battle. One feels that Voltaire, had he lived to hear of the Grand Secretary's loot, would have torn up all his glowing pages on the high morality of the Chinese administra-tion. That the Civil Service, which during the reign of K'ang Hsi was tolerably straight, should have reached such a pass of corruption proves that Ch'ien Lung, for all the remarkable achievements of his long reign, had allowed an evil to grow which must in the end destroy his dynasty. The façade, how-ever, was still glorious. Macartney had no idea, when he was ushered into Ho Shen's apartment on September 11, which had, he says, 'nothing magnificent in furniture or appearance', that he was in the presence of the most corrupt official of all time. Had he been allowed to wander through the private rooms of his Peking residence, however, he would not have found them so modest. He could hardly have failed to notice, for instance, that the wash-basins, spittoons and chamber-pots were of solid gold, and that the 144 beds were of lacquer inlaid with gold and gems. Had he been taken to the vaults, he would have seen gold bars worth eleven million sterling and 28,000 articles of jewellery. Somewhere about, too, was that rock of jade, eight feet long, and now in the Metropolitan Museum, New York, on which poems by the second Ming Emperor, Yung Lo, and by Ch'ien Lung himself were engraved. These objects might have set him thinking, but they were a mere bagatelle to what Ho Shen had stored in his other houses. For example, the con-tents of his antique and pawn-shops were valued at twenty millions sterling. And then there was his pearl, the Cheng Ta Kuang-ming, 'of Glorious Good Omen', the purest largest pearl in the world, and the famous pearl cape, afterwards worn on great occasions by the Empress-Dowager Tzu Hsi.[1]

When Macartney saw him on September 11, the conversa-tion turned at once to the matter of the kotow. It had already been intimated that for a Mandarin to kotow the portrait of George III was out of the question. Macartney had then sent Van and Chou to tell Ho Shen that he was ready to pay the same form of respect to Ch'ien Lung as to his own sovereign. 'What precisely is that?' they had asked. 'To kneel on the right knee and kiss His Majesty's hand,' he had explained, at the same time kneeling to show them how it was done. Chou had reported this to Ho Shen, and there was a long conference. The Legate was then sent to explain that in China one could not kiss the Son of Heaven's hand: it was a capital offence even to touch him. That must, therefore, be omitted, he said, but so that Macartney should not pay to the Emperor of China less respect than to his own king—surely the most reasonable of stipulations—he should substitute for the hand-kissing some other token, such as bringing down his left knee to the level of his right.

This would have amounted to half a kotow or, rather, the first movement of the ceremony of the kotow and, if imple-mented by a low bow, several times repeated, might have been called—allowance being made for the *gaucherie* of Red Bar-barians—three-quarters, even nine-tenths if the bow were low

[1] It consisted of 3,500 pearls, perfectly round and matched, and each the size of a canary's egg. She was often photographed wearing it.

enough, of the veritable Court Prostration. But saying this was not English etiquette, Macartney told the Legate he would not do it.

Negotiations were at this stage on September 11. The Grand Secretary received him with great affability. He looked about forty-five, and was handsome, quick and fluent. After the usual exchange of compliments he announced that it had been decided to agree to the Ambassador's proposals and that the customary prostration would be waived. The Emperor would receive him in audience on the 14th. Much relieved Macartney thanked him and withdrew, full of hope that his mission might now be successful.

Unfortunately this was not the right inference to draw. Readers of this book will by now have seen so much more of the working of the Chinese system than had Macartney, that it will be clear enough to them why his confidence was mistaken. There can be little doubt, I think, that one reason why Ho Shen consented to waive the kotow was that by doing so he was able to put Macartney in the wrong and so easily to reject afterwards all his requests. The position must have appeared to him something like this. On Macartney refusing to kotow, it was open to the Emperor to refuse audience. That would have meant, right enough, a negative answer to his petition, but such a course lacked finesse, because, for one reason, it placed the Court in the undignified position of having elaborately welcomed a man who repaid all their courtesies by refusing to conform to established procedure. The more subtle course was to modify the procedure, sanction the audience and then find suitable reasons for rejecting the petition. In this way the Court could be represented as having done everything which was humanly possible to meet the Barbarian. Moreover, it must have been calculated that the sight of him going through his foreign antics in the sacred presence would shock many spectators and make them feel that the Son of Heaven had carried his benevolence too far. And those—there were, of course, a few—who held that certain reforms in the Canton customs were desirable—needless to say, they were not members of the Court party who profited by the present exactions—would shrink in the circumstances from coming forward. There was even a further advantage. It would be bungling to offend the English past all bearing by refusing their Ambassador audience and so rejecting his pleas unheard. Far less irritating, after receiving him with every show of affability, to refuse what he wanted for reasons stated. Moreover, there were the presents. They could not be accepted if no audience were granted. Why throw away thirteen thousand pounds' worth?

How much of all this the old Emperor was told we can only surmise. The favourite knew well how to handle his master. No doubt he gave him a convincing reason for what was a change without precedent in the ceremonial.

The practice of holding audience at dawn had not altered, so that on September 14 Macartney was obliged to set out for the Court at four o'clock in the morning. 'I proceeded in great state,' he says, 'with all my train of music, guards, palanquins, and officers and gentlemen of the Embassy on horseback.' He himself wore the mantle of a Knight of the Bath over a suit 'of spotted mulberry velvet . . . with the hat and plumes of feathers which always form a part of the costume', as his valet, Anderson, noted professionally in the book he published afterwards. Staunton had the scarlet gown of a D.C.L. (Oxon.). Robed in this way they would fit better into the Chinese scene, it was thought.

Jehol had been built by K'ang Hsi partly as a hunting lodge and partly as a place where he could conveniently meet and entertain the nomad chieftains of the Steppe. It was also a Summer Palace, a garden city, but it differed from Yüan-ming Yüan in this important respect that while the scenery of the latter was artificial, Jehol was naturally a beautiful place. Its streams, hills, waterfalls and valleys, provided without much further labour a magnificent park. About it the Imperial residences were dotted. 'In harmony with the natural contours of the Country,' declared K'ang Hsi in an Edict, 'I have built pavilions in the pine groves, thereby enhancing the natural

278

beauties of the hills. I have made water flow past the summer-houses, as if leading the mountain mists out of the valleys.' There was a large central building, in which was the Hall of Audience, and many other palaces, as at Yüan-ming Yüan, joined by zigzag paths or sometimes by canals.

The Ambassador, however, was not to be received at the Hall of Audience. A group of tents had been erected in some part of the grounds, and it was there that the reception was to take place. We know that the Ch'ing Emperors, when at Jehol, liked to revert occasionally to some of their ancestral customs. The great Genghis had ruled the world from a nomad's tent. But that Ch'ien Lung preferred to receive Macartney in a Mongol *yurt* rather than in the audience-hall of the Jehol palace cannot be dismissed as entirely fortuitous. Audience in a tent must necessarily be less formal than in a palace, and the barbarous ceremonial on which the foreign envoy insisted would not be so conspicuous there. Had the Court been in the Forbidden City, Macartney's refusal to kotow must have entailed his summary dismissal. In those sacred precincts so flagrant a breach of precedent could not have been condoned for any reasons of prudence or policy.

The English alighted at the park gate and were conducted to a tent not far from the great round *yurt* which the Emperor was about to use and inside which was visible a throne on a dais. A length of green carpet led up to it.

An hour passed and it grew light. As the sun rose over the mountains drums were heard and the confused sound of distant voices. Looking in the direction they saw the imperial cortège issuing from a wood on the steep hillside, 'as if from a sacred grove'. The Everlasting Lord was seated in an open palanquin borne by sixteen eunuchs and preceded by a number of others who called aloud his many styles. Behind and about him were umbrella-bearers and musicians, and men holding aloft standards and insignia. As he drew near they perceived that he was dressed in plain dark silk, his silk boots embroidered with gold dragons, and wore a velvet cap, on which was a large pearl, his only ornament. This pearl was the famous K'ang Lung Chiao Tzu, the Azure Dragon instructing Posterity. That Ho Shen had a larger pearl was treason, and one of the many indictments afterwards brought against him.

When the Emperor was seated on the throne in the tent, with members of the Imperial Clan and certain high officers of State ranged behind him, the lesser Mandarinate in kneeling rows without, the President of the Board of Rites, whose department from time immemorial had always dealt with tribute-envoys, conducted Macartney, Staunton and young Staunton, who was acting as page and emergency interpreter, to a position below the throne on the Emperor's left. Macartney then took the gold and jewelled box containing George III's letter and mounted the dais, where kneeling on one knee he placed it in Ch'ien Lung's hands.

In return the Emperor gave him for King George a Ju-i, a token of greeting and good wishes. Macartney had never seen these curiously carved objects before nor white jade, of which this one was composed. Frankly, he thought it a poor present. The white Ju-i was followed by a green Ju-i for himself. For his personal present he now handed the Emperor 'a pair of beautiful enamelled watches set with diamonds'. Such watches were generally French and contained inside their cases classic or gallant scenes in the style of Boucher. They had long been popular at the Court of China; for years the Jesuits had im-ported them on behalf of the grandees. In the inventory of Ho Shen's possessions prepared at his indictment we find that he owned one hundred and forty of such watches. It may not be out of place to note here that he also owned nine thousand Ju-i of gold, five hundred and seven of jade, many of these inscribed on the handle with original poems by Ch'ien Lung, and no less than three thousand four hundred and eleven smaller ones of jade. He himself was kneeling beside the throne at this mo-ment, and took charge of the two watches which Macartney had given. One wonders whether the Emperor ever saw them again. But no doubt he had hundreds such already in his

THE EMPEROR CH'IEN LUNG ARRIVING TO GIVE AUDIENCE TO
LORD MACARTNEY AT JEHOL ON SEPTEMBER 14, 1793

*From a painting by W. Alexander*

treasuries. Staunton then gave him two airguns and got a Ju-i in return. Young Staunton came in for some notice, for the Emperor saw him and called him up, made him speak Chinese, and on being told he also knew Greek, Latin, French and German, gave him a fan and an embroidered bag from his own belt.

Breakfast followed. The Emperor ate his from a table placed in front of the throne, the others at tables on ground level. Macartney had now more leisure to look about him. He could see the Emperor eating heartily, 'a very fine old gentleman', he says, 'still healthy and vigorous, not having the appearance of a man of more than sixty.' When breakfast had been in pro-gress half an hour, he and Staunton were summoned to the throne to receive from Ch'ien Lung's hands a cup of warm wine, 'which we immediately drank in his presence, and found it very pleasant and comfortable, the morning being cold and raw'. The breakfast proceeded with extraordinary propriety. The Manchus had reformed their table manners. There was none of the gobbling the Dutch saw a century and a half earlier, no guzzling with raw meat, no familiar servants snatch-ing chops and stuffing their pockets. The Manchu nobility now ate like gentlemen. 'No conversation among the guests, no bustle among the attendants,' notes Staunton. 'Solemnity and silence . . . like the celebration of a religious mystery,' adds his chief.

The tent was furnished with quiet splendour. There was 'no glitter or affected embellishment,' goes on Macartney. 'The tapestry, the curtains, the carpets, the lanterns, the fringes and the tassels were disposed with such harmony, the colours so art-fully varied, and the light and shade so judiciously managed, that the whole assemblage filled the eye with delight, and dif-fused over the mind a pleasing serenity and repose.' So moved to admiration was this sophisticated and much-travelled noble-man that he adds: 'The commanding feature of the ceremony was that calm dignity, that sober pomp of Asiatic greatness, which European refinements have not yet attained.'

This is a very interesting admission. It echoes and explains the eulogies which for so long the Jesuits had written upon the Imperial Court. In the seventeen-nineties there was still something tremendous in its atmosphere. 'Thus have I seen King Solomon in all his glory,' exclaims Macartney in conclusion, and adds the curious reflection that the spectacle was like a puppet-show.

There the Ambassador spoke with an insight beyond his ordinary apperceptions. The Court of China, in truth, had become like some stage representation, because with the passage of years it no longer corresponded with reality. It had become a spectacle *de luxe*, a perfectly rehearsed ceremonial set in a background of exquisite taste, where no expense was spared to make every detail as soberly gorgeous as possible—the Emperor's boots[1] cost him a hundred pounds a pair, and he never wore the same pair twice.

Macartney's intuition that he was looking at something un-real, something which represented 'the highest pitch of human greatness and felicity', should have warned him that he could

[1] And this was not dear. Compare Tao Kuang's soup. Tao Kuang, the sixth Ch'ing Emperor, was noted for his parsimony. By making cuts right and left he brought down the expenses of his table to £60,000 per annum. The servants were in despair. Their percentages dwindled to a pitiable sum. One day, however, the Emperor enquired about a macaroni soup of a new kind. This gave them an opportunity, and in a memorial stating that the soup could be supplied they submitted estimates for an expenditure of £200,000 (non-recurrent) and £5,000 (recurrent annually). On the assumption that the Emperor might partake of the soup once a week for six months, by which time either he would be tired of it or they would have thought of something else, the cost of each bowl would be roughly £10,000, a figure that left a margin of profit sufficient, not to reimburse them, indeed, for the retrenchments which had been made, but at least to be a partial compensation. Their memorial, however, was rejected, because Tao Kuang was informed by someone that one could get a bowl of this identical soup at a restaurant near the palace gate for sixpence.

It is interesting to note in this connection that when Ch'ien Lung found he was being charged £3 a dozen for eggs, the market price being a penny a dozen, he was annoyed.

no more get into business touch with Ch'ien Lung than could a man in a theatre mount the stage, tell the actors to stop pretending and talk their story over sensibly with him. It was not until later that doubt began to trouble him. The Emperor's manner had been so encouraging, 'dignified but affable and condescending, and his reception of us very gracious and satisfactory'. No doubt Ho Shen would now arrange to see him, and he could discuss with him in detail the British proposals. Perhaps he might have opportunity of speaking to the Emperor alone on some informal occasion. He thought the mission successfully begun.

But he was quite wrong, and the rest of his stay in China was to be a gradual disillusionment. Had he known the classic saying dating from the Han dynasty two thousand years before —'The three cardinal virtues of Government are: to simulate affection, to express honeyed sentiments, and to treat one's inferiors as equals'—he might have been less optimistic. Bearing in mind that old tag we may watch how they balked him with consummate politeness.

The day after the audience in the tent he was invited to the Palace. It was long before dawn when he arrived, to wait patiently with the other lords. At sunrise the Emperor was carried into view on his way to attend early service at a Buddhist church in the grounds. Seeing Macartney he told the bearers to stop, and with great affability said he would not ask him to come because, there being certain differences between the Buddhist and Christian rituals, he did not want him to feel at a loss. Instead, the Grand Secretary would take him over the park.

Ho Shen presented himself and they set off. Macartney hoped it would be an opportunity for a little business. But the Grand Secretary kept the conversation on the objects before their eyes, the splendid avenues, the lake with its lotus flowers, the yachts on which they embarked and the pavilions they visited. These were furnished lavishly with works of art; in each was a suite of rooms beautifully arranged. Macartney saw a profusion of porcelain and paintings, lacquer and carvings in jasper and agate.

But he also saw what disconcerted him. In many of these pavilions were quantities of spheres, orreries, clocks and musical boxes. These were better made, too, he observed with a shock, than the presents brought out by the Embassy and installed with such pride in the Summer Palace. To make it worse, Ho Shen told him that the Emperor had a lot more of such articles in other palaces at Jehol and also at Yüan-ming Yüan. The fact was that from the time of Ricci, two hundred years previously, such things had been presented, imported or copied in profusion. They were novelties no more and had long ago ceased to arouse intellectual interest.

Failing during this excursion to draw Ho Shen into any discussion on the objects of his mission, Macartney asked him for a private interview that day or the next. 'I found, however,' he writes, 'that though infinitely gracious and civil in his manner and expression, I could gain no ground upon him. . . . I therefore take it for granted it has been a settled point from the beginning to do no business with me in Jehol.' The most he could do was to persuade the Minister to receive a short memorandum of the points he wished to raise. 'This is now my only resource, and I must, therefore, set about it without further delay,' he concludes, apprehensively.

Two days later he attended a ceremony which no Englishman had ever seen, the adoration of the Emperor as Son of Heaven on the occasion of his birthday. The classical name for it was Wan-shou Sheng-chieh, the Holy Birthday of the Lord of a Myriad Years. It took place in the Great Hall of the Palace at dawn. While the Emperor remained throughout invisible behind a screen, a slow solemn chant was sung by eunuchs accompanied by an orchestra of gongs, drums and bells. 'During the performance,' says Staunton, 'and at particular signals, nine times repeated, all the persons present prostrated themselves nine times, except the Ambassador and his suite, who made a profound obeisance. But he whom it was meant to honour, continued, as if it were in imitation of the Deity, invisible the whole time.' And Macartney notes: 'In no religion, ancient or

THE EMPEROR CH'IEN LUNG
*Detail from painting facing p. 280*

modern, has the Divinity ever been addressed, I believe, with stronger exterior marks of worship and adoration than were this morning paid to the phantom of his Chinese Majesty.' How was he to do business in such an atmosphere? How fanciful Dundas's idea that he might be able to get on familiar terms with the Emperor!

On leaving the palace he was invited by Ho Shen to view another part of the grounds. His hopes rose. Surely an opportunity for a little conversation would present itself this time. But no. 'I could not help admiring', he says, 'the address with which the Minister parried all my attempts to speak to him on business this day and how artfully he evaded every opportunity that offered for any particular conversation with me, endeavouring to engage our attention solely to the objects around us, directing our eyes to the prospect, and explaining the various beauties of the park and buildings.'

That was September 17. The next day, quite unexpectedly, Macartney saw the Emperor to speak to. It was at the theatre and Ch'ien Lung summoned him, perhaps from curiosity— one cannot tell. He began saying 'with great condescension of manner' how he rarely had time to see a play; he was chained to his desk; reports were always coming in. That was the worst of such a huge empire. Macartney saw his chance and tried by the turn of his reply to lead him towards the subject of the Embassy. But he became inattentive, and making the Ambassador a present of a tenth-century lacquer box and a book of his poems in his own handwriting and illustrated by himself, shook his sleeve as a sign of dismissal.

It was now announced that the Court was returning to Yüan-ming Yüan on September 24 and that the Embassy was to go on ahead to Peking. They left on September 21, no business having been done, for it was impossible to get at Ho Shen or any other member of the Grand Secretariat or the Board of Rites. Macartney found it disagreeable even to go for a stroll, for he was followed everywhere by detectives. All the English were under strict surveillance.

On September 27 they reached Peking and were lodged in a large house in the Tartar city. Macartney got the impression that the Embassy would shortly be sent home, yet so far he had been given no opportunity of discussing the objects which had brought it to China. The only paper of requests which the Government had received was George III's letter, and that was framed in very general terms. For some reason not stated Macartney had not sent in the proposed memorandum. Perhaps he had no security that it would be delivered to Ho Shen, or perhaps he thought a preliminary interview essential.

On September 30 the Emperor was due to arrive at Yüan-ming Yüan. Macartney, though suffering from gout, felt obliged to go some distance down the road to Jehol to pay his respects as he came in. When the Imperial Sedan, a yellow dragon-embroidered vehicle, swept up, the great crowd of waiting Mandarins prostrated themselves on the roadside. The Emperor noticed Macartney, who was kneeling on one knee, halted his porters and sent a civil message to the effect that having learned of his indisposition he excused him from further attendance. Macartney returned to Peking, 'extremely tired and very much out of order'.

On October 2 Ho Shen sent for him to Yüan-ming Yüan. Macartney was ushered into his office and the Minister told him how sorry the Emperor was to hear he was unwell. The climate of Peking was cold for foreigners. His Majesty felt that all the English would be running grave risks if they did not leave before the frosts. Macartney protested they were used to cold, but Ho Shen only smiled and repeated his solicitous remarks. Almost desperately Macartney tried to turn him towards the subject of the mission. 'I begged to recall to his recollection the flattering hopes he had given me when at Gehol that I should have frequent opportunities of seeing him at Yuen-min-yuen, the earliest of which I wished to take, in order to explain to him fully my sovereign's instructions to me, and to enter into negotiation upon the points contained in them; that as yet I had barely opened my commission.' Ho Shen was obviously paying little attention, but Macartney hurried on, urging that he be allowed to remain at Peking for the winter at his own King's expense 'for the purpose of cultivating and cementing a firm friendship between two such powerful monarchs'. Thereafter a Chinese embassy could be sent to London, and he would undertake its safe conduct there and back. 'I then explained to him in general terms the favours I had chiefly to ask, endeavouring to state them in such a manner, and in such terms as to take away any appearance of demand and merely to convey a sense of propriety in themselves, un-attended with the slightest inconvenience of any kind whatso-ever to China; and an assurance to him that they would be received as strong marks of benevolence and friendship towards the Prince who had sent me to request them, and whose sub-jects would always endeavour to render themselves deserving of the Emperor's favour and protection.'

Ho Shen did not attempt to cut short this outpouring; he was too polite. But when Macartney paused and awaited his reply, he merely observed that the Emperor would certainly not have insisted on the Embassy leaving for home at once were it not for his anxiety about their health.

With a sinking heart Macartney perceived the imminent failure of his mission. Ho Shen had no intention of entering into any discussion with him. 'Yet, when I rose to take my leave, nothing could be more gracious or more flattering than the expressions which he made use of.' Almost deceived afresh, he thought that perhaps, when the Minister had consulted with his colleagues, he might be summoned again. But on reaching his quarters in Peking he received information which dashed all remaining hope. The Emperor's answer to King George's letter had already been drafted and was being translated into Latin. Van and Chou, who had continued in attendance, always cheerful, always obliging, but quite useless in any matter of importance, later called to say that the Imperial Letter would probably be delivered the next day, 'in which case they advise me to ask permission to depart without delay'. Both Mandarins looked depressed. They had become fond of Macartney and his staff. They had enjoyed being on special duty, and knew too well that the news they brought would cause distress. Their dejection was more revealing than words. Macartney prepared himself for the worst.

Next day the Legate called at an early hour. Macartney was in bed, suffering acutely from his gout, which was much worse. The Legate left a message to say that Ho Shen expected him as soon as possible, as he had a matter of importance to communicate. Macartney struggled up, hurried into his Court clothes and set out. The rendezvous was an office of the Board of Rites, situated inside the Forbidden City. They passed through courtyard after courtyard, under arch after arch, over bridges of granite with balustrades of marble until they arrived in front of a palatial building. There he noticed a state-chair hung with curtains of yellow silk and on it a scroll covered with the same material. It was the Emperor's answer to King George's letter.

Ho Shen, who came forward to receive him, though more stiffly than usual, explained this, but he did not say what was in the Imperial Mandate. On some tables were a number of bundles, the Emperor's presents.

'Though almost fainting with fatigue,' Macartney made one last effort. Reminding Ho Shen of the points raised at their last meeting, he asked permission anew to submit a memorandum. The Grand Secretary did not forbid him to do so, though he gave his leave in a chilling tone.

There followed the ceremonial of despatching the Imperial Mandate, the details of which hardly differed from those reported by the Dutch in the previous century. It was bound on the back of a Mandarin and, conducted by a bodyguard of sixteen other Mandarins, was paraded in state to the Ambassador's lodging.

Its contents were appalling—there was no other word. When Macartney perused the Latin translation, this is what he found:

'Though you live, King, far beyond the oceans, nevertheless,

inspired by a humble desire to partake of the benefits of civilization, you have despatched to US a mission respectfully bearing
your memorial.

'WE have perused your memorial; the earnest terms in
which it is framed reveal a devout humility which WE find
commendable. In consideration of the long journey undertaken
by your Envoy WE have shown him special favour, even allowing him to be introduced into OUR presence.

'Your entreaty, however, that one of your nationals be
accredited to OUR Court of Heaven cannot be entertained, as
it is contrary to precedent.'

The Emperor then condescends to explain why, apart from
precedent, the proposal for a British representative in Peking is
unacceptable, pointing out, among other things, that no European, other than an Envoy, and he under strict surveillance, is
permitted to enter China, while, in cases where special sanction for him to do so is granted, he is not allowed to return to
his country or correspond with its government. Such being the
law, what advantage could accrue from such a representative?

But if this proposal was prompted, he continues, 'by your
reverence for Our Celestial Dynasty which has filled you with
the desire to adopt our civilization, WE must protest that our
ways have no ressemblance to yours and that even were your
Envoy competent to acquire some rudiments of them, he could
not transplant them to your barbarous land.'

Having thus placed George III at the bottom of the throne-
steps on his knees and elbows, Ch'ien Lung proceeds to admonish him in the classic phrases of Confucian thought:
'Swaying the wide world,' he announces, 'OUR one aim has
been always a perfect governance and WE are not deflected
therefrom by gifts. If WE have commanded that your tribute-
offerings are to be accepted, it was not because WE have any
interest in outlandish objects, but solely in consideration for the
proper spirit which prompted you to dispatch them from the
remote island where you live. As your Envoy will have seen
for himself, WE are in need of nothing, WE possess all things.

'WE have expounded OUR wishes and it is now your duty, King, to respect them, displaying in the future an even greater devotion than has inspired you in the past, so that by perpetual submission to the Dragon Throne you may insure peace and eternal prosperity for your country. Besides distributing presents (of which WE enclose an inventory) to each member of your Mission, WE confer upon you valuable silks and antiquities, somewhat in excess of what is usually bestowed on such occasions (a list of them is likewise appended). Reverently receive them and note the tenderness of OUR regard. A special Mandate.'

Prepared by what has gone before, the reader should find nothing surprising in this epistle. Its sentiments ought to be wholly familiar to him. Ch'ien Lung was expressing himself in the immemorial manner. To Macartney, who had not fully grasped the rigidity of Chinese thought, the letter seemed nonsensical. How could he present it to his sovereign? He felt bemused with gout, fatigue and disappointment.

However, he must neglect no means, and there was not a moment to be lost. He drafted the memorandum, making it as short as possible. It contained these requests—that the English merchants be allowed to trade at other ports besides Canton; be given a warehouse at Peking and a settlement on an island off the coast as the Portuguese had at Macao; and that the authorized customs dues be stated to them exactly in writing, so that they might know how they stood and be able to resist illegal demands.

This was sent off. The Embassy began to pack. They knew they were expected to leave at once. Four days later, on October 7, 1793, they left Peking, still attended by Van and Chou. On their way through the city they stopped by arrangement at Ho Shen's house, when he handed the Ambassador the answer to his memorandum. 'I said I hoped', notes Macartney, 'the answer was favourable to my wishes, as it might contribute in some degree to soften the regret which it was natural to feel on leaving the place of His Imperial Majesty's residence. He seemed as if surprised with the courtliness of such an address, considering the circumstances of the moment, and, feeling himself embarrassed to make a suitable return, changed the subject, and among other things said he hoped our tables had been properly served during our stay. . . . He had a smile of affected affability on his countenance.'

As to their food and lodging, there was no conceivable com' plaint. The Emperor had granted £500 *a day* for the expenses of the Embassy, and the house which had been assigned to them was a palace stated to have cost £100,000. It had been built by a dismissed Hoppo out of his profits from the Canton trade, which included extortions from the English merchants. 'The wits of Pekin had been much diverted with its being allotted for our residence,' observes Macartney.

When on board his house-boat at Tung-chao on the Pei-ho river, he examined the reply to his memorandum. It was similar in tone and as unsatisfactory as the first letter. All his proposals were refused by the Emperor. The letter was directed partly to George III and partly to the Ambassador. Addressed to the former was the following sentence: 'Your proposals, having a tendency to alter the whole system of European commerce, so long established here, WE cannot therefore assent to them.' This is followed by certain explanations, where trifling objections are raised and declared to be insuperable. But the Emperor is good enough to wish to save the King's face, and adds: 'WE cannot, however, believe that the above requests proceeded from your own motion; they appear to have originated from the Ambassador himself.' He concludes by further admonish' ing King George. 'WE have ever shown the greatest con' descension to the tribute-missions of all states which sincerely yearn after the blessings of civilization, so that OUR kindly in' dulgence may be manifest. Above all, upon you who live in a remote and inaccessible region, but who have shown your sub' missive loyalty, WE have heaped benefits far in excess of those accorded to other nations. But the demands presented by your Envoy are contrary to law. WE have accordingly stated the facts to you in detail and it is your bounden duty to obey OUR instructions.' He threatens that if the English should attempt to trade elsewhere than at Canton, they will be expelled and 'in that event your barbarian merchants will have had a long journey for nothing'. The concluding sentences are: 'Do not say that you have not been warned in time. Tremblingly obey and show no negligence. A special Mandate.'

Macartney saw that his mission had been a complete failure. The thing was to get home now as quickly as possible. But even in this he was to be thwarted. On reaching Tien-tsin his conductors informed him that the *Lion* had sailed, apparently for Canton. The reason which had led its commander to depart without waiting for the Embassy is too tedious to relate. Suffice it to say that Macartney and his staff were now faced with the long overland journey to Canton, the river-road over which we have already travelled with the Dutch.

If Ch'ien Lung had dismissed them, his benevolence still held. In addition to Van and Chou he appointed a Mandarin of higher rank and of the most charming manners to accompany them. He gave orders that every honour and courtesy be paid them *en route*. He increased the grant for their expenses from £500 to the quite extravagant sum of £3,666 *per diem*. And, a small point but one which showed the care and thoughtfulness he had enjoined, plenty of milk was supplied, an article of food which the Chinese themselves do not use. But it had been noticed that the English liked it in their tea, and now a couple of cows were put on a boat fitted as a stable, and remained with the flotilla throughout its journey.

All this kindness puzzled Macartney, and he wrote in his diary: 'How are we to reconcile the contradictions that appear in the conduct of the Chinese Government towards us? They receive us with the highest distinction, show us every external mark of favour and regard, send the First Minister *himself* to attend us as cicerone for two days together through their palaces and gardens; entertain us with their choicest amuse-ments, and express themselves greatly pleased with so splendid an Embassy, commend our conduct and cajole us with com-

pliments. Yet, in less than a couple of months, they plainly discover that they wish us to be gone, refuse our requests without
reserve or complaisance, precipitate our departure, and dismiss
us dissatisfied; yet, no sooner have we taken our leave of them
than we find ourselves treated with more studied attentions,
more marked distinctions, and less constraint than before. I
must endeavour to unravel this mystery if I can.'

But his diary does not show that he ever did unravel it, ever
perceived that a tribute-embassy was welcomed because it gave
occular proof to the people that their Emperor was Lord of the
World. A tribute-embassy from a country such as England,
which was reputed to be the greatest of the barbarian states, was
all the more welcome. As long, therefore, as the Embassy conformed to the rules governing its kind, it was fêted. Only when
it departed therefrom did it become subject to a mild correc-
tion. For a tribute-embassy was part of the classical play in
which the chief actor was the Ch'ing Emperor and the scene
the Great Within. Even had they been inclined to do so (which
was far from the case) the Manchu sovereigns could not have
discontinued this play, because only by acting it could they
retain the support of the Chinese *literati*, the guardians of the
Confucian Cult, without whose co-operation they must have
been overwhelmed by nationalist insurrections, for their own
nation only numbered about three million, one per cent of the
Chinese population.

That Macartney refused to kotow might seem to have spoilt
the chief scene of this traditional drama. But in the records he
did kotow. The account of his embassy filed in the archives was
explicit on that point. The future compilers of the Dynastic
History would be unable to blame Ch'ien Lung for a departure from ritual practice. And a further precaution was taken
to meet any immediate criticism. A number of those present at
the ceremony, which, as we have noted, was less public than
usual, undertook to declare that though the English Envoy had
wished to avoid the kotow, he could not when it came to the
point, for on beholding the Everlasting Lord he was overcome

with awe and fell on his knees and to the ground, an involun-
tary homage in some ways more flattering than a genuflexion
practised beforehand.

The journey to Canton took the usual two months. The
Embassy passed along the Grand Canal to the Yang-tse, and
thereafter, skirting the Poyang Lake, halting at Nanking, and
crossing the Meiling Pass, saw the identical places described by
Nievhoff. It was a lazy pleasant journey enough, and the Mandarins in charge did their best to soothe Macartney. He should
not be disappointed with the Imperial Letters. They were sure
the Emperor was in no way annoyed with him. If the Letters
were, perhaps, a little stiff, he must not mind that; it was mere
form. Things at Canton would certainly improve. But he had
no idea whether to believe them or not.

At Hang-chao they were joined by the Viceroy of Canton,
just appointed to that office and on his way to take it up.
Macartney liked him very much. 'He is perfectly well bred, and
the whole of his manner candid and gentleman-like.' As they
proceeded south in company, they had frequent conversations
about the English in Canton. He, also, begged Macartney not
to worry about their situation. The Emperor had directed him
to give them every facility. They should have free access to him
in person or by letter. Macartney began to feel reassured. If the
state papers he had to show his Sovereign were hardly satisfactory, perhaps he would be able to explain that in China
business was conducted in a round-about way. In so far as
Canton was concerned, the Viceroy, who had a wide discretion inside his own province, would give in practice what
was denied in theory. To that extent the Embassy would have
performed a useful task. Perhaps the rest would follow later.
His optimism was increased by some further presents from the
Emperor delivered to him by the Viceroy, trifles perhaps—
silk, purses, and specimens of Ch'ien Lung's calligraphy—but
showing the continued goodwill of the Government.

The slow long journey ended at last, and on December 19
they reached Canton. The *Lion* was waiting at the second bar,

A VIEW INSIDE THE IMPERIAL CITY OF PEKING

*From a painting by W. Alexander*

but for three weeks they stayed in a house provided for them on an island in the river opposite the English factory. Conferences took place at which Macartney, the Viceroy and the Hoppo discussed the grievances of the English trade. It became clear, however, that the Hoppo was opposed to any alterations, and it remained to be' seen whether the Viceroy could overrule him. Macartney does not seem to have understood that the Hoppo got his orders direct from Court and had, moreover, the same official status as the Viceroy, so that the latter had no power to interfere with his administration of the maritime customs. This gradually became clear, however, and Macartney began to realize that the professions of service which had been made to him during the journey had little practical value. Eventually all the Viceroy could or would do was to issue a proclamation threatening punishment for extortionate dealings with Euro- peans. He was transferred six months after the Embassy's departure.

On January 9, 1794, Macartney embarked for home. Van and Chou were in attendance to the last, and when the time came for them to say goodbye to their English friends they burst into tears. Perhaps the grief of these two Chinese gentle- men, 'kind, condescending, unremitting in their attentions, never out of humour', as Staunton wrote, was the most notable result of the Macartney Embassy. Suddenly all barriers between China and England were broken down in a rush of affection mutually felt.

Otherwise it was a fiasco. As a wit has summed it up, 'the ambassador was received with the utmost politeness, treated with the utmost hospitality, watched with the utmost vigilance, and dismissed with the utmost civility'.[1]

But it was the failure of an experienced and intelligent man, asked to perform a task which was not feasible. How cool and penetrating actually was his mind may be judged from certain observations which he jotted down relative to the power of

[1] *China: an Outline of its Government, Laws and Polity*, P. Auber (London, 1834), p. 200.

China and the course England might have to take in certain contingencies.

From enquiries he had learnt that the standing army of the Empire numbered a million infantry and eight hundred thou- sand cavalry, a gigantic force compared with the standing armies of Europe in the eighteenth century. But he had seen a number of regiments and considered them ill-disciplined and ill-armed. 'The circumstance of greatest embarrassment to an invader would be their immense numbers, not on account of the mischief they could do to him, but that he would find no end of doing mischief to them. The slaughter of millions would scarcely be perceived and, unless the people themselves soon voluntarily submitted, the victor might indeed reap the vanity of destruction, but not the glory or use of dominion.' This judgment is so sound and prescient that it is even valid today.

Given that the conquest of China was impossible, Macartney proceeds to speculate on what was likely to happen if the English were provoked by their treatment at Canton to use force. At any time they could seize Macao, he points out, or Lintin Island in the estuary. 'The forts of the Bogue might be demolished by half a dozen broadsides.' Then, the approach to Canton in their hands, they could blockade the city until they were granted all they desired.

Nevertheless, he sees great risk in such a course. The Chinese might not yield, and the blockade of Canton would merely ruin a trade upon which British India largely depended and which supplied the home market with tea, an indispensable commod- ity and not procurable elsewhere. A breach with China should be avoided 'if prodigious inconvenience and mischiefs' are not to follow. At that time about thirteen million pounds of tea were consumed annually by England and her dependencies.

But when he considers the present state of the Chinese Em- pire he feels these mischiefs 'may happen in the common course of things without any quarrel or interference on our part. The Empire of China is an old, crazy, first-rate Man of War, which a fortunate succession of able and vigilant officers have contrived to keep afloat for these hundred and fifty years past, and to overawe their neighbours merely by her bulk and appear' ance. But whenever an insufficient man happens to have the command on deck, adieu to the discipline and safety of the ship. She may, perhaps, not sink outright; she may drift some time as a wreck, and will then be dashed to pieces on the shore; but she can never be rebuilt on the old bottom.'

During the hundred and fifty years which have elapsed since these anticipations were written, they have been fulfilled almost to the letter. Ch'ien Lung's successors were all 'insufficient' men. Under their increasingly weak rule China drifted and became a total wreck. She is now being rebuilt, but not on the same bottom.

Should this break'up of China occur, goes on Macartney with the same brilliant foresight, probably all European nations would attempt to obtain territorial concessions, and he feels that Britain 'from the weight of her riches and the genius and spirit of her people' would get the largest of these.

This also was a remarkable anticipation of the future.

But he was against any violent policy. 'Our present in' terests,' he sums up, 'our reason and our humanity equally for' bid the thought of any offensive measures, while a ray of hope remains for succeeding by gentle ones.' He recalls that while the English merchants had never been liked in Canton, the members of the Embassy made a good impression in Peking, even won the esteem and affection of some of the leading Chinese. That was the right line. Once friendly understanding took the place of prejudice between the two peoples, an arrange' ment between the two governments would be in sight.

Macartney was a statesman, and in these speculations, re' corded privately in his diary, he is thinking like a statesman.

A number of explanations have already been put forward here to explain the Chinese government's rejection of all the Embassy's proposals, the two principal being that the pro' posals were incompatible with the Confucian system, as it had come to be interpreted, and because they would have reduced

the profits, not of the trading class, which would have benefited, but of the officials and the Court. To these explanations
must now be added another arising out of the very questions
Macartney debated in his notes.

The Ch'ing were slightly apprehensive about the English,
whose empire in India was a source of disquiet, while the
audacity and skill of their seamen, their novel inventions and
the superiority of their artillery, were no less disturbing. Many
Manchus argued that if they were not kept down, they would
acquire a dangerous grip on Canton. The inhabitants of that
city were the most independent and the least loyal in the Empire. A rebellion there, abetted by the British for their own
nefarious purposes, would not be easy to suppress. It was therefore undesirable to encourage any great increase of foreign trade.
The Cantonese were already overcosmopolitan. Let the English merchants become too securely installed there, and their
ambitions, independence, their aims and ideas would be a continuing threat to the stability of the realm. The procedure laid
down for the reception of tributeenvoys was a method, conveniently to hand, for sidetracking innovations which to accept
would have been risky and to reject in a blunt manner irritating
and, therefore, impolitic. It avoided the charge that the Emperor was turning a deaf ear to a just cause, and enabled him by
a great show of hospitality and politeness to gild his refusal to
make any changes.

There can be little doubt that these considerations had a place
with the others in determining the Government's attitude.
Macartney, indeed, had foreseen them, for they were in no way
esoteric or foreign to his experience as a European diplomat.
On the few occasions when he was able to speak to the Grand
Secretary or his colleagues, he was at pains to declare that England had no territorial ambitions in Asia, her sole desire being
open trade. The Chinese, however, interpreted her Indian
policy in a different sense. They saw England allying herself
with one feudatory of the Mogul in order to overthrow another,
and in the sequel annexing the territories of both. Their admini

stration was better adapted than the Mogul's to resist such dis-
integration, but the country contained malcontents, many rebellions had occurred in Chinese history, and they conceived the
English particularly fitted to foment another. The prudent
course was to keep such people at arms' length by trading with
them only to a limited extent, by obliging their merchants to
deal exclusively with a guild of brokers under Government
control, and by refusing them permission to reside anywhere
except at Canton, and there only during the few months of the
trading season, when, in addition, they were forbidden to move
beyond the precincts of their own factory.

Such a policy disclosed the weakness of the Ch'ing. They
dared not let too much light into China. The great K'ang Hsi
had been fascinated in the seventeenth century by the new knowledge to which the Jesuits introduced him. But these clerics,
whose love of learning was subordinated to their desire to see
China part of Christendom, overreached themselves and by
offending the Emperor enabled the party of reaction, the die-
hard Confucians, to nip a movement which might gradually
have modernized their country. By the end of Ch'ien Lung's
reign, a century later, that movement was no longer in being.
The mechanical products of the West had ceased to arouse
intellectual curiosity and had become mere objects of luxury.
Studies which had once attracted a number of clever men at
Court were abandoned, and no attempt made to keep abreast
of European developments.

This came out in a striking manner during a conversation
between Macartney and his conductors during the inland voyage. He had been travelling with the Viceroy, Van and Chou
for nearly two months, and an affectionate intimacy had grown
up between them. On the occasion in question, the Viceroy
happened to want to light his pipe, and Macartney took out of
his pocket what he calls 'a small phosphoric bottle', the fore-
runner of the match-box, and lit it for him. 'The singularity of
a man carrying fire in his fob without damage startled him a
good deal; I therefore explained to him the phenomenon and

made him a present of the bottle.' This little incident led the party to discuss chemistry. Macartney reminded them that among his staff were a number of scientists, doctors and persons skilled in various branches of applied mechanics. If he had been given the smallest encouragement or opportunity at Court, he said, it had been his intention—indeed, his Sovereign had so in, instructed him—to make a present to the Government of know, ledge which, he believed, did not exist in China, and he cited a number of examples such as restoring sight by the extraction of the glaucoma. He had brought a balloon with him, too, he added, and a man to go up in it, along with a number of the latest models in field artillery. But when he had mentioned these things to Ho Shen and offered to demonstrate them, the Grand Secretary had politely changed the subject, as if it were now the policy of the Government to keep out of sight anything which might suggest that in certain respects China was less advanced than England. Demonstrations of the kind might have revived interest in Western learning as a whole and have led to a closer contact between China and Europe, a result which the Government seemed to view with alarm.

The Viceroy and the two Mandarins were amazed when they heard this. They seemed, says Macartney, 'as if awakened out of a dream, and could not conceal their regret for the Court's coldness and indifference to our discoveries'. One is reminded of some of Ricci's conversations two hundred years before with the circle he formed of Chinese intellectuals. The movement he started was full of promise. Throughout the seventeenth century there were signs that China was about to break away from its isolation. But those enthusiastic for a wider knowledge were too few. When the reaction came it was too strong. China in 1793 was back again where she had been in 1600. Yet there must have been a large number of Chinese minds ready to absorb world knowledge, if their Manchu con, querors had permitted them to do so. One cannot resist the conclusion that, for all the intellectuality of K'ang Hsi, the Ch'ing domination was a terrible catastrophe for China be, cause the Throne, for reasons already discussed, sided with the most conservative and reactionary elements in Confucian society. But, as Macartney himself notes at this place, 'it is in vain to attempt arresting the progress of human knowledge'. That tide could not be kept out, and because it was pent up until it became a flood it swept away everything when it broke in at last. Had it been possible for Ch'ien Lung—and we have seen how difficult would have been his task—to open relations with eighteenth-century England, those elements in Western knowledge which were essential for the safety and welfare of China could have been gradually absorbed. But here we suppose that his successors were to be able men. In fact, he was the last sovereign of the Ch'ing who succeeded in maintaining peace within his territories and protecting them against foreign invasion. His death heralded a hundred and forty years of increasing ruin. The rejection of Macartney's reasonable proposals was not so much the cause of that ruin as one of the signs of its imminent approach. Its ultimate cause was the refusal to modify a way of thought after it had ceased to bear a proper relation to thought in the rest of the world. Its concomitants were a central Government which grew weaker, a bureaucracy which became more corrupt, a populace which was driven to insurrection, and foreign states which were exasperated until they began to use the superior armed force which had long been theirs.

This book has sought to trace episodically how China might have modernized herself before ruin overtook her, and how she failed to do so. There remains a final episode to relate, which takes the story to the point where England, for a century China's admirer and would-be friend, began to see her definitely in an opposite light, lost all patience and helped to compass her destruction.

That the resurrection of a new China is today of paramount interest to England, that she must contribute to it by every means at her disposal, and that China can hardly hope to achieve it without England's co-operation, is an extraordinary instance of the whirligig of time.

# IV

# Lord Amberst is refused sight of the Face of Heaven

Maybe some readers will have paused over this narrative to exclaim that surely the Chinese had every right to live as they wished in their own country. They threatened no-one. If their Sovereign arrogated to himself the title of Lord of the World, what harm did it do? He never sought to give it practical effect. And if he turned plenipotentiaries, who came to do business with him, into envoys bringing tribute, again, why should he not, if that were his whim?

And, further, were not the Chinese justified in isolating themselves from the rest of the world if they had discovered a way of life which perfectly suited them? In support of their claim to self-sufficiency, they could point to the persistence of their civilization through four millenniums, to the size of their territory, to the triumph of its art, the variety and weight of its literature, to their enormous wealth, the propriety of their manners, the comparative absence of crime, to the industry, intelligence, the happiness of a vast population.

As we know, there is much substance here. And how much more interesting was China because of her dissimilarity, because she had sought to solve in her own way the problem of living. This was precisely what had attracted Voltaire and the other thinkers of the eighteenth century. Was it not, therefore, an historical misfortune that the West sought to break down the wall? Could it not leave that lovely garden to go on blooming by itself for ever?

To these arguments we must reply that, in the world as it is and always has been, a nation can only maintain its civilization by force. China herself had in the past given due weight to that truth. Situated in Asia, she had prevented any other Asiatic race from destroying her culture. True, she had lost campaigns against the Nomads of the Steppe, but in the long run had converted them to her ways, or overcome and driven them back to their wastes. But now European races had sailed to her ports and she was not taking practical measures to protect herself. The sea frontier was open, but she built no navy. Nor did she bring her land armaments up to date. Yet in spite of her weakness, she was not prepared to accommodate herself, to make any concessions, to adjust her attitude to foreign nations. The progress of the world had carried her, against her will, into the main stream of life. She would have either to compromise or to fight, but she had made no preparations to fight and she refused to compromise.

How inextricably she was already in the toils of a new international dispensation can be illustrated by an event which occurred fourteen years after the departure of Macartney. In May 1808 Joseph Buonaparte was proclaimed King of Spain and all the Spanish possessions passed under the control of Napoleon. This meant that the Philippines became a base for the French fleet. Manila was only a few days' sail from Macao. Portugal was England's ally, and there existed reasons for supposing that the French would attempt to occupy Macao and interrupt British commerce with Canton. To counter this threat Admiral Drury was ordered to land a force at Macao. The place, as we know, did not belong to Portugal. It was owned and administered by China, the Portuguese having only the permission to live and trade there. The Chinese Government protested against the landing and the troops were withdrawn. It was no more than an episode, for Napoleon had already been worsted at sea, and his defeat on land began soon afterwards when our expeditionary force, based on Portugal, invaded Spain, and ended when it entered France. But there is interest in speculating what would have happened to China had Napoleon beaten England. Portugal being his, he would have taken over her rights in Macao. Instead of their lessees there being the remnant of a once vigorous empire, the Chinese would have seen them suddenly transformed into the vanguard of a new world conqueror. The French would certainly have adopted a forward policy. Flushed with the conquest of the West, Napoleon would have set out at once to conquer the East. With India, the Dutch Islands and the Philippines in his possession, he would have moved upon China, and on dis-covering her undefended state have occupied her ports, fo-mented a rebellion and, continuing his European practice, have placed his nominee on the Dragon Throne. In the result, China would have been opened to Western conceptions of progress and, on her overlord's death, when his dominion split up, have led a new Asia as she had formerly the old.

But this was not to happen. Instead her Government endured for a century a series of misfortunes, none of which singly was sufficient to overset it, but which cumulatively brought it to ruin and the country to its present era of desperate misery.

With the defeat of Napoleon at Waterloo in 1815, the British Government had leisure to turn its attention again to the China trade. During the twenty years which had elapsed since the Macartney Embassy, though the volume of that trade had not declined, the disabilities under which the English lived in Canton remained as before. The question arose, what was to be done? After so exhausting a war, the Government was in no mood to pursue other than an amicable policy. But would any advantage follow a new embassy? If Macartney had failed, was anyone else likely to succeed? Was there reason to expect him to get a better hearing? Would he be able to open negotiations, or would he also be turned away unheard? It was impossible to say. Some argued the chances of success were so slender that it would be waste of time to send another man. But what alter-native existed? Only demands backed by a threat of force. But an armed expedition to China was the last thing which impoverished Britain desired. So, *faute de mieux*, it was decided to try again with an embassy. George III was now mad and his son, the Regent, addressed a letter to the Emperor in January 1816.

Ch'ien Lung, having taken the title of Super-Emperor (T'ai Shang Huang) in 1795, created one of his sons Emperor under the reign-title[1] of Chia Ch'ing, High Felicity. He himself retired into the Ning-shou Kung, the Palace of Tranquil Old Age, in the north-east corner of The Great Within, from where he supervised the government. In 1798 at the age of eighty-seven he became paralysed, and at 8 a.m. on February 7, 1799, while in the Hall of Mind Culture, discarded mortality and ascended into Heaven.

Chia Ch'ing's first act was to cause the Grand Secretary, Ho Shen, to be impeached by the Censorate, not only because he had accumulated three hundred millions by corrupt prac-tices, but also on the ground that he aspired to the purple. He was found guilty on innumerable counts and permitted, by a signal act of grace, to commit suicide. His enormous fortune was confiscated by the Emperor.

This move to purify the bureaucracy—if it were such and did not owe its inception to the Emperor's desire for Ho Shen's wealth—should not be taken as showing that Chia Ch'ing was a reformer. Far from it. A weak and unintelligent man, he clung to the ancient forms, was far narrower than his father. His ex-treme conservatism was a sign of nervousness, for he had an uncomfortable feeling that the Goodly Heritage was beginning to disintegrate. The year of his accession was marked by a for-midable rebellion in Hupei, when the White Lily Society sought to overthrow the dynasty. In 1803, when he was being carried in the Sacred Chariot along the Summer Palace road, a fanatic, called Ch'eng Te, had tried to assassinate him. And

---

[1] Following current practice I have called the Emperors by their reign titles as if these were their own names. But instead of writing 'the Em-peror K'ang Hsi' or 'the Emperor Ch'ien Lung', it would be more correct to say 'the K'ang Hsi Emperor' or 'the Ch'ien Lung Emperor'.

in 1813 the Society of Divine Justice had actually seized the Gate of Azure Thunder leading to The Great Within before its members were arrested. These events proved that the Chinese people, who had not ceased to hate the usurping Ch'ing, thought that dynasty was weakening and might now be driven out.

To return to the English Regent's letter, it pretended to be dictated by the necessity of reporting George III's 'lamented and continued illness' and of improving the friendship which 'so happily subsisted between our Royal Fathers and their respective Empires'. To make this report and cement this old fellowship, Lord Amherst, a member of the Royal Household, was being sent out. As conceivably His Imperial Majesty might direct his Ministers to discuss with him matters of mutual interest, he was empowered on his part to make certain representations.

A short and non-committal letter. But the reply to the last Embassy had been so very crushing.

Lord Amherst left Spithead on February 8, 1816, and reached the bar of the Pei-ho on July 28. His colleagues were Mr. Henry Ellis, from whose diary of what transpired we shall be quoting, and Sir George Staunton, Bart., the son of the Staunton who had accompanied Macartney and who had died in the interval. From being a precocious little boy of twelve he had become a man of thirty-five who held the appointment of Chinese interpreter at Canton and was, perhaps, the greatest authority of the day on things Chinese.

Mr. Ellis was a pessimistic sort of fellow. His diary shows him to have entertained little hope of the Embassy's success. In his very first entry we find: 'Those who have perused the ac-counts of the former embassy, commenced too as it was under better prospects, can scarcely anticipate either public success or private gratification from any events likely to occur during our progress through China.' A few days before reaching the coast he speculates on what the future has in store. Arrogance he expects and 'a nation, satisfied with the hereditary mediocrity of ages, resisting the introduction of foreign, but superior knowledge'. So depressed is he at the prospect that he declares a visit to the Bedouins of Arabia would be preferable.

What actually happened, however, far exceeded his worst apprehensions.

The Government of China, when informed that a new Embassy was coming, had not been entirely pleased. For the reasons given in the last chapter, which still held, they did not want to discuss the Canton trade. No doubt if Lord Amherst could be turned into a tribute-bearing Envoy, the visit might be represented as a compliment to the Throne—and the Throne was in need of compliments at the moment. But was that possible? If he insisted on following the Court ceremonial adopted by the last Embassy, there would be no compliment. Though officially Macartney had kotowed, it was generally known or suspected that he had not, and many people had been deeply shocked. If the Amherst visit was to be of the smallest use to the dynasty, a genuine kotow was essential. It would be impossible to hoodwink or shock the public twice. Macartney's modifications would never have been sanctioned had it not been that he was already at Peking before they discovered his intentions. It was then too late to send him back without a disagreeable scandal, after the great honours with which he had been received. Lord Amherst, therefore, must make clear on landing whether he proposed to comply with the ceremonial. If not, he would be ordered to re-embark at once.

Such were the instructions issued by Chia Ch'ing, and the officials he deputed to meet the Embassy were directed to carry them out.

Now Lord Amherst and Mr. Ellis were not entirely convinced that to comply with the ceremonial would be bad policy. Both of them arrived with an open mind, and were prepared to kotow if thereby the success of the Embassy were assured. Staunton, on the other hand, was quite certain that to kotow would get them nowhere, because in the procedure for a tribute-embassy there was no place for negotiations, and the kotow, far from lifting that procedure, would settle it tighter on their shoulders. If they stood firmly on their dignity, it was conceivable the Government might be induced to discuss reforms at Canton, but if they gave way over the kotow, they would be hurried through the rest of the procedure and dismissed.

The reader will perceive it was a dilemma. But neither Amherst's nor Staunton's hopes were realizable. The Embassy could not succeed. The sole question was whether the Emperor would receive it if the kotow were withheld. But even if he did, that would have no practical importance, for nothing could come of it.

The fact that Amherst and Ellis had not entirely made up their minds led the Chinese officials to believe that after a little persuading they would agree to kotow. At the last moment it was discovered that they would not. A very curious scene resulted, one of those Oriental comedies where servile subordinates undertake more than they can accomplish, and finding they have failed attempt a desperate remedy out of fear of their master.

The Embassy was met at the Pei-ho by two Mandarins, Chang and Yin, corresponding in rank to the Van and Chou of the last occasion. By these men they were conducted in boats up the river to Tien-tsin. There two Imperial Commissioners received them, Su-leng-e and Kuang Hui. The first was President of the Board of Works and the second Director of the Salt Department. The Emperor had ordered them to give Lord Amherst an Imperial Banquet, at which, according to custom, he would be called upon, with the rest of the company, to kotow the Imperial Chair. If the obeisance were duly performed, the Mission was to be conducted to Peking. If not, the officials would memorialize and await further orders.

They did not, however, obey these instructions. After a long debate with Lord Amherst they seem to have persuaded themselves that, though unwilling to kotow at the Imperial Banquet, he might consent in the presence of the Emperor. It seemed a pity to terminate the Mission by an adverse report at this early stage, should there be reasonable hope of success later on. Accordingly, at the dinner they allowed him merely to bow, and did not tell Chia Ch'ing what had happened. More-over, they took the responsibility of permitting the Embassy to proceed up river.

During the voyage they returned frequently to the subject. The Ambassador had encouraged their persistence, for, in an effort to meet them, he had bowed to the Imperial Chair nine times. They knew this was no European ceremony and thought he was weakening. Now they worked him round till he agreed to perform before the Emperor three genuflexions on one knee, each accompanied by three low bows. As the kotow consisted of three genuflexions on both knees each accompanied by three bows to the ground, they had succeeded in bringing him a cer-tain distance. So sure did they feel of being able to bring him the rest of the way, that they sent a courier with a report that all was going well and that His Majesty could count on the full etiquette being observed.

In reply an edict was received directing them to continue the journey to Tung-chao, the port of Peking, where two legates, officials of the highest rank, would meet them with further in-structions. These were Ho Shih-t'ai and Mukdenga, the one an Imperial Duke and Comptroller-General of the Household, and the other President of the Board of Rites. Their instructions were to rehearse the Mission in the ceremony of the kotow.

On arrival at Tung-chao six Mandarins of the Court party subordinate to the above personages came on board and in an abrupt manner informed Lord Amherst that at noon next day their chiefs would instruct him how to prostrate himself. Their manner was meant to be intimidating, as if they thought it only required this to turn the scale. But there they miscalculated the English character, because as soon as Amherst saw himself threatened he decided to make no concessions whatever. If he had hesitated before out of policy, his courage now prompted him to harden his mind. Nor did the blandishments of Yin and Chang in any way deflect him. In character these two

Excellencies were not unlike their predecessors Van and Chou. That night they were all 'intimacy, friendship and humility', says Mr. Ellis, and confided ingenuously that the Court Mandarins had also been extremely rude to them.

On the following day the Ambassador went ashore to meet Duke Ho and His Excellency, Mukdenga. These men had consulted the Embassy's four conductors and knew that Amherst had offered to kneel thrice and bow nine times and, convinced they could persuade him to concede the rest by a show of severity, continued the stiff line which the Court Mandarins had been instructed to take the previous evening. It should be pointed out that they had strong professional reasons for wishing to reach an agreement. If they succeeded it would be something of a diplomatic triumph; if they failed they all ran the risk of incurring the Emperor's displeasure, particularly the two Imperial Commissioners on whose assurances the Embassy had been permitted to advance as far as Tung-chao.

On being ushered into the room where Duke Ho was waiting, Lord Amherst found that no chairs had been set for him and his staff. When he protested, the Duke announced that he himself proposed to stand, and immediately began in a lofty tone to speak of the kotow, using such expressions as: 'The regulations of the Celestial Empire must be complied with', and 'There is but one sun and but one Emperor: he is the universal sovereign and all must pay him homage.' Amherst remained calm, but would not promise to do more than the agreed ninefold bow. The Duke trembled with rage, real or affected, and told him he must either comply or be sent back. The meeting broke up on this note.

The grandees then seem to have realized they were employing the wrong tactics. They had completely failed to intimidate their man. During the following seven days a long discussion was conducted through messengers, the Duke using every diplomatic device to bring the English round to his view. When Amherst found himself no longer threatened, his native stubbornness began to give place again to uncertainty. Perhaps it would be more politic to comply. After all, there was very little difference between what he proposed and what was required of him. Ellis had all along been of this view and took the opportunity to press it again. Staunton, however, declared it a mistake. But in a meeting with the Duke on August 26 Amherst told him that if the Emperor declared in writing that Lord Macartney had kotowed, and that if he gave some assurances that the requests the Embassy had to make would receive sympathetic attention, he would reconsider his refusal.

Ho was delighted and gave him all assurances, adding that if he complied with the ceremonial he might count on his fullest support with the Emperor. It seems that he thought all won, for he sent off an express to Court, stating he had reason to believe the matter settled. The Emperor accordingly gave orders that the Embassy should come on at once. He was in his Summer Palace at Yüan-ming Yüan, some twenty miles away.

But when Amherst returned on board his houseboat after the interview with Ho, Staunton told him that the delegates from the Canton factory who had come with them were unanimously against the concession because, they said, it would injuriously affect the Company, whose standing at Canton depended largely upon the inflexible way it had always maintained the national dignity. If they began copying the Portuguese and the Dutch, their reputation as resolute upholders of their rights would be destroyed. The Chinese would take advantage and increase their exactions, thinking the English were becoming afraid. Amherst from his recent experiences saw the truth of this and immediately wrote to the Duke, stating finally that he could not kotow.

By the time he got this letter, Ho had his orders from Peking. It was an awkward position. He had been too sanguine and precipitate. But how could he now memorialize the Emperor that, after all, the Ambassador had refused? To do so would certainly lead to his disgrace. He consulted his colleagues, who were no less involved than he. They came to the conclusion that the only course was to comply with the Emperor's decree and send the Embassy to Yüan-ming Yüan. When there, perhaps, the Ambassador would change his mind again. He had already changed it several times.

The Duke, therefore, called on Lord Amherst and told him that the Emperor expected the Embassy immediately. They must be ready to leave the next day, since His Majesty had fixed an early date for his annual tour to Jehol. Amherst pointed out that, as it was already late afternoon, it might be difficult to get all the luggage and the boxes of presents loaded in time. The Duke said the presents were mostly landed; it should be pos-sible to get off next morning. 'But have you read my letter?' now asked the Ambassador, anxious there should be no mis-understanding about his attitude over the ceremonial. The Duke bowed and said he understood the position perfectly. Here he rose to go, a confidential smile on his face, as much as to say: 'Do not press me for details now: but take my word for it, the affair is settled.' And he added aloud: 'The Emperor is a man of the most liberal mind: the matter of the kotow will not be mentioned again.'

After all, it was impossible for him to tell Lord Amherst the truth. Had the Ambassador known he was being brought up on false pretences, he might have refused to go and asked for his dismissal. And a sudden rupture of that kind would have been difficult to explain to the Emperor in the circumstances.

By the greatest efforts the boxes were packed and loaded dur-ing the next morning. Lord Amherst's carriage, which he had brought with him, was put together, but it was 5 p.m. before everything was ready. The distance to Peking, as has been stated, was only twelve miles and, not counting the traverse of the city, six miles more brought you to Yüan-ming Yüan. Amherst did not realize it would take the Embassy very long to cover the distance, and though he thought five o'clock rather late to start, yielded to pressure and they set out. Duke Ho had gone ahead early in the morning. The journey, how-ever, was to take much longer than expected. The many palan-quins set the pace; the paved road, though well suited for carts, pedestrians or horsemen, was too rough for the carriage to go faster than a walk. When night fell they were no great distance beyond Tung-chao. About half-way to the capital a halt was made at a rest-house for refreshments. The Imperial Commis-sioners, Su-leng-e and Kuang Hui, were waiting to meet them. This caused some delay, and an hour or so passed before they took the road again. One of the Commissioners remarked casu-ally that he had just heard the audience was arranged for the very next day; otherwise they might have slept where they were. But Amherst did not pay any attention to this, for Ho had given him to understand that the day after was the date fixed.

Another three or four miles took them to the eastern suburb of Peking outside the walls. As they passed through a shopping quarter, crowds of people approached the procession holding lanterns and peering at the foreigners. On reaching the East Gate the gongs sounded the hour of midnight. It had been rumoured that by a special order of the Emperor the gate was to be open and they would be enabled to pass through the city by the route taken by Macartney. But it was shut, and the cavalcade turned north to skirt the walls. All night long the vehicles slowly went forward, Yüan-ming Yüan not being reached until after dawn. Very exhausted by their sleepless night and the rough passage, Amherst, Ellis and Staunton were set down under some trees before a line of buildings. The servants, the baggage and all but six of the staff had not come up. Where they were, no-one could tell.

Duke Ho and his colleague, Mukdenga, who had twelve hours' start of the Embassy and went on horseback, had arrived at the Summer Palace the previous day at noon and were summoned by the Emperor at 1.30 p.m. The audience took place in a minor throne-room known as the Hall of Diligent Government. Chia Ch'ing, who wanted to know precisely what had happened at Tung-chao, for, as he com-plained afterwards, the Duke's message that Lord Amherst was ready to perform the kotow had been expressed in very vague terms, began to examine and then to cross-examine his Comptroller-General. Had the Ambassador been rehearsed or not? Had he actually performed there a specimen kotow? The ques-tions were so sharply framed that the Duke suspected the Em-peror of private information, and, despairing of a lie, blurted out that it had not been possible to hold a rehearsal. 'If the Ambassador refused, why then did you not denounce the Mission to the Throne?' demanded Chia Ch'ing. By this time Ho and his companion were panic-stricken. They had torn off their hats, a sign of the utmost contrition, and kept on knock-ing the floor with their foreheads. At last the Duke summoned up courage to say: 'I guarantee that when the audience takes place the ceremony will be performed in its entirety.'

This satisfied the Emperor. He gathered that Lord Amherst had made difficulties, but eventually had consented to do what was necessary. He therefore fixed the audience for 6.30 a.m. the next day.

When the Duke had left Tung-chao that morning he be-lieved the Embassy would be following immediately and would arrive at Yüan-ming Yüan that night. The Ambassador could then be informed that the Emperor was receiving him next morning and, though the notice would be short, it would not be too short. The probability is that Ho told the Emperor when he saw him the time the English were expected to arrive. Quarters had been reserved for them at Hai-tien, a village some three miles outside the Summer Palace enclosure. They would sleep there and come on early next morning to the audience. Ho must have sent word of these arrangements to the Imperial Commissioners. It does not seem that they let him know in reply how late the Embassy was in starting, and how it could not arrive until the next morning. As he did not hear, he assumed all was well, and circularized the officials to be present at the appointed hour.

The Emperor rose the next morning at 4 a.m. and partook of breakfast. At 5 a.m. he was dressed in the Dragon Robes, and shortly before 6.30 issued a Decree that he was about to proceed to the Palace of Light and Splendour, as the main audience hall of the Summer Palace was called. The Imperial Clansmen, who were Princes and Dukes, and the great officers of state, such as the Grand Secretaries and the Presidents of the Boards, each in his appropriate dress, stood waiting on both sides of the Hall. The Imperial Body Guard, in leopard-tail uniforms, took its position and the Imperial Band watched for the signal to strike up the tune called *Lung-ping*, a sort of national anthem, whose title suggests 'peace after conquest', and which was always played at the approach of the Emperor. It was the sacred moment known as *Sheng Tien*, when the Son of Heaven is about to ascend the Dragon Throne.

Duke Ho, who had been looking out for the Embassy and was expecting to see it arrive any moment from its quarters at Hai-tien, was now informed that it had started late from Tung-chao, had not reached Hai-tien in time to sleep, but had travelled all night and was still some distance down the road. This was disconcerting news with the Son of Heaven waiting to begin the audience. The position was altogether very delicate, for while the Emperor believed the Envoys would kotow, Ho was painfully aware of the opposite and had been counting on sufficient time in which to make a final appeal to Lord Amherst. It did not look as if he would have any time. The question was what to do. One thing at least was clear. The Emperor must be warned that the Embassy was late. For him to mount the throne and then have to wait, would be accounted shocking mismanagement. The Duke, therefore, sought private audience and reported that the Ambassador had been unexpectedly delayed on the road. Somewhat put out, the Emperor directed the audience to be postponed, and desired the Duke to report immediately the Embassy arrived.

It was shortly after this that Lord Amherst and his companions, heavy-eyed, unshaven and in their travelling clothes, were conducted from their vehicles to a waiting-room in the group of buildings which contained the throne-room. The apartment was not large and it was crowded with Mandarins, both official and of the Court nobility, who on hearing that the audience was to be delayed had left the throne-room and were idly chatting there. As the foreign Ambassador entered, there was a general silence and they all stared at him. The occasion was so unrehearsed that it was nobody's duty to come forward and welcome him. His conductors found him a chair, and there he sat in his crushed clothes, unwashed, unbrushed, while the Court dandies and fops eyed him, as their opposite numbers at the Court of St. James would have eyed a dirty-looking Chinaman.

In a few minutes Chang, friendly pleasant Chang, came in with a message from Duke Ho to say that the Emperor wished to see the Ambassador and his two colleagues immediately. 'But', exclaimed Lord Amherst, 'I thought the audience was fixed for tomorrow!' 'I am instructed to say', repeated Chang, 'that His Imperial Majesty expects you at once.' 'How can I present myself in this state?' urged the Ambassador. 'My King's letter, my Court clothes, the presents—they are all with the baggage. Besides, I am excessively fatigued. Have the goodness to ask the Emperor to give me time to prepare.'

Chang at first replied that he could not take such a message, but was finally prevailed upon. During his absence the English-men remained the target of the courtiers' glances. Some of these came up close and coolly examined them. None made any at-tempt to address them politely, though there were interpreters in attendance: Staunton, moreover, could speak Chinese.

An exchange of messages now took place between Duke Ho and the Ambassador, but the latter persisted in declaring that for him to present himself before His Majesty, overwrought and unprepared as he was, remained impossible.

It seems that when Duke Ho saw the lamentable condition to which His Britannic Majesty's representative had been re-duced by a night in an English carriage on Chinese roads, an idea had struck him. If he could get the fellow into the Presence, he should be able to jockey him into a kotow. A man so fatigued as he appeared to be could no longer be very tenacious about dignity. A little pressure, a little horseplay even—we

THE HALL OF AUDIENCE AT YUAN-MING YUAN

*From a painting by W. Alexander*

must remember that Ho was a Manchu, a big bluff Northerner, whose Chinese manners were only skin-deep—a little jostling at the right moment and the Englishman's resistance would give out. When, therefore, Ho's messages were met with refusal, he appeared himself in the waiting-room and, accosting the Envoys and roundly declaring that His Majesty could not be kept waiting any longer, seized Lord Amherst by one arm, a Mandarin taking the other, and assuming a jocular breezy manner, tried to hustle him from the room. His intention, presumably, was to get him across to the audience-hall and into his position in front of the throne, give the signal for the Emperor to take his seat and, at that solemn moment when the assembled grandees fell face downward, either by a last minute appeal to the noble lord's sense of what was proper or by pulling him down with him or tripping him up cause him to perform some sort of a prostration, hardly a graceful one, no doubt, but lack of grace could be attributed to his barbarian lack of culture. But Amherst, who seems to have guessed they intended to manœuvre him into a kotow, though Ho protested he need apprehend no trick of the kind, 'with a great deal of firmness and dignity', says Ellis, who was watching the scene with indignation, 'shook them off, declaring that nothing but extremest violence should induce him to quit the room for any other place but the residence assigned to him'.

Worsted, the Duke left the waiting-room. He was now summoned again to the Presence. Chia Ch'ing, who knew that the Embassy had arrived, enquired the cause of the further delay. Ho was afraid to tell him that the Ambassador desired a postponement, being unprepared for an immediate audience. To have done so would have been to confess that he had mismanaged the business which had been entrusted to him and exposed the Emperor to inconvenience. In desperation, therefore, he declared that the barbarian Envoy had got stomach-ache. 'But that should not prevent him from making a short appearance,' said the Emperor. 'He is so bad that he cannot move,' said Duke Ho with solemnity. 'WE directed', wrote the Emperor later, 'that the Ambassador be taken back to his lodging and supplied at once with medical aid, after which WE desired the immediate attendance of his deputies.' The Duke, who knew well that Staunton and Ellis would also refuse to appear, could do no more in answer to the second order than mutter unconvincingly: 'The two subordinate Envoys have also the stomach-ache.'

The Emperor was furious. Believing that he was being trifled with by men whom he knew had already made trouble over the matter of the kotow, he immediately issued a decree commanding the Mission's expulsion. 'China is lord and sovereign of the world,' he wrote in an Edict describing the event. 'Was it possible for US to submit calmly to such a calculated display of irreverent arrogance?'

While the Emperor was dictating the decree, the Duke returned to the room where Lord Amherst was waiting. There he repeated to him only the Emperor's first order, saying that he had been excused from appearance and would be conducted to the quarters reserved for him at Hai-tien. To tell him the rest, and before witnesses, was obviously impossible. There followed a little scene which Mr. Ellis found indecorous and somewhat puzzling. The Duke, when seeing Lord Amherst to his carriage, drew his whip and began laying about him to clear a way through the crowd of Mandarins. These were Manchu manners, and we think he was in roaring good spirits because he believed his troubles were at an end. What a stroke of luck that the Emperor was getting rid of the Embassy, for now he need worry no more about the kotow. But he was being too sanguine again. His troubles, alas! were only beginning.

Amherst drove off. He, too, was relieved, thinking that the Emperor had seen the reasonableness of his request for a postponement, and expecting that a fresh date would be communicated to him in due course. When the carriage reached Hai-tien village, it stopped before a delightful country-house, pleasantly situated among trees and flowers. Here was found the rest of the Embassy. The baggage-carts had just arrived.

Amherst went indoors to rest, telling them to bring the boxes in. His first intimation of something untoward was the news that the cartmen refused to unload. On enquiry it was learnt they had orders not to do so. Soon afterwards some Mandarins appeared with the Emperor's Decree and desired the Embassy to leave at once. It was a shocking surprise. When Amherst pleaded that he and his staff were in urgent need of refreshment and repose, he was told that the Emperor's commands allowed of no delay. But why were they being expelled? It could not be the kotow; the Duke had assured them that was settled. And surely the Emperor was not so unreasonable that, informed of their all-night journey, he should punish them for having refused to appear. To these questions they could get no coherent answer from the Mandarins.

However, in China the unexpected always happens. When in much dejection they were preparing to re-enter the carriages, a body of servants appeared bringing a magnificent breakfast, a present from the Emperor! Though we know all that had happened at the Palace, which was more than poor Amherst did, it is doubtful whether we can adequately explain that breakfast. Yet anyone with experience of the Chinese will see in it their feeling for appearances, their dislike of carrying a scene à l'outrance and their innate caution which disposes them to hedge. Yet, of course, the breakfast may have been ordered before, and it was no-one's business now to cancel it.

Tension was relieved. They sat down to eat, and not till four o'clock did they begin the journey back to Tung-chao. To avoid the jolting Lord Amherst had himself carried in a palan-quin. So did Staunton, but Ellis gave up his to an invalid and got into a cart. When they had been going some time, he could stand the shaking no longer and decided to walk. Jaded as he was from the previous night, stumbling into pot holes and drenched with heavy showers, his annoyance became acute. 'I never felt so irritated in my life,' he says. Yin was with them, one of their original conductors, and he, in a way characteristic of his nation, tried to soothe them by saying—a loyal prevarication or a half-glimpse of the truth—that it was not really the Emperor's intention they should have gone back. Haggard and low-spirited they reached Tung-chao at three o'clock the next morning, August 30.

The following day, surprising to relate, the Emperor sent down some presents—a white and a green jade Ju-i and ten embroidered pouches—and announced that he would be pleased to accept some trifles in return. Accordingly, portraits of the King and Queen, a case of maps and some colour prints were despatched. On September 2 the Embassy left Tung-chao for Canton by the overland route. They had not seen Duke Ho or any other important Mandarin, nor had they received an official letter stating the grounds for their dismissal. Though every sort of rumour was current, they were not sure to what to attribute it.

Leaving them to their slow journey—it took four months instead of the more usual ten weeks—we must now return to Yüan-ming Yüan and enquire what happened there after their expulsion.

It seems that on August 30, the day after, the Emperor gave audience to the Court nobility and officers of state out of a desire to elicit further information about Lord Amherst's be-haviour, and perhaps to sound official opinion on the Edict of expulsion. In the course of the audience he learnt of the true state of affairs, that the Envoys had only just arrived after an all-night journey and were without their Court dress or papers, that the application for postponement was made on that ground and that stomach-ache had nothing to do with it. Deeply per-turbed by this information, which showed him to have passed orders under a misapprehension, he published in the *Peking Gazette* of September 4 an Edict in which he gives an account of the whole episode. 'If at that time', he writes, referring to the moment when the Envoys arrived, 'Duke Ho had addressed to us a true report, we would certainly have issued a decree and changed the date of the audience.' He goes on to blame the other officials present. 'All the Court nobility and great Officers

320

of State were waiting in the anti-chambers and must have been eye-witnesses. Yet, though it was their duty to report to US when they saw Duke Ho mishandling the situation, and to petition for a postponement, they sat immovable and speechless in their chairs.' Such officials were useless, he continued. If they hesi-tated to report, they should at least have protested to the Duke that the Ambassador had reason on his side. Their complete indifference to the obligations of their high station made him sigh, he confessed, and in conclusion he lectured them thus: 'Whenever you perceive failure of loyalty or of public spirit let no-one plead that it does not individually concern him. Let all of you look up diligently to the Face of Heaven[1] and regulate your conduct by the admonitions WE have repeatedly given you. Respect this.'

Here we have the explanation of the presents sent after the Envoys, an action which puzzled them, for it was unaccom-panied by any letter or message, nor was there any suggestion that they might be recalled. But we perceive that, though the Emperor now knew the truth, he was not prepared to cancel his expulsion order.

Shortly after the publication of the Edict in the *Gazette*, he addressed a Vermilion Edict, that is to say a State Paper written by his own hand, to the Civil Service. In this he details the misconduct of the Imperial Commissioners, Su-leng-e and Kuang Hui, and of the Legates, Duke Ho and Mukdenga. Its terms show that he had made certain enquiries and was at last fully aware that his instructions to rehearse the Embassy in the ceremonial had been disobeyed and, so, that it ought never to have been permitted to come up. That was one dereliction of duty on the part of all the four officers. Then came Ho's false insinuation that the Envoys were feigning illness, when in fact their reluctance to appear was due to their night journey. By thus deceiving him, Ho, and by collusion Mukdenga, were respon-sible for the expulsion order, which should not have been issued on such grounds. They had therefore caused the Emperor to lose

[1] One of the styles of the Emperor of China.

face. 'I am astounded at the way my stupid officials have mis-managed this business,' he concludes, adding that the Board of Civil Office will be asked to recommend appropriate penalties.

When the recommendations were made, he relieved Su-leng-e of the Presidentship of the Board of Works, reduced him three grades in the Civil Service and appointed him Super-intendent of the Imperial Gardens. Kuang Hui was trans-ferred from his Directorship of the Salt Department, reduced to the last grade but one and posted to officiate as Magistrate in a frontier district. Mukdenga, who was very old, was retired from his appointment as President of the Board of Rites. As for Duke Ho, by far the most active culprit of the four, he was relieved of his Comptrollership, fined five years' emoluments as Duke and had his decoration, the Yellow Riding Jacket, taken away.

While these transfers and penalties were being debated at Court, the English reached Canton, where the Emperor's letter to the King of England was delivered to them. Though in the *Gazette* and in his Vermilion Edict Chia Ch'ing had openly declared his mistake and how it had arisen, he did not believe in the propriety of frankness to a barbarian. In point of fact, he had to be circumspect, for if he were to write that he would not have dismissed the Envoys had he known the cir-cumstances, he risked the riposte—why did you not recall them when the circumstances became known to you? The reason, of course, was that he had also discovered they should not have been allowed to come at all, because they had refused to re-hearse the kotow. But he was disinclined to lay bare to foreign eyes the mistakes which had been made, and composed a letter which hushed them up by recounting only part of the truth and containing besides a quantity of mis-statements.

The letter begins by recalling the previous Embassy and not-ing that Macartney had performed the kotow (a statement which was true only in so far as it corresponded with the Chinese official records). For the new Embassy, says the Em-

peror, exactly the same ceremonial was prescribed. The Am,
bassador, however, early showed a perverse disposition. At a
banquet given at Tien,tsin, he failed to conform with etiquette.
'Nevertheless WE bore in mind that the lowly official of an
outer barbarian king could hardly be expected to show fami,
liarity with our ceremonial usage and were pleased to pardon
his remissness.' This was, as we know, a mis,statement, for it
was precisely because the Emperor was *not* informed of what
happened in Tien,tsin that the Embassy was allowed to
proceed.

Chia Ch'ing then alleges that, when on approaching the
metropolis Lord Amherst's attention was again drawn to the
kotow executed by his predecessor, he promised to perform a
like prostration. Satisfied that all was well, 'WE decreed August
29 for the audience. On August 30 WE fixed a dinner,party in
the Hall of Perfect Rectitude and Enlightenment, with a further
entertainment in the Garden of Universal Joy. On August 31
there was to be the Farewell Audience, followed by a conducted
tour over the grounds of the Summer Palace. Finally Sept,
ember 2 was fixed for the reception of OUR Mandate at a
main Hall of The Great Within, with a banquet that night
at the Board of Rites.'

What could have been more handsome, more condescend,
ing than such a programme, asks the Emperor. It was com,
municated in its entirety to the Ambassador, who expressed
himself as greatly honoured and pleased. 'Yet on his reaching
OUR Palace gate on the day appointed long beforehand, when
WE were about to take OUR seat on the Dragon Throne, he
suddenly announces that he is unwell and unable to move.'

The Emperor then goes on to say that his first impulse was
to believe this statement, that he at once excused the Ambas,
sador and ordered a doctor to attend him. But when he com,
manded the presence of his deputies, they sent in the same
message that they were unwell.

Barbarian though you are, continues the letter in effect, you
must admit that this was rudeness. The whole Court was

assembled, WE were waiting in OUR Dragon Robes, when deliberately to slight the Throne your Envoys refused to present themselves. 'Such discourtesy is unprecedented. Nevertheless WE administered no reproof, WE ordered no punishment, but merely directed their immediate departure.'

As for you, poor King, your motives were good. 'WE fully recognize the spirit of reverent submission which animated you. Your Envoys are alone to blame for their gross breach of respect. WE accepted your tribute and, to acknowledge your devotion, have in turn conferred presents.'

The letter ends with a sympathetic admonition. 'Living at such a distance these embassies must cause you great trouble. Nor are they less troublesome to US on account of the indecorous scenes to which they give rise. The presents they bring are of no interest or use. In future do not bother to despatch them, for they are merely a waste of time. You will be better employed admonishing your subjects and improving your defences. If you loyally accept OUR sovereignty there is really no need for these stated appearances to prove that you are indeed OUR vassal.'

This letter is dated September 11, a week after the Edict in the *Gazette*, in which Chia Ch'ing showed himself to be in possession of the truth. But in all the circumstances it was hardly possible for him to have written in any other way.

If Lord Macartney's Embassy had been a failure, Lord Amherst's was a fiasco. The first Lord's requests were all refused, but he was treated with a magnificent condescension; the second, whose requests never reached the stage where it could be said they were refused, for his letters were not presented, was met with a bare civility which degenerated into rudeness when the officials responsible for conducting him became alarmed after bungling their instructions. The judicious reader, however, will have perceived that he was responsible in some degree for the fate which overtook him. Both he and Ellis, not being quite certain in their own minds about the kotow, led the Emperor's delegates to believe they might be persuaded, and it was that vacillation which was the cause of all that followed. Had they made it unmistakably clear from the start at Tien-tsin what ceremonial they intended to follow, they would either have been allowed to come up on their own terms or have been turned back from the port of entry, and the latter would have been preferable to expulsion from the capital.

The Embassy, however, served its purpose, for it made abun-dantly clear, what had been suspected, that no negotiation was possible with the Court of China. The issue was therefore clear. Either the British would have to continue to trade at Canton under the conditions to which they had submitted for over a hundred years, or they must take the risks which Lord Macartney had sketched and by a show of force endanger what in spite of insults and exactions remained a highly lucrative and vital commerce.

But, in fact, the breaking point had been reached or was very close. Ellis's remark, 'I never felt so irritated in my life,' summed up not only the feelings of himself and his companions but of the British Government. It marked the end of one epoch and the beginning of another. The Embassy of Lord Amherst was China's last opportunity of effecting a peaceful and dignified change in her relations with the Western world.

# V

# *The Lord of Ten Thousand Years flees from The Great Within*

The fall of the Great Ming was an episode in Chinese history: the fall of the Great Ch'ing was an event in world history. The first was a dynastic change which did not fundamentally affect the country's structure, her policy or her civilization; the second revolutionized all these three things. The Great Ming fell because the Government was weak and corrupt, the people rebellious, and because a military state, outside the political but inside the cultural boundary, saw its opportunity and entered the realm. The Great Ch'ing fell for the same reasons, with the important difference that the military force which entered belonged to a distinct civilization. The fall of the Ming was one of many such dynastic changes, none of which modified the Confucian conception of The Great Within as the centre of the world. But the fall of the Ch'ing meant the end of the Confucian universal state, both in practice and theory, and so the end of Chinese civilization as the cradle of that idea. Thus the fall of the Ming was not, but the fall of the Ch'ing was, equivalent to the fall of China as it had been known for millenniums.

Could China have saved her old self? This book suggests the answer. Confronted with the dynamic civilization of the West at a moment when her condition was static, she could have saved herself, in the sense of a political and military salvation, by methodically selecting those elements in Western civilization which made for political stability and military power, though by so doing she would gradually have modified her Confucianism out of existence and so deliberately have abandoned the particular ideas which had made her a distinct entity. In a philosophical sense, therefore, the West was inevit, ably fated to deal her a mortal blow, because in order to prevent that blow ending her sovereignty she was bound to abandon her political philosophy. But, as we have seen, she refused to abandon it and so, in the event, lost both philosophy and sovereignty.

So much of this book has been devoted to depicting the tragi-comedy of a universal state persisting into an age when it had become a curiosity, that it may be well to recall how it was founded to meet a very practical situation. In the centuries pre, ceding the third century B.C. the immense area afterwards known as China was a continent containing as many separate nations and governments as does the continent of Europe to, day, and these nations were as constantly and as fatally at war with each other as are now the nations of the West. In the remoter past there had existed a sort of Holy Emperor of the whole continent, and this historical tradition was revived when in 221 B.C. the King of Ch'in after a series of wars absorbed all the other states and united China under one sovereign govern, ment, with an administration which displaced feudalism by introducing bureaucracy. The success of that unification was extraordinary, because since then nothing has been heard of the original separate nations and their rivalries. Whatever tur, moil or misfortunes afterwards afflicted the united nations of China, none was due to nationalist wars between them, for absolute peace in that sense reigned inside the continent for ever afterwards. It was the constant policy of the Chinese Govern, ment to extend the incalculable benefits of that peace to all bordering nations and beyond them as far as knowledge went. The whole of what we call the Far East was stabilized in this manner, and thereby was enabled hundreds of years before Europe to develop and preserve a civilized way of living. Hence the reason that the nations of Europe, sailing from beyond knowledge when they appeared on China's coast, were invited to join the universal state, for, in theory, they were being offered the greatest blessing imaginable. But they were in that stage of development which precedes the universal state, the stage which had obtained in China before the second century B.C. Their interests were national, not universal. Yet they possessed knowledge of so potent a kind that, pressing their own interests rather than the interests of the world as a whole, they destroyed the universal state of China and plunged all farther Asia into a turmoil.

Such is the long view from which the events we have been describing may be judged. This turmoil, which was in an oblique manner caused by Europe, must now be cured by it. And this cure, strangely enough, must be the integration of a new universal state, but this time co-terminous with the world. In this we are all agreed, and our agreement makes us Confucians, for Confucianism is a universal political philosophy: in the *Li Chi*, one of its original classics, the ideal stage of civilization is called the 'Great Similarity' and defined as a universal state animated by the common aim of each for all regardless of race or language or creed. That ideal is not peculiar to China, it has always been the stuff of mortal dreams, but China is the only living country which has sought to give it practical effect, for there alone was it woven into the political structure. In Europe it had its home in the Papal City, and here we are reminded of the colloquys between the Jesuits and the Son of Heaven. They were both speaking of the universal state, the *Civitas Dei*, but using terms the other could not understand. Now, though the state cult of Confucianism went with the last Ch'ing Emperor, the old Confucian truths and ideals remain, and we begin to see how the universal terms used by the Holy Father and the Son of Heaven can be made to agree and can be put into practice.

If then China and the Western World have found at last that their political aims are the same, the union of East and West is feasible, and that union is the establishment of a new

*Civitas Dei*, which is the grand elixir in the field of government. That was my meaning when I remarked further back
that the Western World must rescue China from its present
misery, for not otherwise will it be able to realize its own desire.

If this book were to be perfectly balanced it should contain
an account of the final ruin of the Great Ch'ing, comparable to Part I on the ruin of the Great Ming. But that is
impossible. Space forbids, the reader's patience would not
stretch so far, nor is there pressing need, for a multitude of books
have been written on the subject. But clearly a memorandum
at least of what happened is required, and so I shall note the
salient dates of the rest of the story, lifting the curtain once to
obtain a close view of the Son of Heaven at the moment of his
greatest humiliation.

Lord Amherst left Canton in January 1817, and for sixteen
years the British Government took no further steps to enter into
relations with the Court of China. In 1833, when the monopoly
of the East India Company was abolished, Lord Napier was
sent to Canton as Chief Superintendent of the China trade.
He was to act as British representative, to claim the right of
direct and equal dealings with the Canton authorities, using
reason not force to obtain his ends. But he completely failed.
On August 21, 1834, he wrote home: 'I feel satisfied your
Lordships will see the urgent necessity of negotiating with such
a government having in your hands at the same time the means
of compulsion. To negotiate with them otherwise would be an
idle waste of time.'

This letter may be said to have turned the scale in favour of
force. The British patience was exhausted at last. In 1839-40
the armed conflict between Britain and China began. Though
mixed up with a dispute over opium, which led to it being
called the Opium War, the real object of the operations was to
force China to trade in a modern way. Naval action obliged
her to agree to those requests which Lord Macartney had made
forty-seven years before and to throw open to trade four more
ports, allow Consuls at each, cede an island, Hongkong, as a

trade emporium, abolish the Hong merchants and publish a uniform tariff.

The effect of this treaty was to reduce the monopolist profits of the Cantonese officials and merchants, and they sought to evade its terms where they could. The Throne was unable to prevent this. It became greatly weakened by the Taiping rebellion, comparable to Li's rebellion against the Ming, which broke about 1855, the rebels taking Nanking, the second city of the Empire, and establishing a dynasty there. So impotent did the Government become in the south that the Portuguese were able to declare Macao to be their property and to expel the Chinese authorities.

In 1857 the British, after the Cantonese had burnt their factory and committed other outrages, were so angered that they decided to take the city. This was effected on December 25, 1857, by the fleet and a landing force of 5,000 men. The French gave some assistance.

Lord Elgin, who was in command, had instructions now to press for diplomatic representation in Peking, another of Macartney's points. In spite of the capture of Canton, he was refused, and a British force, assisted by a French contingent, advanced up the Pei-ho River to the capital in 1860. The Emperor, Hsien Feng, the seventh of the Ch'ing, accompanied by the Imperial Concubine Yi, afterwards Tzu Hsi, the famous Empress Dowager, fled to Jehol. The metropolitan army was utterly defeated. As a reprisal for the murder of certain British prisoners Lord Elgin burnt about two hundred of the buildings in Yüan-ming Yüan, including the curious baroque halls built by the Jesuits, the contents being first looted. He then seized the Anting Gate of the Tartar City of Peking, and on October 24 went in state to the office of the Board of Rites. His demand for a legation was accepted. Canton was then returned.

This ended the period of conflict which had begun in 1839–40. The English had now acquired what they wanted. Political and commercial relations between Britain and China had

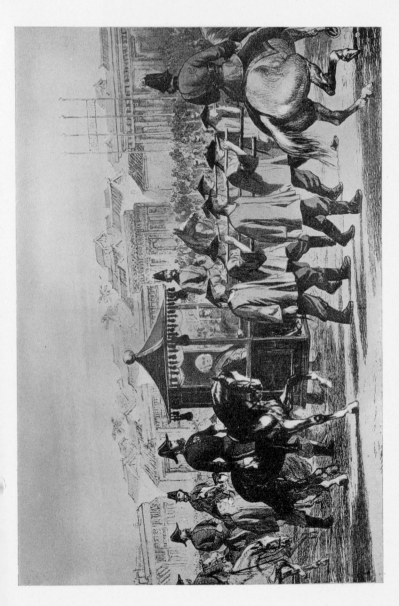

ENTRY OF LORD ELGIN INTO THE FORBIDDEN CITY IN 1860

*From a chromo-lithograph*

been placed on a modern footing. But the forceful methods employed to obtain this result had so shaken the credit of the Ch'ing with their own people that further troubles were inevitable.

It was thought by some observers that what was called an awakening of China would now take place. But no reform party emerged at this time, either at Court or among the bureaucracy. But Japan woke. In 1868 the feudal system of the Shogunate was swept away by a Liberal movement which restored the Emperor to an active place and opened the country to all the knowledge of the West. Thus Japan suddenly did what China might have done any time during the previous two hundred years. The miseries which have since afflicted the latter are the measure of her mistake in allowing Japan to pass ahead. England's ambitions in China were only commercial, as were those of Republican France and all other European nations. But Japan's were also political. She desired from the first to dominate the Asian continent. By equipping her with its knowledge, Europe armed her to realize her aims. Danger- ous as was to China the new knowledge of Europe while manipulated against her by Europeans, that knowledge was infinitely more dangerous in the hands of the Japanese, for they were on the spot, and from 1914 onwards, when Western nations were fighting each other in Europe, had an increasingly free hand to do what they liked.

In 1864 the Taipings were crushed with British assistance and the tottering Ch'ing was propped up. Not only the British but all the principal Western nations and the Japanese now possessed legations outside the wall of the Imperial City near the T'ien-an Men, the Gate of Heavenly Peace. And the Euro- peans had Treaty Ports all down the coast in which the Chinese writ did not run. This state of affairs continued till 1894, China remaining complacent and inactive. Then came the shock of the Japan war. The Japanese, by this time armed like a modern European power, believed that China was breaking up, and planned to obtain a footing on the Asiatic mainland so as to be well placed to insist on a share of the spoil. They seized the Liaotung peninsula, part of Manchuria, the home-land of the Ch'ing, easily defeating all the Chinese armies sent against them and sinking the Chinese fleet. The Western powers had looked on during the war, but when it was over, alarmed at the idea of a Japanese army stationed on the mainland, forced Japan to give back Liaotung.

This defeat by the despised island dwarfs roused the Chinese people to the imminence of their peril. Kuang Hsü, the ninth and last ruling Emperor of the Ch'ing, occupied the Dragon Throne. In 1898 he was twenty-seven years old, but so mentally undeveloped as to be hardly more than half-witted. The Empress-Dowager, Tzu Hsi, who had placed him on the throne when he was four and had acted as Regent until his majority, watched him from the side with her implacable eyes.

Told by certain of those who had won his confidence that China must reform or perish, he issued in frantic haste between June 20 and September 16, 1898, no less than thirty-eight reform edicts, sound enough in idea but far too numerous to be capable of execution, and in any case futile without the support of the Civil Service and the Court. He also became mixed up in a conspiracy against the Empress-Dowager, and that was the end of his freedom, for his redoubtable aunt had him detained in semi-custody for the rest of his reign.

The common people, convinced like the Emperor that some remedy must be found or China would be eaten by the foreigners whose teeth were already in her flesh, took action after their kind and in 1900 broke into the frenzied insurrection known as the Boxer rebellion, the object of which was simple —to exterminate all foreigners. The Empress-Dowager, in whose character was something naive and ignorant, encouraged the Boxers, in the belief that they could drive the barbarians into the sea, and allowed them to besiege the legations in Peking. To relieve their compatriots a cosmopolitan force drawn from the various Treaty Ports advanced on the capital and occupied it, sacking the palaces of The Great Within. The

Empress-Dowager, taking her prisoner, the Emperor, with her, fled north at dawn on August 15, 1900, as the foreign troops entered.

We are enabled to take a look at her and her party, because a Mandarin called Wu Yung, who was District Magistrate of Huai-lai, seventy miles north of Peking, has given in a book published in English under the title of *The Flight of an Empress* a vivid account of what happened when they passed through the town. A Confucian scholar and a regular member of the Civil Service, he had been at Huai-lai for two years when the Boxers began their depredations. They were curious ruffians, half-ecstatics, half-tricksters. They came flooding to Huai-lai and took possession of the town. They did not, however, depose Wu Yung, but his position as guardian of law and order was very anomalous, and was made more so when the Empress-Dowager gave the Boxers face. He could, in fact, do no more than sit and watch the bandits turn the administration upside down. They were capricious to a degree, and he daily expected his office to be burnt and himself decapitated. Many of the neighbouring villages were deserted, supplies were difficult to get, robbers infested the roads, deserters from the metropolitan army pillaged and murdered. But he kept up his courage and did what he could. The local people were devoted to him.

For some weeks he had had no official news of the outside world, when suddenly on the evening of August 16, the day after the fall of Peking, he received a letter from the Magistrate of Yen-ch'ing, a district contiguous to his on the way to the capital, stating that the Empress-Dowager and the Emperor, together with the Empress, five Princes, two Dukes, a number of high Court officials, and many soldiers, attendants and eunuchs, were on their way to Huai-lai and would require food and lodging. The Imperial fugitives were likely to reach a little posting station called Yu-lin, eight miles distant, on the following day.

It was a tall order to receive the Court of China at Huai-lai with less than twenty-four hours' notice. Some of Wu Yung's subordinates were so terrified at the idea that they advised him to flee. How could an adequate welcome be provided for their Majesties in the time and in such difficult circumstances? They would only incur blame and punishment. But Wu Yung declared that it was his duty as an Imperial official to do what he could. During the night the Government rest-house was put in order. The walls were papered and the ceilings repaired. Lanterns and red draperies were hung over the gates. The floors were swept and a few works of art arranged to advantage. And a message was sent to the petty official in charge at the posting station of Yu-lin, telling him to have refreshments ready.

At dawn on August 17 Wu Yung, dressed in his official robes, set out on horseback for Yu-lin to meet the Imperial cortège. He had had a very unpleasant scene with the Boxers before he could get away.

'The head boxer', he records, 'asked me why I was leaving.

' "I am going to meet the Sacred Chariot of the Empress-Dowager and the Emperor," I answered.

' "How is this?" the Boxer leader cried in a loud voice. "They have fled long ago. How can you still call them Emperor and Empress-Dowager? They are not worthy."

'I replied: "The Emperor has the responsibility of making a tour of investigation once in three years. He can go where he likes in his own country. If, as a District Magistrate, I go out of the District privately you can say that I have fled. But you cannot say that of the Emperor. If I go to the country parts of Huai-lai district on my official business, can you say that I have fled?"

'The head boxer looked at his associates, and said: "This is breath from the mouth of a Secondary Hairy One. He should be killed." '

A Secondary Hairy One was a convert to Christianity or an associate of foreigners, and the Boxers had murdered large numbers of such persons. Wu Yung knew he was in imminent danger of seizure and death, but he managed to frighten the Boxers and they left him. They were, in spite of their impudent words, nervous of what might happen to them when the Two Palaces, as the Dowager-Empress and the Emperor were styled in Court language, arrived, for the utter failure of their society against the invading foreigners had stripped them of the Imperial favour.

When Wu Yung with his guard were three miles out of the town, it came on to pour with rain. Fortunately, he had with him his purple cloth overcoat to put over his official robes and an oiled silk covering for his tasselled hat. A high cold wind was blowing, and hunched on their horses the little troop pressed on. After a while the rain stopped and they perceived coming towards them a mule litter, preceded by a guide on horseback. Wu Yung, guessing the litter must belong to the Imperial party, drew to one side of the road, quickly took off his overcoat and the oil-cloth on his hat, and waited respectfully. On coming up, the guide informed him that the litter contained a Court Chamberlain named Chao, who immediately put his head out and, on learning that he was addressing the District Magistrate, enquired what accommodation had been arranged. Wu assured him he had done all possible in the time.

'If there is but a room, it will be sufficient,' said Chao. 'The Two Palaces have suffered hunger and cold for two days and nights. Their appearance is very pitiable. The foreign soldiers fought their way into the Forbidden City. There was nothing to do but leave. . . . The Sacred Chariot is immediately behind. You had better go forward to meet it. I will not say more to you.'

Wu reached Yu-lin by ten o'clock, while there was yet no sign of their Majesties. All the shops were shut and the place seemed deserted. At the barracks he found one man on duty. This man said that when orders were received to provide refreshments, he had told the innkeepers, of whom there were three, to make the requisite preparations. They had done so, but there had been a rush earlier that morning of fugitives from the battle area, and everything was eaten except one cauldron of millet and bean porridge. This cauldron, said the man, was now in the principal inn, not too bad a house. There were chairs, tables, beds, windows and the doors were still in place. There were even pictures on the walls, he added. But the inn-keeper and everyone else had fled.

Wu hurried to the inn, a courtyard with buildings on the four sides. It was empty, but he found the porridge and set a guard over it.

Hardly was this done when an Imperial Prince named Su arrived on horseback and announced that the Two Palaces were close at hand, the Empress-Dowager in a four-man chair and the Emperor behind in a mule litter.

Wu Yung stationed himself at the gate of the inn compound. Presently he saw a blue sedan carried by four men. He knelt as it reached the gate and in a loud chanting voice gave his name, rank and district, and formally welcomed the Empress-Dowager. As the Emperor's mule-litter passed he repeated the same formula. He then rose from his knees and sat by the gate, watching the arrival of a long line of grandees. There passed the young Empress, the Heir-Apparent, the Chief Eunuch, Li Lien-ying, and Princesses, ladies-in-waiting and women, with Princes, Dukes and officials of all kinds, some in country carts and some on horseback. They came on in disarray, their appearance was dilapidated. It was the third day of their flight. On the first they had covered twenty-three miles, on the second thirty miles; that morning they had done fifteen more. They had had no proper lodging and very little food, and they had suffered from the cold winds because their clothes were too thin. Amherst's journey from Tung-chao to the Summer Palace was nothing in comparison to what they had endured. Springless carts on such roads average hardly more than two miles an hour. A journey of thirty miles is twelve hours of jolting. The admini-stration having broken down and the villagers dispersed, there was hardly a cup of tea to be had.

When as many as could crowd into the courtyard had entered and the commotion was subsiding, suddenly a eunuch came from the building on the north side of the courtyard to which the Two Palaces had gone, and cried in a loud and arrogant voice: 'Which is the Magistrate of Huai-lai District?' He stared haughtily and stood with stomach and chest stuck out. This man was the Deputy Chief Eunuch, Ts'ui.

When Wu Yung heard himself called, he stood up and acknowledged his identity.

'Those above call you to audience. Come with me,' said the eunuch in such a loud fierce voice that Wu Yung, not yet fully understanding how thankful the Court was for any sort of a reception, feared his arrangements had been found inadequate.

'Is the Imperial summons dangerous?' he whispered to the eunuch, as he went with him.

'How do I know? This is your fate,' said the fellow, rudely pulling him by the arm.

But Court eunuchs were rude to subordinate officials on principle. It was their way of getting tips.

Wu Yung was taken straight into the presence of the Empress-Dowager. She was seated at a table dressed in the blue cotton clothes of a poor country-woman, her hair done in a simple knot at the top of her head. Wu Yung knelt at once and then kotowed. He found that Her Majesty was not annoyed with him. She asked him quickly the ordinary routine questions which are always asked, his name, rank, length of service and so on, and then came to the point: 'Have you prepared all that we will need?'

Wu Yung answered with deference and humility: 'Reverentially, I have prepared. But I received word only last night. Under the circumstances I could not prepare fully. What I have prepared is not complete, and therefore I am afraid.'

The Empress-Dowager was greatly relieved to hear that he had made any preparations. And she was touched by his devotion and burst into tears.

'The Emperor and I have travelled continuously for many hundreds of miles,' she said. (The seventy miles had seemed an eternity.) 'Not only have we not seen a subject, but we have not seen even the shadow of a Magistrate. Now we have come to Huai/lai. You, dressed in official robes and hat, have come to meet us. We can say that you are a faithful official. I never thought that the country's affairs would come to the pass they have. But seeing you, who have not discarded ceremony, I feel that there may still be hope for the country and the dynasty.'

She spoke with such emotion that Wu Yung also could not restrain his tears.

After a moment, drying her eyes, she went on: 'Day by day we fled and had nothing to eat or drink. We were both cold and hungry. On the road we were thirsty. We told the eunuchs to get water. Though there were wells, there was either nothing with which to draw water or else the wells would be filled with floating human heads. . . . Last night the Emperor and I had only a bench between us, and we sat shoulder to shoulder watching the sky for morning. . . . Look at me! I am like an old country woman now. The Emperor, too, is very tired. It is two days since we had food. Have you prepared food for me?'

Wu Yung told her then how he had tried to prepare, and how only one pot of bean and millet porridge remained, too coarse a food for Her Majesty to eat. But the old lady replied: 'Can I at this time say what is good and what is not good?' and told him to bring it quickly. But first she desired him to see Kuang Hsu, the Emperor.

The Chief Eunuch, Li Lien/ying, took him into another room. There the Son of Heaven was standing by a chair. He was wearing a much/worn black silk wadded coat, without overcoat or sash. His hair, where it should have been shaved, was an inch long, and his queue was disordered. His face was covered with dust, through which his skin showed yellow and dry. He was quite speechless.

Wu Yung kotowed and withdrew to get the porridge. It was sent in without delay with a pair of ivory chop/sticks which he had in his belt and which he wiped clean with a piece of paper. He waited outside the curtain of the door and presently, he says, 'I heard the sound of swift eating, and of porridge being drunk with inhaling of breaths, as if the food were good.'

Then Li Lien-ying, the Chief Eunuch, came out, a great ugly scoundrel, a most infamous person, as we know, but there was a cheerful smile on his evil face. He held up his thumb in approbation, saying: 'You are good. Old Buddha likes you very much. Serve her with all your heart. Good will come to you. Old Buddha has a desire to eat eggs. Could you find any for her?'

Wu Yung said the village was deserted, but he would go and see. In an empty shop, after searching everywhere, he pulled out a kitchen drawer and found five eggs. These he brought back, and as his men were all occupied, drew water himself, built a fire and boiled the eggs. Then placing them in a coarse bowl with a little salt he handed them in through the curtain.

After a while Li came out again. 'Old Buddha enjoyed the eggs very much,' he said. 'Of the five you sent she ate three, the remaining two she gave to the Lord of Ten Thousand Years. The light was shed on no-one else.'

A little later the Empress-Dowager appeared on the veran-dah. Wu Yung was waiting in the courtyard and she called him over. He did not presume to enter, but knelt in the mud of the courtyard below her. She was smoking a pipe.

'When we left the Palace we were in a great hurry,' she said, 'and did not bring many clothes. I have only what I am wear-ing. I am cold. Could you get me a few garments?'

Wu Yung had been close to the Holy Mother, boiling her eggs and weeping with her, and so now he did not find it strange that she should ask him for clothes, she who had so many, for it is said that she never wore the same robe twice. It was on that very day that a Mrs. Ker, one of the ladies of the British Legation, penetrated into her room in the Forbidden City. It was just as she had left it. On the bed a coat of black satin, beneath a pair of Manchu shoes, camphor-wood boxes filled with coats and trousers, gold-embroidered or sewn with pearls, or lined with sable or white fox fur—those were the things Mrs. Ker saw while their owner was asking Wu Yung for something to protect her from the cold.

The faithful Magistrate promised to do what he could when they reached Huai-lai. The Two Palaces set out soon afterwards to cover the eight miles. Wu saw off the Imperial Sedan—the blue chair which had been supplied the previous day by the Magistrate at Yen-ch'ing, who does not seem to have been able to supply anything else—and mounted his horse and by using by-paths reached Huai-lai first. After satisfying himself that the Government rest-house was ready and telling the people to kneel in front of their houses and burn incense—the Boxers had fled—he began to search for clothes. His wife had recently died and her clothes were at Peking. He found, however, a lined broadcloth coat which had belonged to his mother and some clothes of his which he thought would fit the Son of Heaven. For the Princesses, too, he found clothes, for they had come away in silk gauze and were very cold. These and a toilet-set he made up into a parcel and had them delivered when the Two Palaces arrived. Later on, when he was summoned, he says: 'the Empress-Dowager and the Emperor were both wearing the clothes I had sent, and I saw that dignity had returned in some degree to their appearance. The two Princesses, also, had on my long coats. . . . They no longer looked like dejected jackals.'

That is the end of my story. As we know, the Great Ch'ing did not, and could not, survive such a humiliation for long. The foreign powers withdrew their troops from the capital, but the Court, when it returned, remained in subjection to them. In 1904 Japan laid the foundations of her future operations against China by turning Russia out of Manchuria, and establishing herself firmly on the mainland. The Chinese, however, did not perceive the drift of this, though the spectacle of an Asiatic beating a European power persuaded them at last of the value of European knowledge. A Reform Party, which had been slowly organizing itself, gathered strength. In 1908 the Empress-Dowager and the Emperor died, and a child of three, Pu-yi, was enthroned under the reign-title of Hsüan T'ung, Wide Control. We have met him already in the last chapter of

Part I. Four years later the Reform Party led by Sun Yat-sen terminated the rule of the Ch'ing Dynasty and inaugurated the Republic.

On January 5, 1912, Sun Yat-sen issued a proclamation in which, after denouncing the Manchus for closing the country against world-knowledge with the deliberate object of keeping the Chinese in ignorance, the better to hold them in perpetual subjection, and thereby bringing into contempt an Empire which once was admired by all, he outlines the policy of the Republic. 'We will remodel the laws, revise the civil, criminal, commercial and mining codes, reform the finances, abolish restrictions on trade and commerce, and ensure religious tolera-tion and the cultivation of better relations with foreign peoples and governments than have ever been maintained before. It is our earnest hope that those foreign nations who have been stead-fast in their sympathy will bind more firmly the bonds of friendship between us, and will bear in patience with us the period of trial confronting us and our reconstruction work, and will aid the consummation of the far-reaching plans, which we are about to undertake, and which they have long vainly been urging upon our people and our country.

'With this message of peace and goodwill the Republic cherishes the hope of being admitted into the family of nations, not merely to share its rights and privileges, but to co-operate in the great and noble task of building up the civilization of the world.'

But, alas! the long drama was not to end on this note. China's miseries had been great, yet they were destined to be ten times greater. The nations of the West might very well have listened to this her plea for fair play. But her fate was not to be in their hands. An Asiatic island power, as strong as any of them because they had given it the means and stronger than most because it was not separated like them from China by ten thousand miles of sea, had fixed itself upon the mainland. Its policy was not peace and goodwill. It did not seek to build up the civilization of the world. Long before the dictators of the

West appeared, its statesmen formulated a new theory of aggression. The young struggling Republic, inheritor of so much weakness, corruption and ignorance, could not reform China fast enough to meet that menace. Soon, too soon, the West was involved in internecine warfare. There came a time when it could no longer restrain Japan as it had sometimes in the past. Now for three years the Republic has been half swallowed.

Yet Sun Yat-sen's was not a false vision. The great and noble task of rebuilding civilization is at hand and will be undertaken with the help of China.

# Principal Authorities Used

## PART ONE

*Annals and Memoirs of the Court of Peking.* E. Backhouse and J. O. P. Bland. 1914.
*History of Burma.* G. E. Harvey. 1925.
*Twilight in the Forbidden City.* Reginald F. Johnston. 1934.

## PART TWO

*An Embassy from the East India Company of the United Provinces to the Grand Tartar Cham, Emperour of China,* by John Nievhoff, translated by John Ogilby. London, 1669.
*Le Père Matthieu Ricci et la société chinoise de son temps.* 2 vols. R. P. Henri Bernard, S.J. Tientsin, 1937.
*L'Apport Scientifique du Père Matthieu Ricci à la Chine.* R. P. Henri Bernard, S.J. (English translation. *Matteo Ricci's Scientific Contribution to China.*) Peiping, 1936.
*La Chine en France au XVIII Siècle.* Henri Cordier. Paris, 1910.
*Lettres édifiantes et curieuses.* Paris, 1729.
*China and Europe.* Adolf Reichwein. London, 1925.
*L'Orphelin de la Chine.* Voltaire.
*Essai sur les Mœurs.* Voltaire.
*The Analects of Confucius.* Arthur Waley. 1938.

## PART THREE

*The Travels of Peter Mundy in Europe and Asia.* Hakluyt Society, Vol. III, Parts I and II. These volumes also contain relevant transcripts from the State Papers, the Marine Records and other material in the Records at the Hague and Lisbon.

# Principal Authorities Used

*The Chronicles of the East India Company trading to China*, 4 Vols. by H. B. Morse, 1926.

*International Relations of the Chinese Empire*, 3 Vols. by H. B. Morse, 1918.

*A Voyage Round the World in the Years M.D.CCXL, I, II, III, IV, by George Anson, Esq.*, compiled by Richard Walter, M.A., Chaplain of His Majesty's Ship the *Centurion*. London, M.D.CCXLVIII.

The Diary of Lord Macartney, reproduced in *Our First Ambassador to China*, Helen H. Robbins, London, 1908.

*An Authentic Account of An Embassy from the King of Great Britain to the Emperor of China*, Sir George Staunton, Bart., London, 1797.

*Travels in China* by J. Barrow and *Narrative of Embassy to China* by Ænaeas Anderson, who were both attached to the Macartney Embassy, have also been quoted.

*Journal of the Proceedings of the Late Embassy to China,* Henry Ellis, London, 1817. This volume has an Appendix containing translations of the Chinese documents quoted in this chapter. Some of these documents are also to be found in Morse, *The East India Company Trading to China*, and in *Annals of the Court of Peking*, Backhouse and Bland.

*The Flight of an Empress*, by Wu Yung. London, 1937.
*China and the Manchus*. Herbert Giles. 1912.

# Index

# Index

# Index

# Index

# Date Due